Reminiscences

of

Captain Glyn Jones, CHC, USN (Ret.)

U. S. Naval Institute
Annapolis, Maryland

1978

Preface

We have here the transcript of some taped interviews with Captain Glyn Jones, CHC, USN (Ret.) These interviews were held at the Mt. Hermon School, Mt. Hermon, Massachusetts and at the U. S. Naval Institute, Annapolis, Maryland over a span of two years (1975-77).

This is a valuable memoir and contains many highlights. A good part of the Captain's career was spent with the U. S. Marines - ranging in time from Guadalcanal to Korea and with stops in between at LeJeune, Parris Island and Pendleton. He served also in various naval assigments including that as Fleet Chaplain with CincUSNavEur.

The natural bent of the Chaplain has been, seemingly, the educational field. His efforts have been fruitful. From time to time he has involved himself with burning contemporary issues: compulsory chapel attendance, civil liberties, the rule of law in society, the draft, freedom of the press, and of course the position of the chaplain in the hierarchy of command. His observations on these subjects and on others are sharp and telling in their impact - and almost always they are controversial.

Captain Jones has made minor corrections to the original transcript. The MS has been retyped and indexed. An assortment of documents is included in an appendix for the convenience of the user.

John T. Mason, Jr.
Director of Oral History
U. S. Naval Institute

February, 1978

DEPARTMENT OF THE NAVY
Bureau of Naval Personnel
Washington 25, D.C.

Ecclesiastical Relations
Chaplains Division   LIberty 5-6700   Ext. 4-1696

INFORMATION FOR PUBLIC RELATIONS
Biographical Sketch

Name: Glyn Jones
Rank: Captain
Born: 12 Feb 1915
Denomination: American Baptist
Home Town: Poultney, Vermont

Education	School attended	Location	Degrees	Date
College	University of Vermont	Burlington, Vt.	PHB	1937
	Harvard U.	Cambridge, Mass		1947-48
Seminary	Andover Newton Theol. Sem.	Newton Centre, Mass	BD	1940

Ordination:

DATE   1 Nov 1940
Place   First Baptist Church, Woonsocket, RI
By Whom   Permanent Council, RI State Baptist Convention

Previous Military Service

Appointment to Chaplaincy

First Duty: Mar Bks, New River, June - Jul '42

Subsequent Service:

Afloat	Ashore
3rd Mar Reg Jul - Dec 42	12nd Dec 42-Jan 44
USS LOS ANGELES Nov45-Aug 47	Chap Sch Feb 44- Oct 45
2nd MarDiv, Cp Ljn, NC Sep 49-Jul 50	Harvard U. Sep 47 May 48
1st Mar Div, FMF Pac Aug 50-Nov 50	NAS, Quonset Pt., RI Jan 48-Aug 49
ComDesLant, Newport, RI Aug 54-Aug 56	BuPers Dec 50-Dec 51
NavActs, Italy Sep 59-Aug 60	MCRD, Parris Is. Dec 51-Oct 53
CINCUSNAVEUR Sep 60-Sep 61	Dir, Mar Corps Educa Cntr, Mar Corps Schools, Quantico, Va. Oct 53-Aug 54

Present duty: BuPers, Chaplains Division, Navy Dept. Wash. DC

Married   Ruth Muriel Johnson
Date/Place   24 Nov 1940, Woonsocket, RI
Children   4

Items of interest (use reverse side if necessary)

Duties Ashore

Nav Adm Cmd, Armed Forces Staff College
    Norfolk, Va Aug 56-Aug 59
NH, San Diego Oct 61-Feb 62
AdCom NTC, San Diego Mar 62-Jan 64

Medals & Decorations

Silver Star
Bronze Star (Combat "V")
Pres Unit Citation
Navy Unit Citation
Korean Presidential Unit Citation

Campaign Medals and Ribbons

World War II Victory
Atlantic Theater
Asiatic-Pacific Theater (2 stars)
China Service
National Defense Service
Korean War (2 stars)
United Nations

DECLARATION OF TRUST

The undersigned does hereby appoint and designate as his (her) Trustee herein, the Secretary-Treasurer and Publisher of the United States Naval Institute to perform and discharge the following duties, powers, and privileges in connection with the possession and use of a certain taped interview between the undersigned and the Oral History Department of the United States Naval Institute.

1. Classification of Transcript.

   (X)a. If classified OPEN, the transcript(s) may be read or the recording(s) audited by the qualified personnel upon presentation of proper credentials, as determined by the Secretary-Treasurer of the U.S. Naval Institute.

   ( )b. If classified PERMISSION REQUIRED TO CITE OR QUOTE, the user will be required to obtain permission in writing from the interviewee prior to quoting or citing from either the transcript(s) or the recording(s).

   ( )c. If classified PERMISSION REQUIRED, permission must be obtained in writing from the interviewee before the transcribed interview(s) can be examined or the tape recording(s) audited.

   ( )d. If classified CLOSED, the transcribed interview(s) and the tape recording(s) will be sealed until a time specified by the interviewee. This may be until the death of the interviewee or for any specified number of years.

2. It is expressly understood that in giving this authorization, I am in no way precluded from placing such restrictions as I may desire upon use of the interview at any time during my lifetime, nor does this authorization in any way affect my rights to the copyright of my literary expressions that may be contained in the interview.

Witness my hand and seal this 16th day of November 1977

Capt. Glyn Jones CHC

I hereby accept and consent to the foregoing Declaration of Trust and the powers therein conferred upon me as Trustee:

R. T. E. Bowler Jr.

Interview No. 1 with Chaplain Glyn Jones, U.S. Navy (Retired)
Place: His residence at Mount Herman School, Mount Hermon, Mass.
Date: Monday evening, 13 October 1975
Subject: Biography
By: John T. Mason, Jr.

Q: I've been looking forward to this series of interviews with you, having heard so much about you and your career as a chaplain in the Navy. Would you begin, Sir, in the proper way by telling me the date and place of your birth, something about your family background.

Capt. J.: My parents were Welsh immigrants, both father and mother. They came from Wales, met in this country, married, and settled in a little town in Vermont called Poultney. I was born in Poultney on the 12th of February 1915.

Q: Unusual that Welsh people would settle in Vermont. Many of them went to Pennsylvania.

Capt. J.: Many did, and to Wisconsin and Ohio, but settling in Vermont took place because there were in this little town and outside of it a number of slate quarries and the northern Welsh

G. Jones #1 - 2

had large deposits of slate and had worked them at home. So, by the nature of the case, they ended up in Poultney.

Q: Very interesting. How many children were there in the family?

Capt. J.: Only a sister besides myself and she is now in Fargo, North Dakota.

Q: So you went to the public schools in Poultney?

Capt. J.: We had, as many New England towns had at that time, a local private academy, which took the town children on a tuition basis into the high school, Troy Conference Academy. I attended that.

Well, you probably got a better education because of that?

Capt. J.: I probably did, as did many New England youngsters in those days when these schools preceded the public high school.

Q: What was the course of study?

Capt. J.: It was what we called in those days the College Preparatory Course. You had to complete certain courses to qualify to enter college, so many hours in English and history and maths, and that kind of thing. They had another course that was called a commercial course. This was designed to produce secretaries.

Q: It must have been quite interesting growing up as a youngster in Vermont?

Capt. J.: It was. It was roughly in central Vermont. There's no greater boyhood than to grow up in a New England small town. In due course, you know almost everybody in town and everybody knows you. You can't stray too far from the straight and narrow without it being noticed, you know, which may not always be an advantage. Later on you look back and feel that it was.

It was an interesting town, divided in three parts in terms of people. One group of native Yankee people, Yankee stock, another third Irish, and another third Welsh. The people got along very well.

Occasionally on Saturday night there would be a few fights between the Irish and the Welsh. The Yankees would get off the streets on Saturday night. On Sunday morning you'd sometimes see the Welsh going to their little Presbyterian church, passing the Irish going to St. Raphael's, and you'd say, "Oh, Mrs. Higgins, how are you? How are you Mr. Higgins?" Maybe Mr. Higgins would have received a black eye the night before, but by and large it was a very close town and the people felt very close to one another.

Q: What ambition did you have as you grew up there and went to the academy?

Capt. J.: I think maybe at that time in my life my father had ambitions for me. He had had rather unhappy experiences in his youth. Our family had been for a long, long time in the British Army and it was sort of taken for granted, when he came along, that he would in due course enter the army, but he didn't want to do this. One of the pressures that was put on him was by the local Anglican rector of the church that my family attended. He believed in the same kind of thing so my father took a rather abiding dislike to the church and this is one reason why he migrated from Wales and came to this country. He felt that there wasn't the kind of freedom that he wanted.

He felt that I should be, perhaps, a lawyer and in high school and in college I took courses designed basically to try to prepare me for law school.

Q: And you agreed with that?

Capt. J.: I did. I accepted it rather uncritically. I was very close to my father and my feeling was that for me he probably knew better. I wasn't inclined to dispute him, but then in my senior year in college I felt called to the ministry. This was a rather dramatic change for me for a number of reasons.

Q: What were some of those reasons?

Capt. J.: One was that I had been making my living for a number of years working in dance bands and belonged to the FA of M.

Q: What instrument did you play?

Capt. J.: I majored in brasses and doubled on strings. I was a trumpet-player, and in those days this made one quite a good living. There were many people unemployed. It wasn't the most promising life for an adolescent in many ways, and one wouldn't expect many ministers to come out of this kind of thing.

When I announced to the band that I was leaving them, they wanted to know where I was going, and when I told them I was going to seminary it caused a minor convulsion. Everything stopped, everybody stopped and wanted to hear about this because it was regarded as a very unusual thing.

Q: They'd had no indication of it at all?

Capt. J.: No. I hadn't said anything to them about this. I wrote my father a very long letter telling him about this change in my mind and about this commitment that I was going to undertake. He didn't take it well. He sent me a telegram that ran, "Come home immediately. Are you well?" I went home and explained it and he accepted it.

Q: What was the real reason that you had this change of heart?

Capt. J.: Basically it was that for the first time I had come to think for myself about what I would like to do with my life and the issue of using my life well had finally come to the fore.

Q: How old were you at this time?

Capt. J.: I was then twenty-two. There were some emotional concomitants. I wouldn't say any unusual ones. A sense of comfort and commitment came; I was settled on something and I knew this was what I was about to do.

Q: Had you met a very engaging clergyman?

Capt. J.: Yes, I had met several, and the entire question of serving people started to become important to me. I had been brought up in the church. Curiously enough, in a Baptist church. My father didn't want me to go to the Episcopal Church because of his bad experience with the rector at home and he didn't want me to go only to the Welsh church because he felt I should adjust culturally to this country. I had been raised to speak Welsh in the home and I learnt to speak English easily enough, as anybody would. I was taken as a child to the Welsh church in the evening for services.

Q: And was that Baptist or Methodist?

Capt. J.: No, that was a Presbyterian church.

Q: Presbyterian?

Capt. J.: Yes, and, of course, I learned the great Welsh hymns there. Beside the Episcopal parish there were only Baptist and Methodist churches there. He selected the Baptist for me because he liked their freedom and he felt that no one basically would interfere with my process of making my own decisions, so that when the time came for me to make my own decisions I would make them for myself. He was the only one who may have had the temptation to interfere but he was too wise to do that.

Q: That's a very unusual characteristic of his, the insistence on freedom.

Capt. J.: Yes, indeed. This was a great passion in his life. He was never a notable person. He was a highly effective person in our town. He was, for example, known for one period as the town Democrat. In Vermont, you may recall, that was to say he was one who stood on his own feet and held his position, which he did in the life of the town.

Q: He was fiercely independent?

Capt. J.: Fiercely independent.

Q: And yet very cooperative?

Capt. J.: Yes, but cooperative basically on terms that were satisfactory to both people, not terms set by someone else.

Q: So he came around to your point of view once you explained it to him?

Capt. J.: No, he never did. He accepted it basically because he felt I had to have the right to choose, but he couldn't, I don't think, have imagined anything worse from his standpoint than my fate as a minister.

Q: Than being a clergyman?

Capt. J.: Yes. My mother, of course, was simply delighted, as most mothers tend to be. So the old man accepted it but never agreed with it. The nearest, I think, he ever came to agreement was when he visited one time in the one parish I had. He followed me around for a couple of days, watched me teach an adult class, heard me preach. I guess at that point he came reluctantly to the conclusion that for better or for worse I was doing this and, as far as he could see, I was doing it reasonably well. Probably he settled for that.

Q: Interesting! Tell me about your career in the seminary. You had college, did you?

Capt. J.: Yes. I went to a junior college in my home town and had my last two years at the University of Vermont. I graduated in 1937, went to Andover-Newton theological school, near Boston, and spent three years there and graduated in 1940. I graduated in June and was ordained in November.

Q: Tell me a little about the three years you spent there.

Capt. J.: I found them a very exciting part of my life, first, because as a latecomer to the vocation many of the preparations that other students had made I had still to accomplish. I found quite exciting many aspects of the academic course. Then, I was sent to do field work in my first year. I was sent to a big Baptist church in Fall River, Massachusetts. The pastor there promptly assigned me as pastor of one of the chapels of the church, in the northern part of the city. It is a mill city and these were mill workers.

Q: A kind of a mission chapel, was it?

Capt. J.: It was a mission chapel, exactly. I came down, the people accepted me gladly. Just a block up the street from us was a very, very beautiful little Methodist church, right on the corner of the North Park. In due course, I got to know the young student pastor there. My building was falling apart and I had about 400 members and the largest attendance on Sundays. His building was in a beautiful condition, well located, had a manse, had a parish house. He had an attendance of only fifteen people. And, in addition, he had a large endowment.

So, it seemed obvious to us that we should have a federation here of this congregation and of that building, so to speak. We worked at it and persuaded our people that this was the only sensible thing to do, to create a federation where the Methodists could remain Methodists and the Baptists Baptists. They could follow their respective liturgical traditions, as in baptism, for example, but they would have a pastor in common and he could be not a student but a fulltime pastor.

Q: I imagine it was more difficult to persuade the small group of Methodists than it was - ?

Capt. J.: Actually, no. Both groups were surprisingly easy to persuade, especially when I said to my people, "Think of the people you know who go to this little church. They're all neighbors." It was not at all a matter of joining up with strangers if you follow me. And so they became convinced that it was the most natural thing in the world.

But, at this point, we ran into the Methodist bureaucracy.

The young student pastor said, "I must go and see the district superintendent. You come along and we'll talk with him and get his approval." The district superintendent said yes, but, he said, "we must always have a Methodist pastor because we have this system whereby we can't have more pastors than charges and it's all got to come out even." So I said I'd talk to my people and ask them if they would be willing to accept this, although we were by far the larger element. The people did gladly accept it.

We established as our requirement that this person be reasonably young and physically vigorous so that he could do active pastoral work, pastoral calling and that kind of thing. We'd wanted a person about thirty-five years of age. It turned out that the new church would be able to offer a minister in 1940 a manse and $2,750, which at that time in that place was considered to be a reasonably good salary. We brought this proposal to the district superintendent and he agreed. So, in June we had our first common worship together, with the student pastor and I officiating together. By the next Sunday the new pastor had come. They had named a man who was over sixty years old, whose wife was a battle ax, to take over the new church. I went over there and complained bitterly to this man.

Q: To the pastor?

Capt. J.: To the superintendent. His reply was to me a classic of its kind, the death knell of the church, if ever I heard it. He said, "Well, when it came to comforts, it became very clear that we couldn't send a $1,500 man into a $2,750 church. I had to select from among those who deserved and rated that salary on the basis of seniority, and that's why I had to send him."

And I said, "Why didn't you tell us? Once we had made the agreement, why didn't you call us and say you'd had to change your mind, in which case I could have gone to the people and told them there was a new ball game and asked them what they wanted to do."

As it was, this man came in and he was a fine person, but not active physically, and his wife tore the whole church apart in two years.

Q: That's rather sad!

Capt. J.: Oh, very sad.

Q: An opportunity missed!

Capt. J.: Yes. Here was a priceless opportunity. Had that church survived, we would have had in the north end a strong Episcopal St. James's Church, a strong mainline Protestant witness and a strong Roman Catholic one. This would have served people in the most economical way possible in terms of personnel and finances, and would have given them also a considerable degree of choice.

Q: The plans you and the other chap made with this amalgamation certainly indicated wisdom and maturity.

Capt. J.: There are many things in my life on which I can look back with not very much satisfaction. I look back on this with considerable happiness. It seems to me that we did envision the general welfare of the community ahead of other considerations that were perfectly valid in themselves but which shouldn't have come first in that instance. I talked to my people about accepting a Methodist minister permanently and they were bothered by this, as you might expect, but their Christian priorities were in order.

My Methodist colleague and I were agreed that neither of us would be named pastor so the church would have a fresh start.

Q: Well, as it turned out, it must have been terribly disappointing to an idealistic young student pastor?

Capt. J.: Oh, it was and to our parishioners as well. My Methodist partner has been dead for many years. I was angry and he was angry. He was also vastly embarrassed because it was the system of his church, as he saw it, that had gotten in the way. He did not remain long in the ministry.

Q: But it didn't deter you from continuing your course?

Capt. J.: No. I think it made me in some ways a wiser man and less prejudiced.

Q: Tell me about your career as it developed from that point.

Capt. J.: Ruth and I were married in the same month in which I was ordained, but before that month, November, I had gone to be the pastor of the First Baptist Church in Woonsocket, Rhode Island. This was a small church in a town that was 95 per cent Roman Catholic, heavily French-speaking. I was received there by the Catholic clergy and the Protestant clergy with great warmth. Across the street from our manse was the rectory of the Catholic church, and the old pastor, a Frenchman in his seventies, came over to greet me and offered me welcome to the town. This was in 1940 when this kind of thing was not commonplace. Often during the short time, a little over a year, that I was there we talked together, to my great benefit. He acted toward me as a father and guide, as he should have acted toward me. Very few people were doing that in those days.

Q: How many people did you have in your congregation?

Capt. J.: About 150, but the curious thing was that there were very few men. Actually, 150 was the membership, I guess the attendance in those days would have been about 30. That gradually grew and the number of men grew quite dramatically, not because, I think, of anything that I had to offer so much as because the other churches were offering very little to men. Almost by accident I started a men's instruction class in the Christian faith. Well, I found that there was almost a hunger on the part of many men in the city for this. First, the men's instruction started with maybe four and then in a few weeks there were ten and then about thirty or thirty-five coming every week. Some of the discussions were doctrinal, some then had to do with the implications, especially the ethical implications, of the faith, some had to do with the nature of Christian nurture and Christian devotion. Some of these subjects the men didn't have much interest in. About others they had great interest, especially those which had to do with Christian doctrine.

It seemed to me then, and later in my Navy experience tended to verify this, that Protestants, generally speaking, are not well taught with regard to any systematic Christian doctrine. They have a little bit here and a little bit there. Christmas, of course, they know and Easter after a fashion, but because they don't have the church year, a way in which to preach a rounded gospel for the year, they end up getting as their nourishment things that the pastors are interested in. A pastor may be considerably interested in one thing and not in many other things that the people should be fed.

Perhaps, at that point, the class met some needs, and then the men gradually began to come to church.

Q: This was also on the verge of World War II, wasn't it? Was this a factor, perhaps?

Capt. J.: I don't know. I don't think so. I don't recall that it was a factor. Indeed, if I had any feeling at that time, it was that my people were not abreast of the situation in the world as I thought they should be. I was, as you might expect, an active proponent of intervention, and this of course shocked my father. He didn't like the military, largely for the reasons that I've mentioned. He knew that this was my position. I made my position public in town and in the pulpit. I felt that my people were not so much active isolationists as simply not au courant with what was happening in the world. It seemed to me at that time that one of my tasks was to make them aware of some very dangerous trends that were abroad not only in Germany and Italy but in this country.

I think there was a degree of response to that. There was also a degree of negative feeling, of people saying this young man should preach religion in the pulpit, he shouldn't preach politics and economics.

Q: But it does indicate that you were a vigorous preacher and this, in turn, may have attracted the men?

Capt. J.: I don't know. I don't think I was a very good preacher. If there was any value in my preaching, I think it had to do with the strength with which I felt things and my communication of the things that I believed. I would be shocked, I'm sure, to read now the sermons I was preaching in those days, not so much that I would disagree with what they said then, but because of what I think must have been a general lack of skill in the homiletic art. I was a poor preacher.

Q: But the conviction was the overriding thing?

Capt. J.: I think so, I think that one way or another I communicated this, either to the edification of the people or to their occasional anger and unhappines..

Q: Well, controversy in the pulpit sometimes is a very engaging thing!

Capt. J.: It is. I don't know who it was who said that the function of the minister was to set himself on fire in the pulpit. I don't know that I did that, but I was deeply involved with the things that I preached during that phase of my life.

Q: How did you take to the pastoral life?

Capt. J.: Poorly, I think. My predecessor had been a saintly man whom I could never in several lifetimes hope to equal. He cared for people, one by one, picked up all the women for the women's meetings and drove them to the meetings, and went to the meetings. Let's face it, women very frequently are the heart of the church. I can understand why he did this. When I went to that church and saw this, I talked to the leader of the women. I said I shall be glad to visit you once a year or on call if there's something you want me to do, but I'm not going to be a regular attendant at your meetings. You run your own show. Also I asked them not to give my wife any honorary positions. She's a twenty-year-old girl I said. Let her belong to the church and enjoy being one of your sisters without thinking she's going to run things. They were very pleased about this.

I think I would not have been a success if I had remained a parish minister. I was zealous in my caring for the sick, called on people and all of this, but I think that in the parish I was probably a square peg in a round hole. I think in the providence of God it was a good thing that I was taken from there into the Navy, where I felt that my own shortcomings would be compensated for by the nature of the life.

Q: That's a very interesting analysis.

Capt. J.: Well, I could be mistaken but I don't know what contribution I would have made to a civilian parish.

Q: You said that quite naturally you were an interventionist, but it wasn't so natural, at least in certain parts of our country. What induced you to be?

Capt. J.: I don't think I had any more interest than many people in the affairs of the world until, of course, I got to college and, started to do a little history. I read about Versailles and I began to look at events of our time with some of the perspective that history gives. I saw in Nazism and in Fascism some very, very old phenomena come back to life in our time. These feelings of mine were then set ablaze by the Spanish civil war.

I contemplated the possibility of joining one of the international brigades to go over there. From that time onward, I was increasingly aware of what was happening in Europe and in the nation. It seemed very clear to me, after the Czechoslovakia thing, that war was only a matter of time. I remember being very angry at Roosevelt for refusing during that period of time to build up armaments, for telling people that somehow we could participate in this world and still escape going into the war, which I thought was not possible. In 1940, of course, the thing came to a head and the country had to make up its mind. It had to decide basically whether it was going to let Britain go down.

I believe the country, in spite of America First and the Bund and the newspapers -

Q: George Sylvester Viereck!

Capt. J.: Viereck, indeed! In spite of all this I think the country concluded that this thing may have elements we don't completely understand but we are not going to let Britain go down. I think it came down to something as simple as that. I don't think the country still saw all the issues that were at work in this.

So, I think at this time a process of education began which culminated in those very remarkable five years after the war which were to me five years of creative sanity with the Marshall Plan, rebuilding Germany and Japan. I don't know any other country at any other time which had moved so quickly from the passion of war, and it was a passionate war, to the necessities of peace and had seen them as necessities. When I think of Clemenceau, Lloyd George and the old realpolitik at work in 1919 of Henry Cabot Lodge and Wilson, then when I think of 1946 and President Truman and George Marshall, it is to marvel at their greatness. These men suddenly found a world for which they had not been fitted but in which they chose to fit, suddenly growing into the demands of the world, as men have seldom done.

Q: Yet it hadn't started out that way. We had unconditional surrender -

Capt. J.: That was so stupid.

Q: And the Morgenthau Plan for Germany.

Capt. J.: All of this you remember.

Q: Yes.

Capt. J.: And so stupid. I've become rather philosophical about our stupidities, having seen them then.

By this time, too, I had begun to read some military history and this was one reason why I became so excited about this short five- or six-year period when I saw that we finally had learned something. We had learned that Morgenthau was wrong. Germany would never remain an agricultural society. And the unconditional surrender thing was stupid, simply stupid, and it made the war last some eighteen months longer than it otherwise would have. If you don't leave a hole for them to climb out of then you're going to have to fight. It cost us hundreds of thousands of casualties. And I was against it them. It was simply bad strategy, a stupid strategy. Roosevelt I could understand, but Churchill! That Churchill should have bought it amazed me, because Churchill, supposedly, had a world of experience, but he went along.

Q: Well, let's go back to 1940 now.

Capt. J.: Yes.

Q: You were still in Rhode Island?

Capt. J.: Still in Rhode Island. Then the church there was lucky to lose me! Although I must say we enjoyed that parish, very, very much. We loved the people and the people were much better to us than I deserved. We had all of the difficulties that young ministers have. We had the water bust in the manse and water all over the decks -

Q: And lack of money!

Capt. J.: Oh, lack of money, indeed. Ruthie said to me some few years ago - she had found a piece of paper on which she had written "We can either go to the movies on Saturday or bowling, but not both." That's the way it was, and I don't think that life was any the less rich for it. In some ways, we had some wonderful experiences there.

Q: Had she had any experience in church work and the ministry?

Capt. J.: She'd been a very devoted member of the Union Methodist Church in Fall River. We'd met, as a matter of fact, through this. The young people of her church were having an Easter sunrise service and they're the bane of my life. I hate them with a passion. Anyway, they invited me to speak at this Easter sunrise service and arranged that I would be picked up. So half-asleep at 5:30 one morning I boarded her automobile. She said that I scarcely looked at her, which is probably true. I spoke and had breakfast, then I had to go and have services in my own church.

I saw her again the following Sunday and before long it occurred to me for my own welfare that I should have her as partner for life. We were married in November two years later in my little parish in Woonsocket.

Q: So she had some kind of an introduction to the life of a church?

Capt. J.: Oh, yes. She'd also been close to the minister and his wife in her own parish. The daughter of the minister was her best friend. So she had over a number of years seen what happens in a manse and gotten a general idea of what the life was like. She was only twenty when we were married. The great thing that happened was when I said to the ladies, "Leave her alone" they agreed. They let her alone, and they were very proud of the young wife of the young minister, and she very much was a part of things without having to be the boss of everything.

Then when Pearl Harbor came - I tried to get into the Navy before Pearl Harbor and wasn't accepted because I was underweight.

Q: You tried to go in as a Navy chaplain?

Capt. J.: As a Navy chaplain. I tried to go in as any kind of a chaplain. Bob Coe, now retired in California, was our very dear friend, our best man, a seminary classmate. He came down one day and said, "You must join the Navy." He said, "I have just joined the Navy and I'm going down in a couple of weeks to Newport." If you join the Navy, you go on all the big battleships and you have beautiful silver and clean linen and that's the only way to fight a war.

I don't know how much I was impressed by that, but I was impressed by seeing the chaplains at Newport. So I tried the Navy and got nowhere. But after Pearl Harbor I tried again and I was accepted.

Q: There was a need then?

Capt. J.: Yes, the whole situation had changed.

I told my parishioners I was trying to do this. Their attitude was one generally of approval. Even those who disagreed with it said basically "Your position is well known, what you're doing is consistent with what you believe."

Q: Sounds like a very intelligent congregation you had?

Capt. J.: It was a very wonderful congregation. They were great people. Finally, when I was accepted by the Navy, I told them, and I gave them my resignation. They wanted me to promise to come back -

Q: You mean after serving?

Capt. J.: After the war. I said "It's going to be a long war and you don't know how you are going to feel at its end. I think it is just fairer all around to sever our pastoral relationship and to retain our personal friendships."

Q: You couldn't have done that, anyway, could you?

Capt. J.: Oh, I don't think so, although I think they would have tried to do it, but it simply couldn't have worked in any way.

Q: Well, as it turned out, with the war lasting as long as it did, you would have been in the service?

Capt. J.: I would have had to write from some place and say, "Hey, I'm resigning, you'd better get a pastor." It worked out well as it was. They got a pastor reasonably soon. He and his successor are very good people and served the church proudly. It was a good thing I left.

Q: So, you went into the Navy very shortly after Pearl Harbor?

Capt. J.: I entered the Navy in March of 1942. I had applied and I hadn't heard anything, weeks went by, and finally I said to Ruthie "I'm going down and see the Army." I wrote to BuPers and said, "I've had my application in all this time and nothing has happened. I guess you aren't interested, so I'm going down now to see the Army." And within forty-eight hours I had my orders.

Q: How did your bride feel about this?

Capt. J.: She accepted it. I think her basic thinking was that I had to do what I felt I had to do. I don't think she was happy at the thought of my going to war but she accepted its necessity.

Q: So, you got your orders?

Capt. J.: I got my orders to the chaplains' school at Norfolk. It had just been made into one school. They'd had a school up in New York run by Stan Salisbury.

Q: That was at ?

Capt. J.: It was at Fort Schuyler. There was a school down at Norfolk, too, and they decided that they would do better if they united the schools, and they did.

When I started in the school, it was an eight-week course, but I didn't finish. Before I got through it there was a curious situation. When we took our physicals there, among other things they checked us on push-ups. I did an amazing number of push-ups, so they figured I was ready for some kind of physically demanding action. It turned out that I did set a record that wasn't broken till 1945. It may not be the greatest thing to be remembered by, you know, but there it was!

Q: Had you been athletically inclined prior to that?

Capt. J.: Oh, yes. I'd never been push-ups inclined, gymnastics-inclined, but I played baseball and I played football. I was interested in athletics in general. But when they needed two chaplains for the First Marine Division, which was then in LeJeune, they called out and said who have you got that's physically active. And they said, "Jones, he's not very bright but he is physically active!"

So after four weeks, one day I got called in and Chaplain Neyman said, "You and Sovik have got orders to go to the First Division."

Q: Sovik?

Capt. J.: Ansgar Sovik. I think Ansgar is now the president of

St. Olaf's College. So Ansgar and I went to Lejeune. We were driven down there overnight by a sailor because we had to report in twenty-four hours. The division was already leaving, so they issued our 782 gear. Then it turned out they were only going to take one chaplain. We were called in before the assistant Division Commander, General Rupertuis. He questioned us. He was a Roman Catholic himself, a very devoted Christian. He said, "Well, we need a liturgical Protestant chaplain. Sovic you're the guy." He said to me, "I'm sorry but we're going to have to leave you."

This was a real blow, you know, to me.

Q: Being penalized for being a Baptist?

Capt. J.: It looked that way, and, of course, being stupid and young, I had the feeling, gee, the war's going to be over before I get into it. Of course, Rupertuis knew better than that. I was left in Lejeune. The division shoved off, and I was transferred to the Third Marines, an independent regiment at that time. We were wondering where we were going, but in due course we were assigned as a regiment to the Third Marine Division with the 21st Marines, who were there with us at Camp Lejeune.

Q: Let's lap back for a minute and tell me about the school, where you spent four weeks. What kind of indoctrination did you get?

Capt. J.: I think it was pretty good. A lot of it was irrelevant to my immediate need. In other words, a lot of it was relevant to one who was going to have a career as a Navy chaplain, but I didn't immediately need to know anything about the Navy Relief Society and things of that sort, which we took, and which were helpful in the long haul.

We didn't have anyone at the school, furthermore, who had had field duty with the Marines. As a matter of fact, I had the feeling that maybe I was the first man who had duty in the field and in combat with the Marines who was on the faculty of the chaplains' school. I may be wrong on this. There was nothing about the Marines much, anyway, except a chaplain who served in the Marine barracks at Quantico who said Marines are very unusual people and if you get to serve them you'll find them so, period.

Q: But the school as constituted at that point was still a carry-over from peacetime, wasn't it?

Capt. J.: Yes, indeed, it was. As a matter of fact, as I look back at it, I'm amazed at how good it was. Its origin was rather simple. Chaplain Clinton Neyman, while he was on duty in the Philippines, unlike Roland had ended up with quite a lot of time on his hands.

Q: He didn't have as many jobs?

Capt. J.: Didn't have as many jobs, maybe. Also, he was a reflective kind of a fellow, so he sat down and spent some time preparing a manual for the Chaplain Corps. It's fascinating. I still may have a copy of that document around. He also prepared a curriculum of the chaplains' school that was Neyman's. It was later modified, but during my stay at the school, and I was able to see the modifications and the additions, the thing that surprised me was how much of what he had placed there in 1938 remained in the curriculum. The thing that it really taught me was the importance of imagination and planning in advance. Save for Neyman the Chaplain Corps would have been totally unprepared for indoctrinating the young clergymen at war's beginning. Clergy are very hard people to teach. They're people who, by the nature of the case, are committed to their own beliefs and committed in a profound way, and not likely to take easily a liking to new things that are being told. So I found them and in some ways, it's probably a pretty good characteristic. But it does mean clergy are not easily indoctrinated.

Q: Even in seminary!

Capt. J.: I guess even in seminary they're not. So that's what we had, and I thought it was a good school. I only had half of it.

Q: But you didn't feel inadequate when you went off into the Marines?

Capt. J.: Well, I was too inexperienced to feel inadequate, but I had sufficient motivation to want to do what I could do, and so I went around to seek for things to do and there were things to do.

Q: How much carryover was there from your parish work?

Capt. J.: None. Everything was different, and I had to learn, in a sense, the hard way because the school hadn't taught me, couldn't have taught me at that point, but I gradually and slowly did learn.

I had to make my own way, in a sense. The Marines are my favorite people, I served longer with them than anywhere else, I know them better, and they're tremendous people. The Marines don't expect the apocalypse from a new chaplain. All they ask is "Is the guy trying to learn, is he trying to belong, does he like people, does he want to serve people?" - these are the questions they ask. And if you have the right answers to those questions, then what you don't know is easily supplied. It doesn't matter at all. OK, the chaplain will serve you. And this is the way you put the web belt on, the whole bit, so they take care of you. And the understanding is that when the time comes, you're going to take care of them. If that covenant works out, the chaplain, I feel, has the best of all possible worlds. The Marine Corps is the best place in the world for a chaplain, at least for some chaplains.

I'm sure there are chaplains who don't feel that way. Frankly, I don't really understand how a chaplain could fail to feel like that. They took care of me. I was a babe in arms and I needed to be taken care of!

Q: During that period when you were a "babe in arms," what was expected of you? What did you do?

Capt. J.: There were two things I could have done at that time that were effective. The first was to take care of myself, to make sure that I was equipped to go out, and the second thing was to stay out of the way. These people were combat-loading, they were desperately doing their last training in the field before going overseas.

The best thing I could do was make sure that I had my own equipment and that I trained so far as I could with the troops. There was no one to train a chaplain.

Q: There was no other chaplain available?

Capt. J.: For a time I was the only chaplain at Lejeune. When there were other chaplains available they were as green as I was. As a matter of fact, in due course they became greener than I was because I was one of the few chaplains - my regiment was the only one down there for a while, for a couple of weeks - so I got some landings and field training. In due course, the 21st came in and they got a couple of chaplains.

Then there came to my regiment a Catholic chaplain, Frank Sullivan, a Jesuit.

Q: Had he had any experience?

Capt. J.: Oh, no. As a matter of fact, I don't Frank ever gained any experience. Apart from what he did, which was priceless. In a sense the only thing he needed to do, was to be himself. He had to be cared for from hand to mouth all the time he was with the regiment. You never knew where he was, he couldn't read a compass, you know, he was lost. Well, many of those things I could take care of and help him with, but in the basic things he was taking care of me. He was the pastor pastorum and once he saw that these were things I needed to learn, he set about to help teach me. He was willing himself to learn the things that I could teach him about functioning in the Marines. There wasn't much I could teach him then, it was more later, perhaps. But he was a priceless companion and we remained bosom friends until his death.

I sent down to you, I think, a letter I had written to The Boston Globe when I read his obituary, which gives you a little bit of the spirit of the man. So I'm grateful that my first senior in the Corps, so to speak, as a pastor was Frank Sullivan.

We had some interesting experiences down there. Frank was not only a Jesuit, he was Irish and he had a rather short fuse and on occasion he would blow up, and sometimes for the good of the community. I had a man, a Catholic, come into my tent - he was a retread - and he used to go every night to the officers' club and he'd really tie one on. Then about two in the morning, he'd come raging in and wake everybody up. The tents in those days had Franklin stoves, something like them, cast-iron stoves in the middle of the tent. I spoke to this officer and said, "Look, next time, if you've got to sound off, don't come to our tent. Shove off some place else. This is my tent." Well, he went out one night and Frank and I were commiserating about being woken in the middle of the night. I said to Frank, "Well, okay, let's find out how well this guy can take care of himself."

Before we went to bed, I took his footlocker and put it right at the door of the tent. And, sure enough, about two o'clock in the morning, he came raging and raving and singing out. Well, he tripped over the footlocker and went headfirst right into the stove. It sounded as if he had scalped himself. We put the lights on to see, and there he was, lying on the deck. He was conscious and he was angry.

Q: Was he sober at that point?

Capt. J.: No, he wasn't sober but he was a lot soberer than he'd been a minute before! He said, "I'm never going to stay with you guys again," and he shoved off and fell over it again on the way out. He slept some place else and then the next morning he took his gear and went away and that was the last I saw of him.

Frank was called up to D.C. by the Jesuits for something and he had a car that the order had given him. So he left instructions for me to have the car to drive around. Well, a motor transport captain found out about this. So he got the keys to the car and he just drove the car around for almost two weeks. About a day before Frank returned he wrecked the car. I didn't know about it, and Frank came in and said, "Where's the car?" I said, "I don't know, I haven't seen it." He chased it down and finally found it.

Then I had to hold Frank down because he had to try to explain to the order what had happened to the car.

Q: Oh, it was owned by his order?

Capt. J.: Yes. He couldn't own a thing. He was a Jesuit. It was owned by the order. So this was the kind of experience we were having. It was making us sort of grow up in a hurry about living and working with men.

G. Jones #1 - 32

Q: What were your clerical responsibilities there?

Capt. J.: For the most part it was counselling.

Q: Counselling?

Capt. J.: Yes, and I think perhaps in all my time in the Navy that has been the single most important ministry for me, and I think for many chaplains. Servicemen turn much more readily to their chaplains for counsel, I think, than civilian churchmen go to their pastor. People whom you couldn't drive into the church, so to speak, at the outset of a personal problem go to see the chaplain.

And so I was busy a great part of the day counseling.

Q: They go to see the chaplain, but not in a religious context?

Capt. J.: Not many of them in a religious context. Many have needs of all kinds, home problems, love affairs, disciplinary problems in the regiment, personal problems of adjustment - not very often religious problems. Some men come in who want to get out of the service, other men come in because they've been told they couldn't go overseas. That's the way I got my clerk in the Third Marines.

This fellow came in one day, he was a Jewish fellow, and he was crying. When I got him calmed down, he said he'd joined the Marine Corps to fight Hitler and now he had just heard that he couldn't go overseas because he was too old, he was thirty-three, and his feet were flat. Couldn't I do something.

I figured if you've got a man who wants to fight, let him go. So I went to see my colonel and I said I've got this man and he wants to fight and everybody in personnel has said he can't go. Well, he said, he shouldn't go but "I tell you, I'll make a deal with you. If you'll take him as a clerk, he may go." So I said check because I wasn't going to be doing an awful lot of typing or anything.

So Fred Stark came to me. In civilian life he'd been a gambler by profession. He was not what you'd call a practicing Jew, but when Hitler started to burn these people he suddenly became aware of his heritage and he wanted to do something about it and he was a great clerk. He took care of my odd jobs and we embarked together. When we were in the transport, going out, we had an awful lot of really green people, it was unbelievable, in the regiment. The old cadre NCQs were fleecing them by the ton, gambling, you know. The colonel talked to me about it and said, "What can you do about it?" I said I didn't think I could do anything.

So I talked to Fred. Well, he was a gambler but he said it was wrong to go after these green kids. He also was manager of Freddie Apostoli, who later became middleweight champion of the world, and Fred knew how to handle his fists. So he said: "You leave it to me. I'm not going to tell you anything, but I'm going to straighten this out." So he sat in on a couple of games and exposed a couple of sharks, and the word quickly got around the whole ship, "Watch anybody with a deck of cards." And so the gambling ceased, almost, just like that, except among the NCOs themselves.

Q: A talent you wouldn't ordinarily expect to find in a clerk!

Capt. J.: You wouldn't but there it was. It's something that could happen in the service and wouldn't happen any place else.

Q: You were talking about the various men who came to you and the kind of problems they had. What power did you have to help solve these problems? What authority did you have?

Capt. J.: Oh, authority, none, not in the sense of military command. A chaplain doesn't have that. Moral authority, quite a lot, and also other things were helpful. I could, for example, once my credentials were established, go down to G-1 and say a kid has this problem, can you do this, can you do that, and if they could they would. For problems at home, the Red Cross was present and tremendously useful. So this was a strong weapon for my use.

Some things worked out. I heard that there were some Third Marines in the jail in Jacksonville, and so I went to call on them. I found out that these were some eighteen-year-old kids. They had stolen a tire and they'd been apprehended. At that time, stealing a tire was something like a felony because of the shortage of rubber and so forth. This judge, some traveling jurist, had given them five years in jail, and the jail in Jacksonville was unbelieveable. There was a little harridan by the name of Ma Elliott who ran it. The windows were open and mosquitoes were coming in and biting these kids. I talked to her about this and her attitude was they deserve anything they get.

So I went to see the judge and I said here's this five-year sentence and a couple of these kids are only a year removed from juvenile jurisdiction, and this five years in jail down here isn't going to do anybody any good, not you, not them, not the country. Why don't you let them go, let them come back with me to the regiment. Well, he couldn't see it. He said, "We've got to make examples." And I was thinking making examples is bad law. This means we don't have equality in law. Some people get hit harder than other people for your local purposes. I was too dull to realize that I was trying to influence a judge!

Q: But you did it selflessly!

Capt. J.: Oh, of course. Well, the old guy got very teed off at me, but I was getting teed off, too, in my own way, and I said, "The best thing you can do is call those kids up in front of you and chew them up and release them into my custody. That's the best thing you can do."

Q: But he'd already sentenced them?

Capt. J.: He had, and he said, "I'm not about to have some Yankee come down here and tell me what's the best thing I can do." Well, I said, "Do you want to get your name in the paper?" and he said "Why?" "Well," I said, "I'm going to put your name in the paper and you're going to be known as the hanging judge who sentenced four teenagers to five years in the clink."

And, do you know, that bothered him. I said, "I have friends in New York," and he stopped and said, "Let me think about it. Finally he said, "All right, I'll do it."

Q: He was going to put them in your custody?

Capt. J.: Put them in my custody.

Q: How could he rescind the sentence?

Capt. J.: He just blocked it off, changed his mind, rescinded it, took it back. Law in the South, you know, is not always an exact science.

Q: When the sentence was given to those lads, did not the Marine Corps take some interest in it, other than examples?

Capt. J.: It didn't. Today, were such a thing to happen, the Marine Corps would be in there with four fists right away to see what the story was, but the situation in Tent Camp at this point was so confused that I think it was only by accident that anyone discovered that these people were absent, to say nothing that they had been tried and convicted.

I remember going to see the legal officer before going to see the judge again, and his attitude was that nothing could be done. They'd been sentenced, which probably was the legally correct thing, and he was quite surprised when I showed up with them in tow. The kids never forgot it and they became solid supporters of mine in the regiment.

Q: I would think so! You made mention of the fact that you had considerable moral authority.

Capt. J.: Yes.

Q: Was this something that accrued to a chaplain per se, or was it something that you had already earned?

Capt. J.: That's hard to answer. I don't know. I'm speaking now of this period. When I went back to the Marines a second time I had money in the bank in terms of moral authority.

Q: A treasury of merits, then?

Capt. J.: For those people, a treasury of merits. I had served with the Marines, I knew Marines, I'd been in combat with Marines, I'd been decorated by the Marines. I arrived and I was known. It wasn't this way in 1942.

Q: No, you were a novice!

Capt. J.: I was, oh, a novice is putting it mildly. But I think that among Marines there is a strong tendency toward fair play, toward making sure that a man has his chance before he's counted out. And, if he thinks that you are doing all you can, he'll give you a chance, then he votes in your favor. This doesn't mean necessarily that he's religious in other matters. It means that he's going to be on your side in terms of you trying to do your job. And this kind of thing happens for many reasons, some of which, you know, you wouldn't necessarily go to the Baptist Convention and boast about it.

I remember we were on Guadalcanal and we had trouble with torpedo juice. We had a Seabee battalion with us in the 19th Marines. Unbeknownst to me they had a still. It had beautiful copper tubing, the whole business. One day I was moving across the division from one regiment to another regiment and I ran across this still, which was well concealed. I looked it over, recognized that it was a still and I went away. The next day, my colonel, who was Speed Cauldwell, ran into me and he said, "Say, I'm going over to the 21st Marines. Where are you going?" And I said, "I'm going to the 21st Marines, too." "Oh, he said, "let's go together," and so we did.

I took him a long way around so that he wouldn't see the still. My reasoning was that torpedo juice, made by straining wood alcohol through bread, had already blinded several Marines. The Seabees can do anything. If there's going to be anything potable on this island that isn't brought in it will be something that the Seabees have made. Why knock in the head, so to speak, a going proposition that isn't basically going to hurt many people or things?

Well, I brought the colonel back after our errands and that day there came to my tent two Seabees. They wanted to know how I was getting along, and I said, "Fine. How are you?" Fine, they said, and they talked about our chapel and said, "Don't you need something?" I said no, not particularly. "Well, do you need an altar?" I was using some table as an altar and it was all right.

"Well," they said, "you ought to have an altar." I said, "OK, where can I get one?" and they said, "We'll make it for you," and they did, mahogany, no less - an altar and a lectern and a pulpit.

We weren't near Henderson. There was a little chapel at Henderson, but here at Koli Point I had these equipages which I've not run into since. Somebody had seen me that first day and then the word had gotten around, you know, that the good deal is over, I guess. Then they saw me the next day escort the colonel all the way round and they figured I wasn't going to blow it. So from that point on nothing was too good for me.

Q: That's an interesting story.

Capt. J.: I don't know that I should feel particularly proud about it, but I felt then, and I was much younger then, that there are times when turning your eyes the other way may not be the worst thing. If the chaplain is aware of every bloody thing that happens everywhere and doesn't have solutions for the problems that they're up against, then until he's called on to do something, it's better sometimes to stand away. If they think he's a policeman, it never works for the rest of them. He's got the wrong role.

So I look back at it and I still don't think I did wrong.

Q: You were down at Jacksonville?

Capt. J.: Yes.

Q: You were learning fast!

Capt. J.: And the hard way, but with a lot of good friends around to help.

I made my first amphibious landings, I was able to read a compass, which many chaplains weren't able to do! I had in a sense grown up being able to use the woods, so that I was not in all ways unprepared for this. I was physically active and was able to stay abreast on the marches.

Q: What was your relationship with the officers when you were still in the States? How did they accept the chaplain?

Capt. J.: There are different kinds of officers. We had young NROTC kids, just out as second lieutenants, and they looked at me pretty much, I think, as they looked at clergy. There were the old retreads who came from the days when there were few, if any, chaplains when it was a phenomenal thing to see a chaplain in the Marine Corps, although they'd had two in particular who distinguished themselves for bravery in World War I. And then there were the old regular Marines, and the old regular Marines were on your side. They would back you up and support you if they felt that you wanted to learn, they'd try to be of help, and they accepted you as being as much a part of the regiment as any Marine was.

So it took some time to get on the wavelength of the Marines and, in some cases, of the retreads, but all the regulars basically had known chaplains. I guess they had varying experiences but basically favorable, so I didn't have any great problems with them.

Q: Did you make any conscious effort with these young ones and retreads, as you call them?

Capt. J.: I did with the young platoon leaders, and I did almost as a function of my pastoral work again and again and again in counseling the men. I'd find that a man would come to me who should have seen his platoon leader. I would send the man back and I would see the platoon leader and tell him that the man came to me when he should have come to him. And basically I said when any of your men want to come to me you make sure they are allowed to, but, I said, I don't want to see any of your men who want to come to me to get away from you. And this philosophy worked so in due course, I think, they accepted it.

Q: What kind of worship services were you required to conduct?

Capt. J.: I conducted basically any kind of services I could, given the situation. They were generally almost always simple. I found that with the exception of the sacraments, this was true of all chaplains. You didn't have the complete liturgy. The Episcopal chaplain didn't have Morning Prayer in the accepted sense of Morning Prayer. You'd have a much simpler service. He'd celebrate the Eucharist and the same with the Lutheran chaplains. A sermon they would not have but they would have a much shorter form of worship for any service but the Eucharist. Later the men tended to celebrate the Eucharist in the brief form.

Q: Before they went abroad, what kind of attendance did you have?

Capt. J.: Very poor. I can remember holding services in messhalls and there'd be ten or eleven. I remember one Sunday, Ruthie played for me. I couldn't find a man to play the piano. She played the piano. When she started to play all kinds of bugs came out of it and she screamed! We'd have very few people, but the worship had been announced and everyone knew I was there.

There were from time to time large weekends of leave and this was the last chance for the men to go home and so they wouldn't be around for church.

Q: Now, to depart with the Marines from the States. Were there any of the boys who indicated a fear of what they were getting into?

Capt. J.: Yes. They didn't constitute a large number. I would say most of the people had a bravado of ignorance. They were entirely confident that they could take care of so many Japs and all of this kind of thing. There were others who were afraid. They could, however, for the most part be talked to.

Q: Did they come to you?

Capt. J.: Oh, yes, they would come, and I think perhaps the thing that helped them most was when I said that I was afraid, too. I hadn't been in combat and I didn't know what would happen. I knew people got killed in this kind of thing. And I think it gave them a measure of confidence to know this. I ran into, as you always do, a few cases that were pathological and you'd turn them over to the doctor. I ran into a few odd balls, people who'd gotten in by mistake. But, basically, the men who were afraid - most of those that I worked with - were not afraid to come to me and we'd talk about how they were afraid.

We left by train. I was, at that point, with the First Engineer Battalion, assigned to go with them by train.

Q: Destination unknown?

Capt. J.: At that point, destination unknown. We went down through New Orleans. My train commander was Lieutenant Colonel Muggs Riley, commander of the First Engineer Battalion. He and I got to be quite good friends. In the middle of the desert one day we were talking to him about the Reising gun, you remember the old sub-machine gun which appeared to have been stamped out of tin. We were saying this doesn't look like too much of a weapon and he was saying it's a hell of a weapon. Finally, he pulled the switch and and stopped the train and he said, "Come on out and I'll show you."

Q: Immediate demonstration!

Capt. J.: Right there, you know. Of course, the train stopped, all the Marines got out and Muggs said, "Come on and I'll show you." He told us how to hold down the strap and keep the muzzle down when you fired full automatic. Then he invited Frank to fire. He forgot to hold down the muzzle and the thing went brrrrr like this and the muzzle rose and the volley cut some telegraph wires. Well, the moment Muggs saw that he said, "All aboard, shove off," and we did. I never heard whether anything happened as a consequence.

It got to be quite a story in the Marine Corps.

Q: You didn't have your chance?

Capt. J.: Exactly.

We arrived in San Diego and took off from San Diego in one of the old Matson liners, the Lurline. She hadn't yet been converted and so the civilian crew was aboard.

Q: This was going to Honolulu?

Capt. J.: No. This was going from San Diego directly to Samoa. The captain was a man by the name of Van Orden, who was a cousin of a battalion commander of ours, of our 2nd Battalion, George Van Orden, who retired as a brigadier general.

It was a new experience for many of us. We ate very well. I held daily services in the early morning and they were very well attended.

Q: What date was this, approximately?

Capt. J.: I think it was August 1942, but I'm not quite sure. We had a very good crew. On our cruise to Samoa we were accompanied by the old Detroit, a light cruiser.

Q: She was the only escort?

Capt. J.: We had the Detroit, two destroyers and a reefer. There were four ships. I forget her name. I should remember her name because she had constant engine trouble. One day everything just conked out and she slowed to a stop. Our captain, who was a very high-geared guy, just about went out of his mind with that thing stopped out there. He was thinking of Jap submarines and all the rest and all we could do was to cruise in circles until they finally got the thing fixed and we got under way again.

We had quite a bit of training on board ship in small arms and in things like that.

Q: You say "we." The chaplain also?

Capt. J.: The Marines, yes. As a chaplain, you could get any training you wanted.

Q: Oh, you could?

Capt. J.: Oh, yes, it was done by the Marines and basically I took what I could. I don't think Sully quite agreed with it - that anything I learned was going to be helpful some time. So I learned quite a bit about weapons.

Q: It was a good pastoral technique, too, wasn't it?

Capt. J.: Yes, it was.

Q: You were a worker-priest.

Capt. J.: I was, indeed, and I got to know a lot of people. Later on when I went back to the 2nd Marines in Lejeune I went out and fired for record with the Marines to qualify every year. This was regarded by the Marines as a very good thing, that the chaplain would come and that he was able to qualify with the M-1.

We arrived in Pago Pago and up at the end of the harbor was Sadie Thompson's Place that had been made famous in Maugham's short story. We unloaded day and night. There was a regiment already on the island. We were sent up to our counterparts so that we ended up bunking with our opposite numbers in the Eighth Marines.

Sully and I bunked with John Magyar, who was the only chaplain with the Eighth Marines. In the morning we went down to see how the unloading was coming and found the saddest of things. A young Marine had fallen asleep on the pier and had been run over by a truck and killed. We went to the morgue to see him and later buried him in the little cemetery there in Samoa. Over the gate to the cemetery was a sign that Joe Burns had there. He was the base Catholic chaplain. The sign read "We live by deeds, not years." Already there were some twenty or twenty-five graves there, and we added another one.

Q: This was a staging area, was it?

Capt. J.: Later it was a staging area. At that point, it was a defense area. The Japanese still had plans to take it and cut the lifeline to Australia. The regiment came under the Samoan Defense Force. Then there was under the defense force the 1st Marine Brigade, and we were the regiment in the brigade. We also had some antiaircraft people and that was about it. We had two antiaircraft batteries, one of which stayed with us and one of which was sent to Wallis Island along with a tank company.

Then we had with us a battalion of artillery, pack howitzers, and these, of course, were sited in various defense locations on the island. So our job at that point was to defend the island.

Q: Was there a real threat to the island?

Capt. J.: At that point, there wasn't. Before, in January, Tutuila had been bombarded by a Jap submarine and ironically the shells landed on the store of the only Japanese family on the island. Of course, the Marines pondered over this, wondering whether the local Japanese had given them the coordinates.

They never found any spies, to my knowledge. We lived in the jungle and immediately started to train. With the training came attrition. Some of our people couldn't do it. We had a number of senior officers who couldn't hack it.

Q: This was training vastly different from what you had in the States?

Capt. J.: Yes, this was training for jungle warfare. As a matter of fact, when we were committed, we were probably the best-trained Marine regiment in jungle warfare. It happened that our colonel had fought in the jungle on Haiti. This was Speed Cauldwell and he was a specialist in jungle warfare. He taught us the rudiments of it, then endlessly drove us, so when we went into combat every man in the regiment knew how to behave in the jungle, knew how to use cover, how to move, and knew how to locate himself, to know where he was, and all the rest. So I think our casualties were relatively lower once we were committed in the jungle.

Q: You'd had no introduction to that kind of training in the States?

Capt. J.: None at all. The one thing we worked on in the States was amphibious landings. The thought at that point was when the Marines get ashore they'll be Marines and they'll fight anybody who's there. Well, it quickly became apparent to the first of us that jungle fighting called for tactics peculiar to this kind of war, and the tactics were not at all unknown in the Marine Corps.

Q: Not unknown?

Capt. J.: Not unknown, no. The Marines had been through the years the country's experts in small wars and among the small wars —

Q: Central America?

Capt. J.: Central America, South America, and the Caribbean, and small wars frequently have jungle fighting. So all at once what the Marines had to do was train their people in something they already knew — something that the officers already knew. That's what Speed Cauldwell taught us.

Q: What about the health aspects of this, malaria and so forth?

Capt. J.: We ran into serious problems there. First, on Samoa, there was no malaria and this was good, but there was filariasis and every man in the regiment contracted it. In its advanced stages, as you know, this becomes elephantiasis. It's a breakdown of the lymph channels that becomes permanent, swelling in the legs and the arms and the testicles.

Q: This is very frightening, isn't it?

Capt. J.: It is, indeed. We heard jokes about men pushing their testicles ahead of them in a wheelbarrow. Well, literally, we saw people doing that on Samoa, and this became the thing of which the men were most careful. And, of course, promptly the myth spread that catching filariasis would make men impotent. Then another rumor spread. Mrs. Roosevelt came down to visit the South Pacific and in due course she won her share of idolaters in our regiment, but at this point she didn't visit us. But the word came out that Mrs. Roosevelt had said that when the Third Marines returned to the States we'd have to wear a black patch because we had filariasis, so the girls would identify us.

It's very interesting how most men are more afraid of being emasculated than of being killed. That is the real working fear of men in combat.

Q: I hadn't heard that.

Capt. J.: This is my theory and it may not be so with other people. No one likes to be killed, either, but many fear emasculation more.

I remember when we went to New Zealand, I think along the same line, the black men were enormously successful with the women and finally the secret came out - it was said, I don't know whether it's true or not, it was said that the black boys identified themselves with the New Zealanders as night fighters! The New Zealanders, and the Maoris, didn't have the racism that we find in our own country.

Q: This medical problem was something the Marines weren't ready to deal with either?

Capt. J.: No. The Marines had seen malaria before but filariasis they had not seen. We discovered that in this country there was little expertise in jungle medicine and tropical medicine. So they promptly established a research group on Samoa to try to ascertain what, in fact, filariasis was. There were a number of theories. Finally, they broke through and ascertained what it was. They performed a number of operations on the lymph nodes and glands and dissected them to find that in people with filariasis there were worms caught in the nodes and causing a mechanical blockage of lymph fluid - making it impossible for the fluid to pass. It could pass one way into your arm and swell it up, but it couldn't pass out.

As a consequence, an instruction was given to avoid getting bitten by mosquitoes. Well, that's a pious preaching. On an island like Samoa, we were living in the jungle and we were getting bitten like mad by mosquitoes.

The sad thing was that when the Eighth Marines were committed, they had been there nine months. A lot of their men fell victim to filariasis. One characteristic of the disease is that when you have onsets in the later course of it, you're unable to work. The pain is too great in your arms, your testicles, and your legs for you to be able to undertake any serious physical effort, especially in tropical climates. So they went into combat, but very promptly under the stress of effort their men came down with recurrences of filariasis and were physically useless. So the regiment, as a regiment, the Eighth Marines were committed for a short time and had to be taken out for that reason.

Q: Is this a disease that afflicted the native people, too?

Capt. J.: Oh, yes.

It was a pity the Eighth Marines had to be withdrawn because it was in every respect a fine Marine regiment and had it been committed four or five months before it certainly would have performed quite as well as any Marine regiment. But it simply had reached a physical point where it could no longer perform.

Q: This crisis - and I expect it was something of a crisis, wasn't it, medically speaking - must have had its reactions on the chaplain and his duties?

Capt. J.: Oh, yes, indeed. We were faced with these stories that I mentioned to you, and a great deal of counseling where individuals came to you to discuss their fears and concerns, sometimes quite young boys who had no present thought of marriage wondered if they could have children. Well, you know, these are deep and long thoughts for a young person to entertain, and especially under the pressure that these young men felt at that time. And, of course, there was little we could say to them. We didn't know the answers, beyond the fact that they would all catch it - many of them did catch it. They had seen the missionaries, the Anglican, Roman Catholic, and Mormon missionaries who were there and all of whom had advanced cases of elephantiasis, none of whom felt any great concern because they intended to live and to die there. So it was a considerable emotional hazard.

Q: Not the sort of thing that would aid you in preparing for combat with the Japanese!

Capt. J.: No, although I must say that later on, especially after the results of the research became available and it became reasonably clear that the evacuation of the unit from the island would end the infection, and that then the occurrences would gradually become less and less frequent and finally would cease, that the men became reconciled to it and felt that no permanent damage had been done.

Q: Was this peculiar to the Samoan islands?

Capt. J.: I don't believe so. I don't think it is peculiar to the Samoans. I think there are other places in the world where filariasis is known. In this country it occurs in New Jersey and Louisiana.

It's very curious. We've had a naval government over these islands since 1917, and one would think that some naval officer - the governors were Navy captains - would have written to BuMed and said "I have an interesting medical situation. Can you send someone to look at it and evaluate it?" And especially since that island would prove strategically important to us in case of war. But no one ever did. The government, even when we were there, was conducted on a very primitive basis, and was not asking some of these questions.

There was a chaplain on the island, Roy Bishop, a very delightful man. Roy ran the schools of Samoa, but the chief target of his prophetic zeal was rats. There were rats all over the island. So he would give the children a piece of gum for every rattail that they brought in. This was one of the main items of interest on the island!

Q: A pretty mundane ministry!

Capt. J.: Yes, indeed it was. Yet he defended it. Roy said somebody has to fight the rats, so it was his job and he undertook it.

Q: How long were you stationed on Samoa?

Capt. J.: From, I would say, September until the next April, mid-March or April.

Q: And training all that time?

Capt. J.: Training all that time, and it was very rigorous training.

Q: Were there new techniques being fed in constantly?

Capt. J.: Well, first we were getting regular reports from the First Marine Division, but the First Marine Division was not jungle-trained. One of the tremendous factors in my admiration of the division at that time was the quality of performance that they gave in ignorance of jungle warfare. Their rapid adjustment to the conditions.

Part of it, of course, was because of Vandegrift, who recognized that he couldn't have the Marines in a mobile situation. He created a cordon defense. He did it for other reasons, too, you remember, because he didn't have many men and he didn't have many bullets. The only Marines that he allowed basically to be mobile were the 2nd Marine Raider Battalion. Evans Carlson's battalion, which he sent on a trek behind Jap lines. That lasted over a month, if I remember correctly. But he had a very realistic understanding of the capabilities and shortcomings of his men. I think he was very wise to use the cordon to minimize Japanese superiority in the jungle.

When we went into action, the situation was the reverse. The Japanese had considerable odds on our men of the First Division. We were much better than the Japanese when we went in, in terms of utilizing the jungle.

Q: In retrospect, had the Japanese had adequate preparation for jungle warfare?

Capt. J.: Oh, yes indeed. They were extremely well trained for jungle warfare. The people who faced the First Division and the people we faced later were well trained in jungle warfare. They had other shortcomings which nullified the excellence of their training. Man for man, in the jungle, they were probably better than the First Marine Division. Man for man in the jungle against us, they were not as good, but the difference was our training. The First Division sent officers back to tell us "watch out for your telephone lines, they were always listening in on them, and ambush, and don't take their dead for granted, they'll turn over and give you a grenade." All of this had happened to them and the information was very useful to us in a tactical sense. They had to learn that themselves the hard way.

Q: What was the state of morale in your division as they trained on Samoa?

Capt. J.: It varied. To begin with, it was never bad, even when these concerns about filariasis were present. Morale was never what you would call low. There came to be an impatience about not being committed.

Q: For such a long period of time?

Capt. J.: It was a long period of time and they became impatient, especially when they knew that their friends in the Eighth Marines had been committed and physically they hadn't been able to take it.

We felt then that the longer we stayed on the island the more questionable we would be from a physical standpoint for commitment. But we did a lot of things that were a lot of fun. The men kept busy. We were very, very fortunate in our junior officers, especially our battery and company officers. They were awfully good – and the men developed pride in their companies. By and large, they were very proud of their company commanders. Then the platoon leaders started to become characters of one sort or another and to become known. All of this bound us together.

At this point, some of the men would drive me around the island to the various detachments to hold services. Attendance at church started to go up dramatically. We had very good attendance, large numbers of people coming to our services. I mentioned hearing Sully preach a sermon where he ended up fighting the war for his wife. I don't know if you remember that story.

Q: Yes. You might tell it on tape, however.

Capt. J.: We used to go together and he would celebrate Mass and if there were a different place for worship I would hold Protestant services. In some outfits we had to use the same place. I used to sit at the back or outside sometimes and listen to his sermon. He was always a fascinating preacher. But on one occasion he overreached himself. He was talking about the purpose of the war and he ended his tirade by saying to the Marines, "And why are we fighting? For your mother and my mother, your sister and my sister, _your wife and my wife._" Then he stopped and there was a silence, and he said, "My God, I've gone too far!" The Marines rolled onto the deck, Mass was stopped, everything was stopped. Finally, when the Marines had laughed it out of their system, he finished the Mass. For weeks thereafter, he would receive solicitous enquiries about the welfare of Mrs. Sullivan!

You can't let the Marines get a step on you!

Q: No, indeed!

Why this long period on the island? Did you discover why?

Capt. J.: I don't know. I suspect that there were a number of reasons. The main reason, I think, was shortage of shipping. They had landed the First Division on Guadalcanal but they didn't possess control of the seas around the island. Then there was a question for a period of time of transports being used both by MacArthur and by Nimitz, being used in both places and not being available in one or the other. Finally, first things had to be put first and Army troops were gotten in to Guadalcanal to relieve the First Division and they were evacuated to Australia. In due course, we were sent down to New Zealand and we staged in New Zealand to go up to Guadalcanal. We were in New Zealand for about six weeks and the country won us all.

There were more men in the Third Division and in the Second Division, which also had staged in New Zealand for Tarawa, who went back to live in New Zealand than you can shake a stick at.

Q: Really. The scenery - ?

Capt. J.: Everything, the people. Scenically, of course, it's beautiful. The people are simply magnificent. They're unpretentious, warm, they're a free people in the best sense of the word. And then there are other things. You go up to Auckland, let's say, on liberty, you might stay overnight and come down and go to a restaurant for breakfast. For 35 cents you could have steak and eggs - such steak! We hadn't had any for all this time and weren't to have it again for a while. Simply everything about the islands was charming.

The other thing, about the people. These were a people who had sacrificed. Their own division was in the Middle East.

Q: The Anzacs.

Capt. J.: Yes. They had taken a lot of casualties and they were defenseless before the Japs until our First Division went in to Guadalcanal. Literally they looked upon us as their saviors. As you would expect, I got to know quite a few of the clergy there, and they felt when we left, in some ways, as perhaps they felt when their own youngsters left. They knew that a lot of our kids would never come back and the ones they had come to know they were afraid about. This communicated itself to our kids, that someone should care that much.

New Zealand, I think, did for us everything that we needed to have done for us, including giving us affection and concern right at the point when it wouldn't be unusual for one to think who the hell cares what's happening to me. We'd been out on these islands, getting Asiatic and so on, and nobody cared and all at once somebody cared.

Q: That's a new slant on the stay in New Zealand. I've never heard that before. I've heard stories of the Seabees going down for rest and relaxation, but that was always just a gay escapade.

Capt. J.: Oh, yes, and there was that side of it. But I think any American, even those who R and R'd, anyway in our division and in the Second Division, if you had asked them what were their deepest feelings about New Zealand, would have answered something like what I have said to you, that they wanted to go back there.

And some crazy things happened there. I was in a tent with our dentist, Smitty, who was six feet six and thin as a rail, and a delightful Marine captain by the name of Dave Mell. Dave was off all religion. He had been brought up by a strict Southern Baptist family and he delighted to tell me he was off it and I delighted to tell him he was going to hell, you know! He liked nothing better than to drink beer. He was not bad about it. He just liked beer and he drank a lot of beer, and he had under his hut a case of New Zealand beer, Waitemata beer. I don't know if you've ever had it. It is much more powerful than our beer, so you had to watch out or it would take you unawares.

One Sunday afternoon after I'd had service was a rainy day. I was lying on my bunk in the tent and Smitty was lying down on his bunk and he didn't have a stitch on. He was just lying there. And David was sitting on his bunk with a big quart bottle of Waitemata beer, and there came this voice from the outside saying, "Anybody home?" We looked at each other, and I said "Yes." Smitty quickly got under his bedclothes, and in came Mr. Orange, the local Presbyterian minister and five or six of his young people. Well, I introduced them around. David's face fell about three feet, and Smitty, here he was imprisoned in bed! The visitors sat around and they wanted to talk. David, now, was left on the outside of things. He didn't know what to say, and he finally said what he said every night when he got home from work. He took a bottle of Waitemata and held it up like this and he said, "Let's get to drinking!"

Well, old Mr. Orange had never run into such people, and David was showing them the case underneath his bunk and saying, "I've got a bottle for every one." So Orange cut short the visit and shoved off. He sent me a very nice letter nevertheless, saying that he certainly should have known better than to take impressionable young people into a military camp.

Q: Then your destination was Guadalcanal?

Capt. J.: We went on to Guadalcanal.

Q: You went over in what transport?

Capt. J.: The *President Adams*.

Q: Was Felix Johnson the skipper?

Capt. J.: He was the skipper. Do you remember him?

Q: I know him well.

You told me off tape that Skipper Johnson was a rather remarkable man on that trip over to Guadalcanal.

Capt. J.: He was indeed, and later he took us to Bougainville. He was, I think, in the minds of our people the paragon of transport skippers, who understood what a transport carrying men should be.

Q: Well, you knew you were getting into something pretty hot, didn't you?

Capt. J.: Guadalcanal was quiet at that time. We had patrols out and they occasionally ran into something but nothing very serious. Basically, again, we resumed training. The big problem on Guadalcanal, the military problem on Guadalcanal, was that there was still some bombing and we lost some people through bombing. But the big problem otherwise was malaria. Almost the whole division contracted malaria and, in some cases, it came on almost immediately, we started to have a casualty list.

Atabrin we took more or less faithfully. I don't know whether it helped us or didn't help us. I suppose the doctors would have to tell us that.

Q: Changed your color a little!

Capt. J.: It sure changed our color and not for the better! But a lot of us caught malaria. I got mine and I spent some time on Guadalcanal, being reasonably sick and having a lot of company in the process. But it was a basically quiet time. We were preparing during a great deal of the time to land at Truk.

Q: You knew that was to be your destination?

Capt. J.: Yes. The first word we had was Rabaul, and then that was cancelled. Then the second word was Truk and at that stage of the game the word "Truk" had connotations - you remember that.

Q: That was a bastion of all bastions.

Capt. J.: Of all the bastions. The information that we had tentatively was that one division was going to go in, and the other information we had was that literally it was a bastion and we would have to take massive casualties on the beach to get in there. So our people were working on that problem when rather suddenly there came a change in plan and the next target was to be Bougainville. The Third Marines and Ninth Marines were to land on 1 November 1943 and we were later to be joined by the Twenty-first Marines.

We went in on the 1st and that night the Japs sent some cruisers and destroyers down to bombard the landing, and Tip Merrill and Arleigh Burke with his destroyers -

Q: The Little Beavers!

Capt. J.: The Little Beavers, you remember them - met them and beat them up and chased them way back past Cape St. George.

The landing was, I think, an easy landing. I landed at the extreme right flank with 1st Battalion Third Marines and then we had in order the 2nd Raiders, the 2nd Battalion, 3rd Marines and the 9th Marines, who had the left flank. We were the only people who got any trace of opposition. We took fire from a little island out in the bay, called Puruata Island.

And then when we came in our mission was to take the peninsula out there, Cape Torokina, and do away with the Japs. We knew that they had some emplacements there.

Q: They had pillboxes?

Capt. J.: Yes. They also had artillery sighted in on the beach, direct fire. Their artillery wasn't from, say, a mountain back there. It was direct fire from a French '75, I think they got two or three boats, maybe more, directing this fire.

Then the men went in, went over the peninsula, and they killed all the Japs who were there, formed a line, and the thing was over.

Q: As a chaplain going in with your men in the battalion, were you armed?

Capt. J.: I was armed. I was armed because we were ordered to be armed. The First Division reported to us back in Samoa that we were not to wear the Red Cross armband because the Japanese snipers picked out first those who were so identified.

Q: As desirable targets?

Capt. J.: As desirable targets. Then, after that at some point, I don't know what the point was, came orders that doctors, corpsmen and chaplains were to be armed with defensive weapons. I don't know how you tell the difference. But I was armed. I carried a Colt .45 revolver that I still have upstairs. They had given me a carbine, an M-1 carbine, and the carbine was no good. If I'd had to run around with that thing strapped on me and banging on the back of my helmet every time I moved, I couldn't have done the job. And so I found a Seabee who wanted a carbine and he had this .45 revolver.

Q: A good exchange!

Capt. J.: We made an even exchange, yes. I had to use an adaptor on my revolver to fire the .45. It took a larger shell than standard ammunition. It was called a police special. Would you like to see it?

(Later)

Q: I do want to ask you, since you've shown me these weapons, about the ammunition. Was the supply adequate when you were down on Guadalcanal and Bougainville?

Capt. J.: Oh, yes. By the time we were on Guadalcanal there was no shipping problem in terms of getting supplies and equipment and that kind of thing as there had been when the First Division was on. There was always an ample supply of ammunition, and, of course, the same thing was true on Bougainville. By that time, we owned the seas around both those islands.

Q: And so there was adequate food, also?

Capt. J.: There was adequate food and we got along very well without any serious trouble at all. When the First Division went in they had seen a lot of their food sail away. They weren't able completely to offload. They offloaded most of the ammunition and all, I guess, of the medical supplies, but they couldn't offload all the food, and so they had to go with very little food for a long time, but we didn't.

Q: You were sick on Bougainville, also, you say?

Capt. J.: Yes. I had recurrences of malaria. Also our regiment in due course began to show the same signs of filariasis that had appeared in the Eighth Marines on Guadalcanal.

Q: Oh, under the strain?

Capt. J.: Under the strain, having recurrences of filariasis. I did myself, and malaria. There reached the point, I would say about the thirty-day point, where the division then began to think that the Third Marines could not continue as a regiment. We were not taking very heavy casualties. We were taking some but we were having so many knocked out by malaria and filariasis that we were in danger of being no longer a tactical unit.

Q: Had the medical corps come up with anything that was effective with filariasis?

Capt. J.: No, they had not. They never did and, so far as I know, there is no known cure. The treatment that they proposed at this time was to take all people suffering from filariasis and to send them to Klamath Falls, Oregon. They felt that living in a cool climate would reduce the chances of recurrence and that then the men would get better faster. I myself was supposed to go there but through the accidents of service I ended up not going.

I had been sent back to a hospital on Guadalcanal in the understanding that I'd be there just a few days and then I'd be brought back up to be with the division. But I got to the hospital then I had a recurrence of filariasis and the doctor said I couldn't go back. Well, I was having arguments with him about this when the Japs came over and landed a bomb on the ammunition dump. Unfortunately, contrary to the Geneva Convention, we had built an ammunition dump completely around our hospital down there, and that thing took three days to go up. There was no way to get in and no way to get out. Lots of our own men were killed and their bodies never discovered.

I don't know whether this constituted a serious loss of bullets, relatively, to our ships or to our artillery or whether it was something we were able to absorb. I do know I didn't enjoy three days with all that stuff blowing up around us.

Q: Not much peace and quiet in the hospital!

Capt. J.: Oh, there was none. You couldn't sleep and no one could move very much because these things were shooting off, sometimes at ground level. Of course, they were all lying horizontally and they'd go off at first in that direction, sometimes they'd take other directions, too.

When that was over, then the doctors felt I had to go back to Noumea, to a hospital there. I went back there and I was able to serve a reasonably useful purpose, considering my condition.

Q: Was the climate any more salubrious on Noumea?

Capt. J.: It wasn't very different. As soon as it became known at the hospital that I was there, lots of Third Marines came to see me and they all had the complaint that the doctors wouldn't believe they had filariasis, although our doctors had ticketed them. The doctors put them to work digging ditches to bring on recurrences. This seemed to me really inhumane and so I went to see the commander of the hospital. His name, I think, was O'Connell. He was a tremendous guy. I objected strenuously to this treatment of my people and he said to me, "We've got to do it, there's no way for us to ascertain whether the man's got filariasis between recurrences except by this."

I said, "Have you ever thought that the only doctors in the Pacific now who know what filariasis is are the doctors who signed these charts? They know, but you don't know. What do you mean? Don't you have that much credence - that much belief - in the capability of your fellow doctors, to accept their word for this?"

He got embarrassed, to his credit, and he said, "Well, I never thought of it." I imagine someone down in the bowels of the hospital had originated this treatment and he had simply retained it. So he knocked it off and from that point on the men were evacuated having filariasis on their tickets. This was accepted as the diagnosis by the hospital, which saved a lot of wear and tear.

Q: I should think it would.

Capt. J.: Oh, it was inhumane. I got well enough in due course to go down to see Halsey's chaplain, who was —

Q: This was his — ?

Capt. J.: Noumea was his headquarters at that time. His chaplain was a man by the name of Pat Rafferty. He was a Baptist, a very flamboyant character, a wonderful guy. By this time I was so broken down that he didn't recognize me. I insisted and he finally accepted the fact that I was who I was.

Q: You mean you'd lost weight and so on?

Capt. J.: I'd lost a lot of weight. This, of course, was very common.

Q: With malaria.

Capt. J.: Malaria and combat in those latitudes. His medical officer saw me and he said, "You've got to be evacuated to the States." I was feeling badly but up to that point I'd had hope I could get back to the regiment. So he evacuated me by flying boat.

Q: Pan American?

Capt. J.: No, it was a Navy flying boat, a PBM, a Martin. We jumped from one island to the other all the way back to Pearl Harbor. At Pearl Harbor we got off and waited a couple of days for aircraft. There were two similar aircraft that were large transports, R4Ds.

We'd had a very hairy time taking off from Noumea. We were taking off from the water, of course, in a seaplane and there was a seacraft proceeding along our course, and all at once he turned port athwart ship. The pilot pulled the stick back. I happened casually to be looking out of the window. It was rather surprising to see us come up at this angle, and all at once I saw something like that. I saw the funnel of one of those things just going past. We did become airborne.

At Pearl Harbor our group was split up between two aircraft. The other aircraft left about a half-hour ahead of us. We found that we couldn't climb so the pilot had to circle the bowl there till we burned off enough fuel to lighten it so we could climb. So another hour later, probably, we got off and headed for San Francisco. In the morning I went up with a couple of cups of coffee for the pilot and copilot. I found that the pilot was absolutely pale. He had just gotten a message saying that our sister aircraft had crashed against a mountain, coming in to San Francisco, and killed all aboard.

We landed at Travis Field and stayed a few days in San Francisco at the Clift Hotel. I had a very embarrassing experience there. I'll bet many men have had this comedown but I don't recall anybody telling me.

Q: At the Clift?

Capt. J.: No. I was walking along the street. All at once a siren sounded and I threw myself flat on the deck. When we were in the Solomons, when the siren sounded it meant not only condition Red, it meant they were right overhead. I looked around and I could see all these feet stopped. I was almost afraid to look up. Here were all these people staring down. I just got out of there as fast as I could get. I never explained to anybody why I'd done that. I've often wondered whether they thought there was one drunk Marine and all of a sudden he got up and got away as if he weren't drunk.

Q: Everybody was conditioned who'd been out there.

Capt. J.: Maybe some of them knew what had happened. We were conditioned, as you say. It was a reflexive kind of action.

I got a set of orders finally telling me to go thirty days later to Klamath Falls and after that thirty days' leave. I talked to the district chaplain at COM 12 and protested bitterly. He had never heard a shot fired in anger, so he got in touch with BuPers. They changed the orders and sent me to the Coast Guard station at Manhattan Beach, New York. This sounded good to me.

I went home and took my leave. Right in the middle of my leave, I got another mild case of malaria, then a set of orders to report to the chaplains' school in Williamsburg, Virginia as an instructor for a period of six weeks, after which I would then be reassigned.

Q: This was more or less recuperation, too, was it?

Capt. J.: I think it was. Also they had a policy of bringing people fresh from combat to the school.

Q: Oh, yes, and that was of some value.

Capt. J.: Indeed, I could see this. Then they'd shove us off and another guy would come in who was from some other place.

Q: As a footnote, why Klamath Falls? You say the cool climate, but why was it selected as a place for the treatment of this tropical disease?

Capt. J.: I don't know. It may have been partly accident. They were probably looking for a general location that had certain characteristics and Klamath Falls, among other places, fell into that category and ended up as being the place.

Q: About your own particular welfare, what happened to the malaria?

Capt. J.: First, to the filariasis, I had only two or three more returns, and they came, I think, after some fairly severe difficulties, and then I never had any recurrence.

Q: Was it thought that the worms eventually died?

Capt. J.: Well, it was their death in the lymph nodes that caused the problem, but in due course they would tend to be washed out.

If you had only one there, the problem was not so bad if you avoided being reinfected. In due course this would clear up and you would not have filariasis, which I think is what happened with me.

Malaria I continued to have - I continued to have recurrences. I remember having one in Camp Lejeune in 1950 and after that I never had a recurrence. But that was a miserable thing.

So I went to the chaplains' school in 1944. Captain Neyman was the officer in charge. Indeed, he had been the officer in charge when I went to Norfolk and he was still there.

Q: He was one of your most able men, wasn't he?

Capt. J.: He was a very able man, yes indeed, very well organized in every respect. A very, outstanding person and chaplain. I imagine he was the best chaplain, the most capable chaplain, in our corps at that point and later in his career. But, as generally happens, or has happened with us, our most capable men generally are not selected to be Chief of Chaplains.

Q: Well, you spent six weeks down there?

Capt. J.: No. I thought I was going to, but they sent word to Washington that they wanted to keep me. I didn't know about this at first.

Q: They didn't ask you!

Capt. J.: No, nobody's ever asked me! Finally, after a couple of months, I went to Chaplain Neyman and asked "What gives?" Then he told me. I said, "I don't want to stay too long in this place. I'd like to get back to the Marines, if I can."

Q: Back to combat?

Capt. J.: Yes, back to combat, if that's what it was. I think basically I wanted to be with Marines. If it was combat, all right. I think I had been disabused of any previous misconceptions I had about combat, so that if I went back I'd have a reasonably good idea about what was going to be happening.

Well, he said, for that we'll have to see what Chaplain Workman says, who was then our chief. And I ended up staying there until the end of 1945, when the war was over.

Q: When you came back, as a man fresh from the field of combat, you obviously had some input to give them in the school. For instance, what were you able to provide them that they didn't know?

Capt. J.: I couldn't provide as much as I would have liked to because there were other things being taught. I think I did give them a feel for the Marines. I think I told them some basic things that could have been helpful to them if they were sent to the Marines.

Q: You were probably the first chaplain who'd been with the Marines to come back?

Capt. J.: I think so. I could be mistaken about this. They had been teaching about the Marines before but the people who had been teaching had only served the Marines in Quantico and not in combat.

So I think I helped a bit at that point. There were just some things, though, that one couldn't do in that context. There are some things you have to learn by going into the field. You have to learn how to use a carbine, you have to learn how to move, you have to learn to ascertain where you are, you have to learn how to find places that you don't see, you have to learn lots of things of that kind that you can't teach in the classroom.

Q: This has to be learned under duress.

Capt. J.: I think it does. Later on in the war they took all the chaplains and stuck them off at Pendleton where they got field training with an infantry regiment, and these things they began to learn out there. In the Korean War the same thing happened. At that time, at one point, I was serving in the chief's office as the detail officer. We would check the records of people and we had to send some of them untrained to the field. So we'd give them temporary duty with an infantry training regiment in Pendleton until they were qualified by the regiment to go out to the FMF commands. In that kind of thing, I don't think that anything I did at the chaplains' school was very helpful.

Q: What kind of recruits did you have at the school at that time?

Capt. J.: We had great people. These were selected clergy. Never did Chaplain Workman let down the standards for the selection of chaplains. There would be rare occasions when someone didn't measure up. Generally speaking, these men were magnificent. They sometimes ran into problems. Generally speaking they would be very good chaplains.

I remember one time having two Baptists from Texas come to see me. They came to see me because I was a Baptist. As they saw it, I wasn't a true Baptist, not a Southern Baptist, but nevertheless I was the nearest thing. And what was their problem? Well, their churches were almost across the street from one another in this Texas city, and now they were being indoctrinated about serving the communion to Christians. They said that in their canon law they couldn't even serve communion to members of each other's churches. They could only serve communion to their own parishioners. How were they going to serve communion to somebody else?

Q: That was a real problem, wasn't it?

Capt. J.: They could care less about denominations. The most moving ministry of the chaplain may come at that moment when he's moving from one hole to another with a chalice and the wafers to those who wish to receive. And that speaks any number of sermons.

Well, these men were saying to me, in those terms, that they were going into combat so to speak with one arm tied behind their backs. I said to them, "You're entitled in the Navy to take this view, but we have to make it a matter of record so that you will never be sent alone any place, which would mean the deprivation of the sacraments for the men."

They regretted this and yet they were honest enough to see that the Navy had to take this view. So they could serve only where there were numbers of other chaplains who were able to offer the sacraments to the Christian people who were there.

We ran into problems of that kind.

Q: When you ran into a problem like that and you were teaching in the school, did you have some optimism about the solution, that perhaps when they had more experience and a larger field in which to operate they might change their minds?

Capt. J.: I don't know personally. With respect to some men, I think I did. With respect to others, I had my doubts. These men would have to go back, most of them, to the environments from which they had been recruited and their people would not have changed and they would have to come to terms with them.

Q: Yes, I can see that, but I mean as they had more service in the Navy, would they become more broad-minded about this particular aspect of the service? Would they be more willing to be ecumenical, so to speak?

Capt. J.: I think you may generalize and say that longer experience in the Navy leads one in the direction of ecumenicity. I don't know that that could be applied in all individual cases. The calcification of the denominational process doesn't always break and sometimes people never completely escape it. I, as you may guess, am not a strong denominationist. I see my ministry as being for anyone who needs me in terms of the symbols to which they are accustomed. I have always been willing to baptize people by immersion and others than Baptists have requested it. Also, I have baptized people by other modes. I cannot see, again, keeping away from people the entry into the Christian community that is provided by infant baptism.

Q: Yes, it does, in a way.

What was being emphasized when you went back to the training school?

Capt. J.: The curriculum of the school -

Q: Had it changed any?

Capt. J.: It had changed in many ways. The core of it was still the old Neyman curriculum. He had foreseen pretty generally what would need to be taught in any case and that was still being taught. There were new things coming in. There were changes in regulations. The role of the Navy Relief Society had changed in degree if not in kind. There were other things happening. Organizations like the USO had come into being. Also, we had learned a lot of things about ministering that had been forgotten since the First World War. Nobody had had a chance to learn them or to use them.

Q: What do you mean by that?

Capt. J.: Ministering to men in combat, beginning to understand the feelings and thinking of men in combat. I think I gave you a little article I wrote for somebody about the role of the chaplain in combat. It had become possible, I think, by this time in the life of the Chaplain Corps at the chaplains' school to describe a chaplain functioning as a professional in combat in the same way as a doctor does. A person who knows and has skills and who has authority for actions, which he knows how and when to perform, a person who is skilled in a situation, who can keep himself alive and kicking and yet, if he has to, put aside his human fears for the sake of what needs to be done.

I think these things were new and I think they brought a new dimension to the ministry that had not been explored. And, of course, there were people with all kinds of experiences who were coming back. While I remained there still came into the faculty every six weeks new people with new experiences.

Q: And that was their purpose in coming?

Capt. J.: That was their purpose.

Q: A constant feed-in?

Capt. J.: Constant feed-in, and I felt it was an awfully good system. There were disappointments among the students. Everybody imagined himself being assigned to the big careers, the battleships, and then you'd get a guy like Bob Fitch, a brilliant guy, who was assigned to the WAVES up at Hunter College. He came to me almost in tears, "They can't do this to me." And I had to say to him very regretfully, "Bob, they can." We had to bite the bullet. We had to go where we were sent. We had to do as well as we could. He was broken but he was committed.

Q: And once you apply yourself to a situation like that, you can see your mission?

Capt. J.: Absolutely.

Q: He had a great mission to perform.

Capt. J.: Indeed. And of course there were the men who felt that unless they were in combat they really weren't doing much of anything. You'd have to talk with them and say, "In combat one can do some things but basically the same ministry had to be brought to men under other circumstances which may be equally trying - absence from home and all the rest."

Q: I'm surprised that point of view prevailed with chaplains. I know it prevailed with many naval officers.

Capt. J.: It was a very common one, and we had problems occasionally and rarely - very, very rarely - but there would come occasionally, once out of a thousand or whatever, a man who was a glory-hunter and I had one or two in my experience in the Navy. One during the Korean War came into my regiment while we were in action in Seoul and having a real bad time. He started to order a lot of people around, including the battalion commander. The battalion commander ordered him out of the place and he wouldn't go, so the battalion commander had me called and I had to go up and order him out. He had come up to a line outfit, while he belonged with a support outfit, several miles back. He later became notorious for public criticisms of the Army that were very much out of place. The Army had performed miserably for reasons that military men knew very well, lack of training and all the rest, and it didn't help anybody to point that out to the general public, or the enemy, or anyone else. But he got some momentary public recognition and one or two media people said immediately yes, he was telling the simple truth that everybody ought to know. I don't know how it helped these people to know that the 24th Division should never have been committed to combat but it had to be because it was the only one in there.

There was that kind of thing but the vast majority of chaplains are not glory-hunters. If I know about this, and I think I do, most of them were tremendously motivated to serve under precisely the same conditions as the men, asking no favors. If out of all these chaplains half a dozen of them were a little off the beam one way or another in that respect, we mustn't be surprised.

Interview No. 2 with Chaplain Glyn Jones

Place: The Mount Hermon School, Mount Hermon, Massachusetts

Date: Tuesday afternoon, 26 October 1976

Subject: Biography

By: John T. Mason, Jr.

Q: It's certainly lovely to see you again this afternoon, Glyn.

You came back to the chaplains' school after a tour of duty in the South Pacific. You came back in February of 1944 to be on the teaching staff there. What were your particular duties? What area did you lecture on, or what did you do?

Capt. J.: I was expected at first to teach about the Marine Corps, but then as my stay lengthened I began to teach in other areas, mainly in counseling servicemen, also, of course, about the Navy Relief Society, and, from time to time, to fill in during the absence of other faculty members in courses that they were teaching.

Q: You say that one reason they brought you back was to talk about the chaplaincy in the Marine Corps. Let me ask in what way does service with the Marine Corps differ from the Navy Chaplain?

Capt. J.: It differs very radically. Perhaps it's best to look at this in terms of the previous experience Navy chaplains had had with the Marines, before World War II.

During World War I there were five or six chaplains who went to France with the Marines and greatly distinguished themselves by their performance under fire. But the Marine Corps, after that war, reverted to its normal complement, which was about the size of the New York City Police Department, and the number of chaplains who were with it went down in number. Very few chaplains were with the Marines. Those tended to stay. People who liked duty with the Marines tended to be allowed to have it.

Sometime in the early thirties what we now know as the Fleet Marine Force was established. At that time there began to be a few chaplains who were attached to the Fleet Marine Force and became something other than Marine Corps chaplains at Marine stations abroad. There had been the Fourth Marines chaplain at Shanghai. Otherwise, there were not many chaplains except with scattered units when they were in action in the banana wars.

By the late thirties, the Marine Corps had begun to organize into a division on the East Coast. I don't recall if there was one in the west. And the concept of the chaplain being in the field with troops began to develop. Then, of course, with the war there came vast expansion in the Marine Corps to two corps of three divisions each, or amphibious forces they were called. It became necessary to man these corps with chaplains as well as to have staff chaplains with each of the six divisions.

So, during those very few years between the late thirties and this time, we found the Chaplain Corps expanding, bringing in new men who'd had no experience of any kind in the service, and at the same time having to learn and absorb and develop doctrine for an entirely new trade, as far as the Navy chaplain was concerned. Some of this trade was already known to the Army chaplain, ground warfare and that kind of thing.

Q: Yes, I suppose it was nearer kin -

Capt. J.: Much more nearly kin to the Army chaplain, but it was different even from that because doctrine in the Marine Corps differed from doctrine in the Army. The Marines majored in a particular kind of warfare which they were able to fight in the Pacific, namely amphibious warfare. There were times when they took over the Army-type role for which they didn't have the doctrine and certainly didn't have the equipment. They didn't, for example, have the kind of artillery that was needed to fight Army-type land warfare. They didn't have tanks and so on. But be that as it may, they had a very distinctive set of needs and there had to be developed a distinctive type of doctrine on the part of chaplains in order to cope. And, I think, by and large, the chaplains did.

Q: This was something that simply grew? I mean through experience in the doctrine?

Capt. J.: Yes. I don't know that it ever got formulated into what we would call a formal body of doctrine. What happened, I think, was the kind of thing that happened in the Chaplains' School, where the expertise hardly bought by individuals then was passed down to other individuals. The Corps made available from time to time opportunities for chaplains to pick up this kind of experience secondhand before they had to go through it firsthand.

Q: Something not acquired in a textbook?

Capt. J.: Precisely. Then, in due course, much more frequently in recent years but even during my time with the Marines, the Marines recognized the need - the Marines were tremendously hospitable to chaplains. In my experience, if the Marine Corps looks for one thing in a chaplain, the first thing it looks for, is whether he is an authentic man of God. Now, they will allow a great deal of leeway in this, but they've got to sense authenticity. The second thing they look for is almost as important, and that is does he like Marines. Now, if those two things are present, there's nothing that a chaplain cannot ask and receive in the Marine Corps. And the Marines came to see in World War II what had been largely forgotten between wars but they had seen in World War I. They came to see again that a chaplain serves a very vital function in the Marines. So the Marines themselves were receptive to the idea of training chaplains for duty in the field. They provided all kinds of opportunities for those of us who were serving with Marines to do this and, in formal ways very largely, this we did when I returned to the FMF. One of the jobs I had again was that of having chaplains temporarily assigned to my regiment for training and going out into the field with them, teaching them how to function in the field, how to read a compass, how to read a map - very simple, elementary things, but nevertheless things that helped you to stay alive and helped you to function when you were in battle, how to find your way around.

Q: Let me ask this. You said that one of the factors that the Marines looked for in a chaplain was did he like Marines. Would you amplify that? Why is a Marine different from a sailor?

Capt. J.: That is a hard one to answer because in some quarters people would say he isn't different at all. In the Marine Corps the answer is self-evident, if you follow me. The fact is the Marine is different from the sailor and the reasons for it I think we may have to find in a number of places. One certainly is the difference in recruit training between the Marine and the sailor. Another is the difference in the function of what we would call in the Navy the senior petty officer and what we call in the Marine Corps the senior noncommissioned officer. The senior petty officer in the Navy is very often a technician. The senior noncommissioned officer in the Marine Corps is a battle leader. The difference in these roles, generally speaking, is immense and the difference, consequently, in the kind of leadership that they show in other situations, non-battle situations, is a very great difference. Everything in the Marine Corps that is done, even in peacetime, is done in the large with an eye to performance in battle. In the Navy that element seems one dimension removed from what is done in peacetime. So that a chief petty officer who is the gun boss of a 16-inch gun in a turret has as his objective the proper functioning of that gun, and that's what he spends his life doing. The notion of its application in battle or the notion of his leading a particular crew in battle is very far removed indeed from his normal type of behavior. He's quite aware that he might have to do that, but it isn't a constant present motivating factor to him, as it is in the Marine Corps.

As a consequence I think the Marines end up recruiting a different kind of person, training a different kind of person, getting a different kind of person after recruit training, and then in the continuance of a man's career, ending up with a person who's oriented differently than the Navy man, which is not to say he's any better, but simply oriented toward a different function in a different kind of a world.

Q: I would think offhand that it would be advantageous for a prospective chaplain in the Marine Corps to serve in the ranks first in the Marine Corps, as Chaplain Workman did?

Capt. J.: Yes, and he was a great chaplain, of course. One of the greatest chaplains in my time in the Navy spent a complete tour in the ranks. Chaplain John Craven. A tremendous man, greatly beloved in the Marine Corps. John is a boy from Kansas, went into the Marine Corps, was converted, became a Southern Baptist minister for the purpose of being a Navy chaplain. He came back in the Navy during World War II and spent a great deal of his time, prior to his retirement two or three years ago, with the Marines, and widely known in the Marine Corps as John the Baptist, as you'd expect.

John was the ideal man for work in the field with troops because he'd learned that part of the trade in the ranks.

We had other chaplains, Ed Jones occurs to me, who served as officers in the Marine Corps and then went into the ministry and returned to serve as a chaplain.

I can't separate the expertise of John Craven in the field in such a way as to say that his service as an enlisted man did great things for him as a chaplain. I know, having been in combat with him, that he knew how to handle himself in the field. Maybe it did help him, but maybe it didn't. That I don't know, and about Ed Jones I don"t know, either.

Q: Since you were at the chaplains' school and were imparting knowledge from the battlefield in terms of Marine Corps service, how successful were you in making an impact upon some of the chaplain students?

Capt. J.: My response would have to be very subjective. I think that to a degree I communicated something of the savor and feel of the Marine Corps to the students and the excitement and interest that I had felt in ministering to the Marine Corps. Now, there were men, I'm sure, who came through the school and had not the remotest interest in serving with the Marine Corps, no matter who talked to them and whether I talked to them about it or not. But there were other men, I think, who heard about this and thought for the first time that maybe the Marine Corps would be the place they'd like to serve. I think some of them did go into the divisions later in the war.

Q: Unintentionally, you were a kind of recruiting agent for the Marine Corps chaplaincy!

Capt. J.: Partially intentionally. One of the important things that happened in the school was an evaluation of the students that was made by the faculty and it was forwarded to Washington. I was directed by two officers in charge of the school to pay special attention to the qualifications of students as far as I could examine them for duty with Marines. And this was a matter of particular interest, as you would guess, to Chaplain Workman.

There came to the school sometime after I another very famous chaplain, alongside of John Craven in the history of the Marines, by the name of Frank Kelly. Frank Kelly was a Philadelphia priest who came in as a reserve. The cardinal of Philadelphia wouldn't allow his priests to join the regular Navy. As a missionary in the Philippines he'd come across a couple of drunken Navy chaplains. He swore he would never let any of his priests, after he became a bishop, enter the Navy, and when he became cardinal archbishop of Philadelphia he lived up to his oath and wouldn't.

Frank Kelly was a man who was ideally suited for the chaplaincy as a Marine. He loved the Marines and they loved him, but then the cardinal wouldn't allow him to stay in the service. So he did his period of time in World War II and extended a couple of years, but he finally went home for a year or two. Then Korea came and he came back in. The cardinal changed his mind a bit. He wouldn't let him become a regular but let him do twenty-two years, most of which he did with the Marine Corps, and in my opinion had a very distinguished career.

Q: When you were engaged in evaluating these records at the chaplains' school -

Capt. J.: I meant to say one more thing when I mentioned Frank. He was on the faculty with me, of course, and this meant that there were two of us with some experience in the Marine Corps. I was not alone in making this evaluation.

Q: In that process of evaluating the records of the student chaplains for headquarters, what were you looking for specifically that would indicate an especially good Marine chaplain?

Capt. J.: Many of the things that you'd look for in any good chaplain, obviously, but some particular characteristics. One would be physical ruggedness. I don't mean physical size. Ruggedness comes in all shapes and sizes.

Q: Durability!

Capt. J.: Durability. The ability to stand the gaff, to take a physical licking and still stay in there. Another, aggressiveness. In the Marine Corps a chaplain has to be aggressive to be effective.

Q: How do you mean that?

Capt. J.: He has to be pushing all the time to advance his cause, and he has to be in the midst of things. He has to be dealing regularly with commands, even at the lowest echelon, as a regimental chaplain - or even lower than that. In a regiment you'd have battalion chaplains. A battalion chaplain normally would be a jg or a lieutenant and he'd be working for the colonel, the regimental commander, but the immediate commander he had to deal with was a lieutenant colonel. In the Marine Corps you get left behind if you're not aggressive. This is true of Marines among Marines and it's true of chaplains among Marines.

And so there has to be, I believe, a rather hard-nosed, pushing quality to a Marine Corps chaplain, an unwillingness to be put down, a willingness to square off - I don't mean physically square off, but to square off with men and with officers, and to stand for something, and to let it be known that you stand for something. Maybe another thing I'm trying to say is moral force.

We were talking about preaching a moment ago and I think preaching is important in the Marine Corps, as it is every place, but fundamentally the thing that the Marines look for, I think, in their chaplains is the fact that situations change when he comes. He must be a man to be reckoned with. Things that might have gone on when he wasn't there have to be pulled in with a sharp rein if he is there because if he morally disapproves in particular there's going to be hell to pay, and he's the kind of a man on those grounds they don't want to tangle with. By the same token, he's the kind of a man with whom they would want to go into battle.

This would tend to suggest that some people who would be admirable, who would have the empathy for life in a wardroom, for example, or who would be very strong in civilian pastorates might not necessarily do a good job in the Marine Corps. And by the same token, a man who might prove somewhat abrasive in a wardroom or in a parish might find that the Marine Corps was the particular context in which he functioned best.

Q: I understand. What about a man's ability to counsel? How was that accomplished in the Marine Corps?

Capt. J.: Pretty much, I think, as it is every place. It is founded there, as I think it is in other places, on the inherent confidence and trust that the chaplain has gained for himself. He won't do much counseling until he has gained that trust. It has to be earned, and it doesn't come all at once. If he goes, let's say in Camp Lejeune, into the regimental area and puts out his shingle and says, "Boys, I'm here, let's all come and talk with me," he will get a few at first and these will be the malingerers, the shirkers, and the people with long stories. He'll be tested out to see where he is, what kind of man he is, and then for a while maybe he won't get much of anybody. He mustn't break his little heart over that, he must just go ahead and do his work. In due course the real pay-off comes. The word gets around that he keeps confidences and is not easily cozened. Then the old first sergeants and gunny sergeants start dropping by for a cup of coffee and want to talk or swap lies. Once in a while they come in and then they say, "Hey, I've got a man and he's got a problem and this is what it is." You may begin at first by telling him how to tell his man what to do, and then in due course you start getting men referred to you by these people. Then you start getting the men themselves.

I don't know that there's any other way in the Marine Corps.

Q: So that means there has to be a semipermanent attachment to a particular group?

Capt. J.: I think so. I talked to Chaplain Workman about the notion of having permanent Marine chaplains. I didn't dislike the Navy, but I like the Marine Corps and I would have liked to spend my whole career with the Marine Corps. He discouraged the notion on the ground that it was essential to the effectiveness of the Corps as a whole that as many chaplains as possible have Marine experience. He cherished the idea, and I'm sure wisely, of the multiplicity of opportunities a Navy chaplain has to work with aviation, to work in hospitals, to work abroad ship, to work with engineers like the Seabees. He didn't want to make the Marine Corps a special preserve that would block other chaplains from the opportunity of serving. From that vantage point, I think he was undoubtedly right.

Q: But all of that means that it is to the advantage of the particular chaplain to get around and experience all these different areas, whereas if he served in the Marine Corps for a longer period of time his benefits would be extended to the men rather than to himself.

Capt. J.: Sure, Now, of course, this was precisely the view that I took and that John Craven took and Frank Kelly took. The Marine Corps, even in wartime, is a relatively small organization. We had six divisions and we had something over 400,000 men in World War II, but the professionals in this group, the cadre, were nevertheless not a large number of men. I got to know a lot of them, John Craven knew most of them, and we got to know the various schools. We got to know the Guadalcanal gang and we got to know the Peleiu gang, we got to know other gangs. After the war, a chaplain would report - I remember my reporting - to Camp Lejeune and, gee, the first night there all my old shipmates came piling in and we had a big party celebrating. They passed the word and they said, in effect, this guy will do to go to the well with, we know him, we'll speak for him, specially if someone had been decorated in action in the Marine Corps, where decorations are rather harder to come by than they might be in some places. That's the thing, I think, you are saying and I personally much more strongly agree with that understanding of benefits than Chaplain Workman's.

Q: You made some statement, I've forgotten in what particular connection, about the man who is always concerned about his promotion, in contrast with a man who's truly concerned with working for people. This is what I was hinting at.

Capt. J.: Yes. I may be jumping the track a little here. I think it's very human and natural for people to desire promotion, so I wouldn't downgrade that as a motive.

Q: Especially when a man has a family?

Capt. J.: Especially when a man has a family, and also especially when he's in an hierarchical organization where promotion means the opportunity for expanded services, for exercise of greater initiative and imagination on his part, greater effectiveness, getting his ideas across. I think there is that legitimacy in a desire for promotion. By the same token I think there are people who want promotion in the wrong way and let it become a wrong part of their lives. They take their eyes off the target, and the target, as you say, is serving people.

I was fortunate about being promoted. I don't know that my record in particular was one that would suggest promotion, but I was promoted. I was glad I was promoted and I felt with every promotion that my arms had been extended a bit, so to speak, and, to the extent I had anything to offer, I was more able to offer it. I faced less ritual opposition than I might have faced, let us say, as a two-striper. My opinions had to be listened to up to a point.

Q: You were a part of an organization?

Capt. J.: Indeed, and as a three-striper they had to make certain assumptions about me. I had been places. I had seen the elephant.

I wasn't looking for the mail buoy any more.

Does that speak to you?

Q: Yes, it does.

Capt. J.: Speaking about illegitmate promotion motives, I think I can say honestly about the Chaplain Corps that we have not more of it, as some civilian clergymen might say and some civilian clergy have written, but we have rather less of it than we find in civilian life and the civilian ministry. Some day, somebody is going to write about this, about the yearning for bishoprics and first churches, and deanships. It is understood in Rome and in the Church of England, but over here is sort of passed off as not really happening. Well, it happens. I think there's at least as much of that yearning for promotion in the civilian ministry, if not more, than there is in the naval chaplaincy.

Naval chaplaincy, I think, is the kind of ministry where if a man is sent down through no choice of his own, he doesn't have much chance to compete for assignment. He is sent, and the ministry fundamentally is a matter, isn't it, of being sent.

Q: You're saying that the military chaplain is a man under authority?

Capt. J.: He's under authority and he's also sent. He's a man who specifically is sent. He doesn't arrive some place as a candidate and say will you buy me. He is sent. Remember the ending of the old Roman Mass, "Ite, missa est." Therefore, go, go forth, right?

Well, he's sent. There's no way to evade that. He may be ever so involved for a time in wanting promotion, but there's no way to evade the fact that he was sent where he is. He's on a mission and he must come to terms with it.

I feel that there's less illegitimate yearning for promotion in the naval chaplaincy than in many other places I have seen, not only in the ministry but elsewhere.

Q: That's a very interesting observation.

Capt. J.: I could be incorrect, but that's my own feeling about it.

Q: Let us go back for a moment to the school in Williamsburg and I would ask you to say a little about the usefulness of training a man in terms of sermons, as a chaplain. What value does this have?

Capt. J.: We did have - I don't recall that I ever taught this course -

Q: But you had some very pointed ideas?

Capt. J.: I had some ideas about it, yes. We did have a course on preaching in the Navy. I think it was taught, if my memory is correct, first by Chaplain Nyman, who in the thirties first had the concept of a chaplains' school, first wrote down - and you may have seen this - what we now call the chaplains' manual, which had no chance then to become an official document, wrote down a curriculum for the chaplains' school. And he it was who felt that preaching ought to be taught in a chaplains' school.

It seems to me that the things he said to us were wise things. I can't say, however, that that was a good place to teach preaching. We were involved in other things and we had other mind sets. I think we came to the school feeling more or less, "Well, damn it all, I know how to preach already. Let's forget this. Let's get with firing the big guns."

Q: Yes, the men came from the ministry?

Capt. J.: Yes, indeed. We had to be ordained and at that time to have had two years' experience in a parish.

Q: So time was a real factor, was it not?

Capt. J.: Oh, it was, indeed. So that I don't know that we paid the attention to the homiletics course that we should have paid. I don't know either, had we paid attention, that it would have made much difference. It seems to me there are some things in life that one doesn't get in a classroom. One can read the Beecher lectures and take classes in homiletics and go through the whole routine and end up with the miserable preaching that characterizes a great deal of the Christian proclamation of our time.

Q: I want to ask what value is preaching in the military chaplaincy and especially in time of war?

Capt. J.: I think it's of great value. This may sound a little contradictory to what I've just said about the value of the preaching instruction in the chaplains' school. The preaching of the chaplain like everything else, like the counseling of the chaplain, is an extension of his character. I'm not saying now that skills aren't important. I'm not saying that theological conviction is not important. All of these things are important. But fundamentally the sermon is the lengthened shadow of a person. The effect of this sermon, I think, depends fundamentally upon how that man is received in the community. If he is understood to be a strong man, authentic in his faith and convictions, compassionate with the gentleness of strength, then I think his preaching can be very effective. It might not pass muster in some terms and in some places.

A man who preached the same sermon in a church that he had used in the field might be regarded as an unmitigated disaster. To sailors and Marines in that circumstance with that message, and the message is basically the message of his own deepest conviction, he can be very effective.

Furthermore, the dimensions of a sermon are never limited to the people who are present. This is something I think we sometimes tend to forget. What a good chaplain says in his sermon sometimes gets repeated in the next thirty-six hours to the regiment. Did you hear what old Joe Doakes said yesterday? So there's a sense in which there's a lengthening shadow that falls from this man in his preaching. I don't know many chaplains who are what you would call powerful orators. I know quite a few who are speakers of deep conviction, who are strong in their proclamation of the Jewish faith or the Christian faith, whose proclamation is thereby respected by men, sometimes by men who don't themselves espouse any formal religion. They expect the chaplain to present strongly the things in which he believes.

Sometimes I think that just as we, when we were children, lived off the faith of our parents, sometimes I think that officers and men, finding themselves in situations where their faith has not been nurtured to the point of coping, find themselves living off the faith of someone else, sometimes the chaplain, sometimes other people.

I had a bodyguard from the Appalachian Mountains by the name of Clem Bolton who could shoot out the left eye of a fly at 200 yards. Clem was a devout, quiet Christian. He made no bones in any company that that's what he was. After a couple of hassles over the issue, it was concluded that he was better left alone. There was a man in battle whose faith became contagious, on whom people leaned because they needed what he had and they hadn't put any in the bank. There come times when that kind of thing happens.

We're talking still about preaching. It's in that context that I think preaching is important.

Q: And talking in terms of living off the faith of somebody else, you said that later, when you were at Camp Lejeune, perhaps 50 per cent of the men were not really related to the Christian or the Jewish tradition and were without any tradition.

Capt. J.: Without any tradition at all. And the central thing about this ministry, you know, comes at this point. One's not surprised that there are Christians who come to the chapel or Jews to the rabbi. The thing that becomes surprising, I think, is to find how the chaplain finds himself as an institution unparalleled in civilian life, sought out by those who don't bear his brand. A civilian minister is pretty well severely left alone, generally speaking, by the gays, by the people at the bars, by the people of the streets - he operates in an orbit. Well, the chaplain in the Marine Corps operates in an orbit and his orbit is the whole regiment. In due course he comes to belong to all the people in the regiment. This is an unspoken thing but there is a feeling among men of some faith and great faith and no faith that when the chips are down, if they want someone to talk to or they want to lean on somebody, that he's a good man to go to.

Q: That is the padre!

Capt. J.: Yes, and I think a test of it - this sounds a little crazy, too - one test of it is how common are the jokes about the chaplain. Here's your TS ticket, here's your crying towel, go see the chaplain! Like the old saying, "Go tell it to the Marines." But underneath this is the implicit assumption that this indeed is what men do when they hurt the worst, and there's something not entirely wrong with doing it. There may even be something right about it.

Q: Going back to the subject of preaching, I would think that it would be less important in the vision of the Marine Corps than would the extension of the chaplain's convictions in a personal way, his moral stature, his faith as a conviction of his own would be projected more readily by not preaching but in a personal contact?

Capt. J.: There are a number of things there. I see no way to separate these things. The only time when preaching becomes rather secondary, and only relatively secondary, is in combat itself.

Q: There's no opportunity?

Capt. J.: Oh, there's ample opportunity and it seems to me a good chaplain takes it as he can. He doesn't do much long preaching but the proclamation is there and the good news is more urgent than ever. Here are men who are literally facing death. They don't know but what it may hit them and they want something by which to live in the face of this.

Q: By way of illustration, tell me how he does preach under those circumstances. I mean what is the opportunity?

Capt. J.: The opportunity becomes, I think, becomes, as you said, highly personal. He preaches as a dying man to dying men. He has to face human mortality or a human predicament in simple terms that everybody can understand - face the reality of fear and get men persuaded that they can live with fear and they can die with fear honorably, especially, I think, he has to offer what the gospel has to offer. The good news of Jesus Christ, the Easter story.

There's the most profound story in the world and it bears repeating on every battlefield, and I think undoubtedly it has been repeated on every battlefield.

So I think preaching has a profound place in battle.

On the other hand, as you say, there are times and circumstances when it is not expedient or not possible. Then there is one thing that seems to be more central even than preaching and that is the sacraments. You, I'm sure, have talked to many chaplains, you will have talked to many chaplains who have spent long periods of time walking under fire, sometimes from one foxhole to another foxhole, distributing the communion. This men will come long distances and endure danger to receive. Here in these very primal symbols is something that speaks to men beneath the level of words at times when words are not always possible.

Q: I would take it that many such men are, as you termed it before, leaning on the faith of somebody else when they come to receive the sacraments?

Capt. J.: I think so without a doubt. I have never, and I would hope no one else has ever refused a man the sacrament. Whoever comes, so far as I could see, was sent of God to come and receive. It may be, I suppose, with many of those men that they never again in their life will communicate. Maybe twenty-four hours before, this was something that they would have decried as childish or superstitious or whatever. But at that moment in that place, in the company of men of faith who came forward to receive, they came forward, too. People can make light of this, talk about foxhole religion, if they want, but my own feeling is that there is legitimacy in human extremities to these ancient practices by which men have been fed in the face of life and death. I see no reason to apologize for the fact that men need at that time or that we are able to provide at that time.

Q: Let me ask, how does a chaplain deal with - the chaplain being a man - his own human reactions to fear, his concern?

Capt. J.: That is a hard one to answer because we all feel fear and there is no such thing as lightly putting fear to one side and saying, "All right, I'm afraid but not for the moment, let's get on with it." I don't think it's that way at all. I think that, for one thing, the chaplain has made up his mind about all these questions before. Most of us, I think, had our minds made up about the question of death, where many of the men to whom we ministered by no means had closed the door on thinking about that issue. There was some worry that we didn't have as deeply maybe as other people. The other thing, I think, that makes a lot of difference and that takes away some of the self-centeredness that fear can cause and does cause is the sight of people in need.

When I first was in combat I was twenty-six years old, old enough to know better, still for the first time, as the Marines say, seeing the elephant, and it was a rough experience for me. I think that one thing that enabled me to tolerate it was to see kids, seventeen and eighteen years old who to me seemed very young, having profound needs, undergoing dreadful experiences, for which no kind of training could prepare them. They could be prepared to take a pillbox but they couldn't be prepared to meditate about death, not even with the sight of their buddies lying about. To see boys with these needs and to be there, how to put it, perhaps to be the only person equipped to understand what the needs were and to have something to offer, to give meaning to what was happening, that is an awesome experience. Not meaning to battles, because there's no way in battle, I don't think, to find significance, but meaning to death.

I don't know. I've been scared so much that I don't know that there's very much left to scare me any more. But I imagine that anybody who's been in battle and is honest is going to say the same thing.

Q: In time, you become inured to it, don't you?

Capt. J.: Yes, in time you do. I don't think you ever stop being afraid. I think that you do develop a certain professional approach to it that you don't have that first day. You go into it expecting certain things and looking for certain things. This is where your training makes a difference.

Q: Yes, and how is that approached in chaplains' schools?

Capt. J.: It is approached only academically in chaplains' school. We didn't take the men into the field in those days. We didn't put them through obstacle courses or have them advance under close fire so that they would know what the sound of fire was like and many of the other things like incoming mortar fire. There was no way beyond saying that these things can be traumatic and you'd be aware of them and so on, but this does nothing beyond giving people a little bit of a set from someone else's experience.

Now they do things much better. At the time of Korea we did things much better and this was not my intention. We sent chaplains going to the First Division out to the West Coast to Pendleton for a month and they went through field training with a field regiment, with a training regiment, including exposure to all these things so that when they heard something incoming they were able, well, generally speaking, able to identify it. They heard a mortar burst and they knew what was happening. They knew the difference between the sounds of our machine guns and theirs, the rate of fire, and that kind of thing.

In World War II we had nothing to compare with that, and the first time many of these chaplains ran into this was when they joined their outfits and went into combat, a hard school.

Q: Yes. Now the element of leadership in a chaplain. How is that approached? How is a chaplain selected in terms of his leadership ability? Is it something that can be imparted? How did the school deal with this?

Capt. J.: You're speaking now of the chaplain's leadership in his ministering to the Marine Corps?

Q: Yes.

Capt. J.: Again, the school was in the position of taking the raw material it received. There was very little the school could do to train people in leadership skills in eight weeks. There were so many things that men had to learn. In effect, men had to try to learn in eight weeks the fundamental things about ministering in, say, sixteen or twenty different situations, to any one of which they might have been ordered and any one of which demanded a great deal more expertise than the school was giving in that particular line.

A great deal of the leadership in those days was, I think, a matter of what was the chaplain as raw material. Was he in the Marine Corps physically rugged? Again, not huge, but rugged. Was he a decisive character who knew who he was? Did he stand for something in the midst of these people? What kind of a person was he intellectually? I've seen tremendously devoted men destroyed in the Marine Corps because they couldn't compete intellectually in that society.

Q: I'm so glad you introduced the element of the intellectual aspect of a man's makeup. It's the first time we've talked about it.

Capt. J.: Yes. I think it's of great importance. Not decisive maybe but one part of a man's character certainly is his intellectual acumen, his capacity to develop wisdom, to a more limited extent the degree of his knowledge of things.

In going to the Marine Corps in World War II he was going to a most unusual society. The officers, the young World War II officers, who came there first were Ivy League men, men from the good Catholic colleges, Holy Cross, Boston College, and men from other fine schools, in their early or mid twenties, a few of them a little over. The intelligence officer in my regiment, for example, had a PhD from Yale, a Dartmouth man, first-class mind, who is retiring shortly from the Foreign Service after a very distinguished career. In the ranks we had men hard to see sometimes because all Marines look alike, we had men of intellectual distinction. One of the young officers in my regiment was a noted playwright. He wrote the play "Brother Rat" as a matter of fact. And I could name others. Two years after the war, one became governor of Arkansas, another the mayor of South Bend, Indiana.

In wartime there were many such as enlisted men. An actor I remember, a professional actor, in my regiment and a professional musician. If the chaplain was not able to hold his own intellectually in that company, he very quickly went down the drain. He went down the drain, because the word would be passed round that really he wasn't running with the program and wasn't intellectually up to standing up to minds of this type among his officers and men.

I can recall seeing men who otherwise were very fine, devoted ministers failing because on that score they weren't able to stay abreast. Sometimes it was because of their lack of a sophisticated Christian theology, not being able to cope with theological questions thrown at them sometimes in sincerity and sometimes in entrapment.

Q: Just to test a man out?

Capt. J.: Exactly. I was amazed, for example, to find out that there were numbers of men and officers in my regiment who had read Niebuhr. Or a man comes up and says I want to talk to you about Aulen's "Christus Victor," so all right we sit down and talk about "Christus Victor." Suppose I'd said "Who he?" Forget it.

Q: He wouldn't come to you again!

Capt. J.: He wouldn't, and worse yet, he'd tell others, "Don't worry about that fellow. All he knows is the plan of salvation from some seminary textbook. He doesn't know Niebuhr or Rahner or Heschel."

Again, I'm not saying that one has to be the Abbot Professor of Sacred Rhetoric.

Q: There aren't too many of them!

Capt. J.: No, there aren't very many of those.

Q: Off tape you were telling me something very interesting about the indoctrination of ex-civilians as Navy chaplains and that is the fact that they had to stand watch. Will you tell me that on tape?

Capt. J.: Yes. In the College of William and Mary building that the Chaplain Corps used there was a long passageway that had classrooms on either side. That was known as the quarter deck. There was a desk attached to the wall there, which was the duty officer's desk. It had his log on it. He had to walk his rounds through the school, check things by the hour, had to answer all calls that came into the school, some of them quite important, the Chief of Chaplains or other people, had to take care of all emergencies that happened during his watch. The model was for some young ensign or JG to stand a deck watch on a ship at sea, even though the chaplain would never have to. I felt then and feel now that it was a very fine educational experience.

Q: That was a bit of realism in terms of the service.

Capt. J.: It was, yes. Some strange things happened. Bob Brown - Robert McAfee Brown - is back at Union. Do you know him?

Q: No.

Capt. J.: Well, he's a well-known theologian now. He taught at Stanford for a number of years and lives up here at Heath in the summertime.

Q: Oh, yes, Heath is quite a -

Capt. J.: A real assembly of theologians. One day he had the deck while he was a student at the school. Pat Rafferty was the officer in charge and that day Pat was being visited by Senator David I Walsh of Massachusetts, Chairman of the Naval Affairs

Committee. Well, Pat took the senator in and out of the rooms abutting the quarter deck and every time they appeared out of a room and back on the quarter deck, Brown would shout, "Attention on deck." Then they'd go into a room and look around and come out and Brown would shout again, "Attention on deck." This really got to Brown and he remembered it during the years after World War II. In 1946 or 1947 he decided he would put it in print. So he wrote a fascinating, charming article for The New Yorker, which published it. The thrust of the article was the anomaly of a clergyman shouting the way a line officer would and playing the line officer's role, so to speak. But it was loaded with humor so no one could mistake it.

Some years later I was out on the West Coast and I ran into Pat Rafferty, went over to see him. I'm very fond of him. As a matter of fact, he sort of saved my neck one time. We got to talking and I said, "Did you ever see that thing Bob Brown wrote for The New Yorker?" He said, "I've got it right here," and he took it out. He read it and he cherished it, and the humor was pretty much lost on him. He had taken it fairly literally and it sounded to him as if Bob Brown were saying to the subscribers of The New Yorker, "Now, look, this is what it was like in the Navy. They really trained us guys." Pat was very pleased!

Q: Might have disabused him.

Capt. J.: Pat's still living on the West Coast, advanced in years.

Q: Well, Sir, you were at the chaplains' school until October of 1945. A year and a half you were there?

Capt. J.: About a year and a half.

Q: Much longer than you expected?

Capt. J.: Yes, indeed.

Q: And then you went to sea?

Capt. J.: I went to sea. I went into Los Angeles, a Baltimore-class cruiser. My predecessor, who had commissioned the ship, was again Ansgar Sovik. A brand-new ship, had never seen action in the war, had just been brought around from the East Coast, training out of Gitmo. The crew had a disastrous experience at Caimanera, and when I arrived on the West Coast, shortly after her arrival out there, they were still sort of picking up the pieces of the crew!

Q: Why? What happened at Caimanera?

Capt. J.: Well, they had a couple of really riotous liberties at Caimanera and things were falling apart. The war was over. If I remember this was about September or October, I'm not quite sure.

Q: You went there in November, didn't you?

Capt. J.: In November, yes. It was the time when they were beginning to send men home in large drafts. We had many men who were very soon due to leave the service and, since we were going to

China, the question was whether we should leave these men or take them with us to China. We were not able to pick up enough long-termers on the West Coast to sail the ship to China, so we had to take these short timers with us. So we had a very unhappy crew, so to speak, out to Wes-Pac.

Q: You mean men who didn't want to go?

Capt. J.: Men who didn't want to go. Their feeling was that if things had been managed better they wouldn't have had to go.

Q: Some of this must have fallen on the shoulders of the chaplain?

Capt. J.: Oh, yes, it did, indeed, and, of course, a brand-new, green chaplain. I'd never been to sea as chaplain of a ship. I'd traveled in a lot of transports, of course, but always as a guest, so to speak. But now I was having to learn a new trade and be out in a new world. I was having to learn a lot of things very rapidly.

I was dealing with men many of whom had had long terms at sea, who knew their jobs very well and their places very well, how to function very well, and so it was a formidable task. We got out of it pretty well. Many of the men, shortly after we arrived in Shanghai, were sent home.

Q: An expensive process, wasn't it?

Capt. J.: Yes, but war is that way. I see no way in which the Navy could have foreseen all of this in the immediate sense. Obviously, they had foreseen it in the theoretical sense. There were operation plans for demobilization and all that kind of thing, but to have them effective in such a way that a particular vessel could be cleared in that period of time of its old-timers and loaded with new-timers, I don't think probably was possible. At any rate, we got the distinct feeling after a period of time that the Navy didn't even know we existed, anyway.

We were going out for four months, two cruisers - Bremerton went with us. At the end of four months, Bremerton was relieved on station and we were told we would be going pretty soon, but then came another four months. I think St. Paul relieved Bremerton and we relieved St. Paul. Then a light cruiser, Duluth, relieved Bremerton and still no orders for us. By this time we had pretty much run out of old-timers. We were not getting new men and we very soon reached the point where the captain was going to be forced to send a dispatch to Washington saying the ship couldn't sail.

Q: You were reduced by what percentage?

Capt. J.: The wartime complement in that ship was 1,600. We had sailed her from San Diego with something like 1,200 and the ship was completely able to sail. What we lost had to do with topside armament and no longer was going to be needed. By the time we got down to Shanghai, we were down to 400, and this was a Baltimore-class cruiser. She was a big ship. We had to go to sea from time to time and these men were having to stand heel-and-toe watches. This ship just couldn't steam unless they did.

Q: Your chaplain's training should have - !

Capt. J.: It certainly did, you know.

Q: Did you have to stand watch?

Capt. J.: No, I didn't have to stand watch, and this question was raised. I pointed out that it was illegal and that I was going to object because I thought that I should not be out of circulation, doing something that somebody else could be doing. Besides, I had serious doubt about my qualification to stand watches, anyway.

Anyhow, Washington finally heard us and we got a dispatch saying we were going to receive 200 men from Okinawa. By this time many of us had been in the service just long enough to start to ponder how could there be 200 men so readily spared in Okinawa, and we suspected what turned out to be the case. These were brig rats. What they did was to empty the brigs and send them to us.

Q: This happened elsewhere in the Navy at that period, too.

Capt. J.: Yes, indeed. So here about a third of our crew was made up of a type of man that undoubtedly in peacetime would not have been tolerated in the Navy at all. All at once our disciplinary problems rose dramatically - all kinds, involving even good men. A chief petty officer was observed by his division officer beating up one of his men. He can't do it, so he gets a court where, from every emotional standpoint, he is amply justified in doing something. That kind of problem was beginning to come up.

Our main mission was - well, we had several missions. We were the flagship, the last one I think too, of the Yangtze Patrol, the old Yangtze Patrol. We were moored in the Whangpoo much of the time, facing downstream, bow down, you know, the Bund was on our left and the Pootung Peninsula was on our starboard side. The communists held Pootung, so you couldn't walk on the starboard side of the ship for quite a period of time. You'd have to duck. They had snipers with telescopic sights, and you had to duck from one installation topside to another when you were moving on the port side.

Q: What sort of counteraction did we take?

Capt. J.: We didn't do a great deal. The problem was the problem of swatting a mosquito with a sledgehammer. We had nets out because they sent swimmers with limpet mines and tried to attach them to our hull. We had snipers ourselves up in the upperworks of the ship looking for these people. We did send some boats over with a landing party but not large numbers of people. Always by the time they arrived these people had disappeared. There was nothing there. So it was a very unpleasant situation.

We spent some time there and most of the time we traveled from Shanghai to Tsingtao, Macao, Hong Kong, Singapore, Trincomalee, and then back up again, showing the flag. Our companion ship of the

Royal Navy during much of that time was <u>King George V</u>. We had some great times with <u>King George V</u>. We were visited by Admiral Bruce Fraser and by Lord Mountbatten, much ceremony, of course, as you'd imagine. Bruce Fraser, as you may remember, was the commander-in-chief, Royal Navy, out there, a very attractive man, and Mountbatten was a very impressive figure indeed.

But every four months passed and we weren't relieved, and morale really was sinking. There was real anger in the ship because by this time it became quite clear that something could have been done. In San Diego nothing could have been done to prevent these old hands from being shipped to China, but something could have been done to relieve us. Finally, while we were at sea, one of the stern tubes of the ship gave way and we were sent to Pearl Harbor for repairs. We believed that they wouldn't send us back to China, but they did. By this time, we had serious morale problems aboard the ship and especially among the officers. Many of the crew had been rotated and those aboard consisted of men who had not been out there for a long time. Almost all the heads of departments had gone out with the ship. Many of them had been away from their families for a long period of time during the war. We had an exec, for example, who had been during the war fifty-six consecutive months at sea. He'd been in command of a DE squadron, he was assigned as exec to us. He was a nice person, but this man, who had an excellent war record, was practically catatonic by the time he came to us. He could barely talk. He was utterly and completely exhausted, and he was given a large and complex naval organization to administer. He simply wasn't up to it. He could have been up to it, but here was a very fine and promising naval career wrecked because of misassignment by BuPers.

Everybody who was present recognized the injustice of this man being assigned. Everybody agreed he had to go. The ship was getting much worse much more rapidly. It wasn't a Captain Queeg kind of thing at all, a man drunk with power. It was literally a man no longer able to make decisions. He had been brought to the point where there was no more give in him. He was brittle, he was breaking. Just the saddest thing, especially when you contemplated what an excellent officer he had been all these many years at sea, and then no real consideration being given either to the needs of the service or to his needs in assigning him to that billet.

Q: How did the personnel of the ship cope with the declining morale? What steps were taken?

Capt. J.: They tried many things, all of the things that you would expect. Many of the things that you wanted to try you weren't able very well to do. Recreation, for example, in circumstances like that has a very limited potential.

Q: With the snipers shooting at you all the time!

Capt. J.: No, not all the time. We were able to run boats to the Bund. We did get parties off to Hangchow, which is a beautiful city.

We'd rented a hotel and sent them there. They could spend a few days there and drink beer and ogle the girls and see the countryside. This was very well received but beyond this there wasn't a great deal we could do.

One of the few things that seemed to help at all was to stress Navy courses, correspondence courses.

Q: Naval War College courses?

Capt. J. No, no. These were courses for advancement in rate, courses for skills of various kinds, and some of them courses for college credits of various kinds. Numbers of men got involved in these and found that these were a useful and constructive way of using their time. An awful lot of men, however, as you'd expect, went on the beach. Shanghai was then, at least, a real riproaring oriental liberty town. We had bad trouble with venereal disease of an exotic type which did not respond to our treatment. Also we lost numbers of men in Blood Alley who were knifed there, a chronic problem. Our people would get liquored up, then they'd wander into these areas of the city where people would be lying in wait for them and would kill them.

Q: Was that in terms of robbery?

Capt. J.: Yes, robbery, and these people liked especially - the custom of many Chinese at that time was to put their life savings into their teeth, as you probably know, gold teeth. Numbers of the murders that took place were murders where you'd find the corpses minus all their teeth. They'd been taken out by robbers.

There was a buoy about 100 yards forward of our ship where they moored the bodies that were picked up every day in the river. Two or three times a day you'd see a small tugboat coming down-river towing two or three bodies. They'd bring them up to this buoy and tie them up. Here these naked corpses would be spread-eagled out round the buoy until late in the day, then there would come a tug that would pick them all up and take them away. Of course, the sight of this kind of thing made quite an impression on these young American minds. They'd never seen human life treated quite so casually. Most of these were postwar sailors, except for the senior petty officers and the heads of departments, and it was simply a new world to them.

Q : What an experience that was!

Capt. J.: Yes, indeed.

Q: Did you touch in at Japan at all?

Capt. J.: Yes. I hadn't been in Japan before. I was in Japan later. We touched in with LA I think only a couple of times, Kobe and Tokyo, if my memory is correct.

Q: You came back in the Los Angeles. She finally was called home.

Capt. J.: Yes. We were called home, relieved out there. While we were out there we saw quite a lot of the Communists. Our First Division was in Tsingtao, had a perimeter around the city. I had numbers of friends there so when we got to Tsingtao I'd see some of them. The Communists quite clearly were going to take over the country. It was equally clear that the Chinese people, so far as we could get to know them and we got to know quite a few of them, wanted no part any more of Chiang. They would take anyone in preference to Chiang, and the only other one in the field, of course, was Mao.

It was a shock to come back to this country and hear talk about General Marshall giving China to the Communists, the talk of the China Lobby, Knowland and Bridges and that crowd, and later McCarthy, about China being given away to the Communists when our experience very directly was that the Chinese people were going to do anything they had to do to get rid of Chiang. None of them knew very much about Communism. They didn't have the kind of fear of it that we had and, for that matter, I suspect, although great loss of life ensued, that the Communist way of life was not vastly different from that which they knew in any case. Probably more honest without the squeeze. This we could see beginning to happen in China before we came home.

Some of these Chinese that we knew felt this way quite strongly. I got to know a man in Shanghai, a man by the name of Li, who was a very intelligent man, a member of the Kuomintang. Until very recently, he may still be there, he was a professor of politics at

Northwestern University. He got out of Shanghai with his life. But he agreed that the Kuomintang was totally corrupt, that it was exploitative of the Chinese people and that the people were not going to stand any more of it. When the time came, Chinese troops would not fight. This is what happened. The old story in the Orient, you know, was the silver bullet. In Chinese wars you didn't find very many people getting killed. Two war lords would approach with their armies, then they would scout around, and the one who had the larger army would send a message to his opponent and say it's all over with you, the thing to do is to join me with the message he'd sent him a silver bullet. If the bullet was returned, it meant there was a deal. This is the way the war lords worked. Well, Li among others said to me "We're going to see the silver bullet when the Communists come," and it turned out that way. The Chinese didn't desert by ones and twos. While divisions changed, as divisions from Nationalist Kuomintang troops to Communist troops. One day they'd be ostensibly fighting for Chiang and the next day they were fighting for Mao. This is one explanation for the rather rapid Communist conquest. They took over probably 50 per cent, if not more, of the Nationalist armies in statu quo, armed, equipped, organized, which had been the custom, of course, in China for centuries.

We came back to the West Coast and spent some time - not very long in our case - there, operating off the West Coast. Then I went to Harvard, went to school.

Q: Was this something you asked for?

Capt. J.: I had asked for it before. Word had come out about a short, one-semester course, and I was interested in going. I applied and got a letter from the Bureau saying, "This is going to be expanded next year and we'd rather that you waited and finished your tour in the ship and then...."

Q: Then it became a two-semester course?

Capt. J.: It became a year course, yes.

Q: What was the course?

Capt. J.: Things changed later, but I was allowed to take anything I wanted to take and so I had a ball.

Q: Like a sabbatical!

Capt. J.: Oh, it was a great sabbatical. I studied history with Samuel Eliot Morison and Arthur Schlesinger. I studied liturgy with Massey Shepherd. I studied the modernist movement in the Roman Catholic Church with Dean Sperry of Harvard Divinity School. We met twice a week and there were only two of us. I was able to move amidst the rich furniture in that great man's mind for a year. Unbelieveable experience! I took a course in situational ethics with Joe Fletcher, studied Shakespeare with Roy Battenhouse the theological implications in Shakespeare. I don't remember what else. I simply went out and signed up for all the things I wanted and didn't bother about a degree or anything.

Q:: And you could have your family there with you?

Capt. J.: We lived in Plymouth. I commuted from Plymouth. We had many old friends, including Bob Coe, whose picture you saw up there, in Plymouth. As a consequence, we had a lot of fun family times as well as my doing the studying I had to.

Q: Did you find it difficult to go back and study in earnest like that?

Capt. J.: Oh, I think if I'd had to take some preassigned course from the Navy - if the Navy had said to me, "Now, you must bone up on Lundensian theologians for a year," I think I would have found it difficult. As it was, I was doing what I wanted to do, I wasn't doing it necessarily with an eye to my advancement in the Navy, or for anything other than my enrichment as a person and stimulation as a minister, and so I didn't find it difficult. I found it highly enjoyable.

Q: Did you make some new friends there?

Capt. J.: Not very many. I ran into a lot of old friends, but I didn't make many new friends. We got to know the students, of course, and got to know - I didn't know Massey Shepherd before and didn't know Battenhouse and didn't know Samuel Morison. I got to see more of him later on. He used to come down to the Naval War College regularly, so I saw him down there when I was with destroyers. But in the way of finding a new circle of acquaintances, I can't say I did. Maybe I should have. Commuting, I think sort of stopped that to a degree.

Q: Did you commute with other students there?

Capt. J.: No, I commuted pretty largely by myself. Bob Coe, who lived not far from us, whose idea it was for us to live in Plymouth, thought that probably we could drive up together and back, but it turned out that we got schedules on opposite days. He'd go Monday, Wednesday, and Friday and I'd go Tuesday and Thursday, so really we didn't drive up much together.

Q: At Harvard, you said, there was an ROTC unit?

Capt. J.: Yes, to which I was administratively attached. But I, as a student, had no duties there.

Q: You got your pay check through them?

Capt. J.: I got my pay check through them, I guess. I don't remember, but I got it from somebody! But there wasn't a big Navy community that I would see by the nature of the case. I tended in the evening to go back home to Plymouth, so I didn't see a lot of Navy people up there, but I had a great experience.

Q: Isn't that great that the Chaplain Corps did that sort of thing?

Capt. J.: Oh, indeed!

Q: Was this universal, across the line? I mean did all of the men

Capt. J.: Not all of them went but many men were selected to go. I couldn't tell you how many, nor could I tell you what percentage of men. A very considerable number of people who ended up being senior in the Chaplain Corps were men who had gone to graduate school. Most of them in recent years have been sent to get degrees for accreditation of one kind or another. It was less so in my day. It was possible to do what I did.

Q: But all this predicated on a promising man? I mean the record indicates his promise in the Chaplain Corps?

Capt. J.: Probably. I would think so. Well, I know so, as a matter of fact, because later on, in the Bureau, I served on the board that selected these people. We would select people who were going to be in the Navy for a while, who showed promise of growing, maturing and becoming leaders. I don't know what percentage of a year group was selected to go.

Q: Well, you went back to the Navy after that?

Capt. J.: I did. I went from Harvard to Quonset Point for a year and saw there my first service with naval aviation and enjoyed it. The first time I ever saw a revolving altar was down in Tent Camp in Camp Lejeune. They were building a chapel with a revolving altar.

Q: Serving different faiths?

Capt. J.: Yes. They have one at Quonset, three sides.

Q: What were your primary duties there?

Capt. J.: I was station chaplain and served as the Protestant minister to the community. My colleague, Francis Timothy O'Leary, was the senior chaplain, the Roman Catholic chaplain. He has been a very dear friend of our family ever since.

We were talking about the problem we had there with fraternal organizations.

Q: Yes. Is this within the Naval Air Station?

Capt. J.: It was at the Naval Air Station. The organization consisted very largely of civilians and workmen. One day a chief petty officer came up to me and invited me to join the Masonic order. I politely refused. I had nothing against the Masons and I still don't, but I said, "Thank you very much, no." And he said to me, "You'd better." Well, I was not accustomed to such arrogance and I said in good Christian terms, "What the hell do you mean?"

He said, "Well, on this station there's only one way to get ahead and that's to belong to the Masons."

I said, "That's all over now. You go and tell the good brothers to call off the dogs."

He shoved off and I went down the hall to see Frank. I said I'd just had this thing from the Masons. I told him about it and he said:

"I've been hearing funny sounds from the Knights of Columbus."

Q : A well-organized station!

Capt. J.: Oh, boy! Anyway, he said, "I'm going to look into this." No one had invited him that way to join the Knights of Columbus. He automatically was the guy who ran them behind the scenes. But he'd heard some funny sounds from them and he checked into it. He found that there was a deadly feud in the repair department - what do they call that department? Overhaul and Repair Department, or something like that - among civilians between the Knights of Columbus and the Masons. He came back and reported this to me and asked what we should do. So I said, "I think we ought to give the unvarnished word to these people, and tell them that you and I aren't buying any of this and it's got to stop." Then he said, "How are we going to do it?"

We talked about it and decided that, first, we'd go to see the skipper, who was a real character. I'd better not say too much about him.

Q: What was his rank?

Capt. J.: He was a four-striper, much passed over. He'd been an island commander during the war for a while and he escaped a court-martial for lots of doings. Anyway, we went to see him together. We told him this was happening and he called in the officer in charge of the O & R. He knew about it, so the captain said to him, "Knock it off. Now. I'm quite prepared under Civil Service to prefer charges against any people who make any noises in this direction."

Well, the average, discreet naval commander shies away from preferring Civil Service charges, as he does from leprosy. But the old man was just the kind of a guy who would do it and all the civilians knew it. So, gradually, they became Christians and stopped the knifing.

Q: What was the crux of the whole thing? Just animosity or something?

Capt. J.: Some of it was. I think some of it also was a projection of individual hostilities, using these organizations as weapons. Also, the old feeling that nobody gets ahead in this place but Catholics or Protestants, as the case may be, and that kind of hatred developing. It was a very sick kind of a thing. I think, during the course of the year, a great deal of that went down the drain.

Q: Did it hamper in any way your ministry to the community?

Capt. J.: To a degree. To what degree, I don't know. There was no doubt that I was persona non grata to a certain group of - certainly to a group of influential civilians - and also to a certain group of influential Navy people, most of whom were CPOs. There were very few, if any, naval officers involved in this, to my knowledge. But there were numbers of CPOs. This is a big thing, sometimes, in the life of a chief petty officer or a master sergeant. Some of them, I think, were turned off me because they felt I had been too aggressive in coping with this.

Anyhow, we didn't hear any more of it, and Captain Case, in due course, reported he thought things were leveling off and that enough people were frightened of the old skipper taking action, so they took it easy.

Q: What about the Roman chaplain? Was he affected in any way?

Capt. J.: I think perhaps to a lesser degree than I was. The Catholics had to go to Mass some place and Dixie Kiefer Chapel is a very convenient place. It had the advantage, too, of not being tied in with a parish, so they didn't have to support a school and other things that you might have in a Roman Catholic parish. And I think some of them were inclined not to lose out on what they thought was a pretty good thing that way. But I don't think it would have bothered Frank in any case. Frank had his convictions and those people knew where to find him. They didn't have to hunt for him at all! - so far as his convictions were concerned.

They had nice chaplains before but I think that they had wrung their hands and felt that this was something about which they could do nothing, and therefore it was something about which they probably should say nothing. And I don't know but what I would have felt that way, except for the manner of this man who came in to see me.

Q: He raised your hackles!

Capt. J.: He sure did.

Q: Is there anything comparable to a situation like that was ever tossed out to the students in chaplains' school, as a problem to deal with?

Capt. J.: I don't know. So far as I can recall, it's the only problem of that type that I ever encountered. It wouldn't be the kind of thing that you would prepare as a case, let us say, to represent something one might expect, because it is something, I think, that normally speaking, in the Navy you don't at all expect. The ecumenical movement in the Navy far predates good Pope John XXIII. It's been a living force since long before I joined the Navy.

Q: It's born of wartime experience, isn't it?

Capt. J.: Yes, and long before World War II the care of Navy chaplains for each other of different faiths was clearly present in the senior people that I knew when I was a JG. Their parishioners, I think, felt that when a Catholic chaplain was friendly with the Protestant, or the other way round, in that they were more Christian than otherwise.

Q: It wasn't a matter of proselyting, was it?

Capt. J.: No, no, I don't think so. There was probably some of that, but it wasn't a big issue, I don't believe. Also, the fact is, and it was then, that in many cases the only chaplain who was around on some occasions was either a Catholic chaplain by himself or a Protestant chaplain by himself, and in those cases in many ways he had to be the pastor for the whole flock and do what he could for everybody. Navy people came to take that for granted. They themselves are, I think, notably tolerant of differences in belief and practice, far more so, I think, than the average of civilian Christians.

Q: Did you find your flock any different from others you had dealt with in the Marines and elsewhere? You were dealing now with flyers.

Capt. J.: Yes, they were different.

Q: How did they differ?

Capt. J.: Again, there was a different ethos. There was the ethos of the man who worked on the line, the mechanic, for example. He was like any good artisan anywhere. Military life to him meant being effective in a very demanding job, and the concept of seeing himself in combat was quite far removed. The pilots, on the other hand, were a very special breed of cat, very different. This was when the jets were breaking in. Most of the pilots, as of this time, were men with war experience, fighter pilots especially - I think of Bob Farkas and some of those guys. They were somewhat of the "wild blue yonder" type with a little bit of the Red Baron, and this was considered not to be out of place. They were entitled to be a little eccentric and, indeed, it was regarded as being better than not if they were a little bit on the bias. We got to know them.

They're great people.

I remember especially Jesse Brown, a black pilot. He used to come to my chapel. We got to know him pretty well. A beautiful boy. I next heard about him a couple of years later. He'd been shot down in Korea and was unable to get out of his plane. A Navy pilot from a family that Ruthie knows, Tom Hudner, from Fall River, landed his plane nearby, got out and tried unsuccessfully to rescue him and received the Medal of Honor. Brown was burned to death in his plane.

Q: The fact that flyers live nearer to the possibility of death than the ordinary citizen or ordinary man in the military service makes them different?

Capt. J.: Yes, I think so, to a degree, and in this, in a way, they might be more like Marines than like other naval officers.

Also, the Marine Corps, you know, is tremendously tolerant for idiosyncracies and eccentricities. I'm thinking of some of our shipmates. I worked with Chesty Puller as his chaplain in the First Marines. And Big Foot Brown was a Marine. I don't know if you know about Big Foot Brown.

Q: I know about Puller but I don't know him.

Capt. J.: Big Foot was a great guy. A former enlisted Marine, a very devout Presbyterian. Very tall. He looked very English. He had a hairbrush mustache and looked like a guardsman, very thin, and had big feet. He got his nickname down in Nicaragua. He was on patrol in the far boondocks and sent a message back to base asking to have a pair of shoes delivered by air. And so this pilot came over in an old biplane, swooped down and dropped the box. It had one shoe in it and a note saying the airplane wasn't big enough to carry both and he'd deliver the other one next time. Of course, at that time, the Marine Corps was so small that stories like this got around. From that point on, he was known as Big Foot Brown. He was a highly gifted officer. He blew up a critique one time. We had divisional maneuvers, then a critique in the theater. Major General Hart was an especially pompous and stuffy, very un-Marine-like officer, division commander. A very brave officer, but awfully stuffy, and he couldn't tolerate these people who were relaxed.

Anyway, Big Foot was commanding the Tenth Marines and it came his turn to give his critique on the maneuvers. He came on stage with an alarm clock in his hand. He announced to the 1,500 people who were there that the alarm clock had been set to go off at the end of his time limit. When it went off he'd stop talking, and he did. But his critique was what really fractured everybody. The burden of it was very simple.

He said, in the Marine Corps we've got tanks. There was a time when we could lay wire from the Tenth Marines (artillery) up to the Second Marines (infantry) and nothing much would happen. Now, he said, we have tanks and the tanks go over the wire and they break it. This severs connections and interrupts important conversations. He said this as if it were all news. Well, everybody sort of sat back and said, well, what's new.

Then he really gave it to us. This has only been true, he said, for twenty-five years and with this assembled talent here, a two-star general - and he named him - a one-star general, and colonels all over the place, nobody has figured out a solution. Next year, he said, we're going out and do you know what we're going to do? We're going to run the tank over the god-damned wire and we're going to cut them again and I'm not going to be able to reach the infantry again. Then the alarm clock sounded off.

Well, the place blew up, and, of course, Hart was furious, absolutely furious, but there wasn't much he could do. Big Foot's time with the 10th Marines was pretty nearly up. Hart couldn't take his regiment away from him, because he'd only told the truth. This kind of a man the Marine Corps cherishes, and to an extent, it seems to me, I saw something like it in the pilots. Many of them were young and maybe not as confirmed in their evil ways, say, as Big Foot Brown was.

Big Foot, you know, retired after thirty-five years in the Marines as a major general. He started as a private in World War I. Then he went to the University of Alabama and got his Ph.D. in history.

Q: Where did you serve with him?

Capt. J.: At Camp Lejeune and in Korea. In Korea, as a matter of fact, later, he took over the regiment that I was in, the First Marines. He became regimental commander. Great old fellow.

A couple of things I remember that are of no great moment but they go to make the life of a chaplain or of the Navy man.

I remember having a Navy Relief show at Quonset Point. It was like almost any show. I was asked to form a men's chorus to sing some rollicking songs. We sang "Stouthearted Men," "Cruising Down the River," and things like that. One boy in the chorus had a lovely voice and I suggested that he sing a solo. He did. He then left the Navy and became a professional. His name was Julius LaRosa. He got involved in a real wingding with Arthur Godfrey some years later. He was singing on Godfrey's show on television and he committed lese majeste of some sort and offended Godfrey, who was god during those two or three years. Godfrey fired him with much unction. But he's conducted a successful career ever since.

The other thing I remember was a beautiful man who used to come down from Providence. He was Dan Byron, of the National Catholic Community Services. It didn't matter that I was a Protestant. He'd come in say, as he did to Frank O'Leary, "Hi, Glyn," sit down, relax, have a cup of coffee, talk and say, "What do you need?" I had the same experience with the National Catholic Community Services down in South Carolina, in Beaufort. They had the USO down there. I was the senior chaplain at Parris Island, came in to visit, and the young man who ran it - this was the beautiful thing about the NCCS - the first thing he'd say to me was, "What do you need."

Anyway, Dan Byron used to run the greatest clambakes. You're a New Englander, aren't you?

Q: No. Well, by adoption, yes.

Capt. J.: Okay. Then you know the clambake. In 1949 we used to have vacation bible schools together, Catholic and Protestant congregations, and we also used to have all our parties together, so they were Dixie Kiefer Chapel parties, Catholics, Protestants, Jews - everybody was invited. Sometimes the Y would do it, but more often Dan Byron did it. When he ran his clambake, everybody really became devout for an evening. Dan would come down and he'd say to me or to Frank, "You know, it's getting near time for a clambake. Why don't you rally the faithful and we'll do it? But I need some lobsters." Well, we got lobsters by getting in touch with a fighter pilot and saying, "Dan Byron's going to have a clambake and we need some of the faithful to provide." So they would fly up to Brunswick, Maine, to get the lobsters. Dan would spend a whole day on that clambake and you wouldn't believe it. I've been to a lot myself, but they were the greatest clambakes I ever attended. And these sailor boys, oh, they loved it. There was no limit to what they could eat. I thought afterwards, wouldn't it be great if churches, whatever churches, could be like that. If somebody could have the sense, well, you know, they're all God's people and, for the moment, one may go to Mass and another to the eucharist over here, but let's have a clambake. An agape meal.

Those people were very close together and I think not merely because of the clambakes. I think they became close together as Christians. I think they started to see themselves doing these things together, not merely as accidental people who happened along but as people who were Christians, shared the same sanctuary.

Q: Is it perhaps, Glyn, because within an organization like the Navy there's more framework to the existence, the regulations hold them together as a unit?

Capt. J.: I think that certainly is one factor. There's nothing in civilian life that says a church here should share a building or a particular church there. Here we had only one chapel and we had to share it. But I think it goes further than that. It seems to me there's something in the Navy community itself, some sense of our having to depend on each other, entirely apart from religion.

Q: On shipboard, for instance?

Capt. J.: On shipboard.

Q: We're all in this together.

Capt. J.: Yes. The fighter pilot has his tail man. His life is in that pilot's hands. Go throughout the service - there's an ultimate dependence. We're talking about life and death. And the wives are very sensitive to this. Ruthie can tell you about what happens when a Marine division gets orders to leave in twenty-four hours for, as it says in the orders, "duty beyond the seas." She can tell you a story that will bring tears to your eyes, of people caring for people.

When they do this in the ordinary affairs of life, somehow their practice, which is above that of religion in many cases, gets transferred to their religious insight and they won't remain content with the Protestant chaplain who runs down his Roman Catholic colleague or vice versa. They're not going to buy this. In some ways they bring us up. We think that we're bringing them up, and maybe we are in some ways, but I think they bring us up, too.

Q: In the larger sense, extending it beyond a unit like the Naval Air Station at Quonset, did you find this same spirit prevailing in the Navy throughout the world, as you went elsewhere, particularly with the chaplains?

Capt. J.: Oh, with the chaplains, yes. You know, chaplains get so used to being a chaplain in the U.S. Navy and it becomes so routine to them that they soon forget that they have a wondrous treasure in their hands, something very precious, because they simply take it for granted. I took Frank O'Leary and John Wissing and David Casazza and George Rosso, name them all, for granted. It never occurred to me to think toward them the way that as, for a brief time, a civilian pastor I had thought about the Roman Catholic priest who lived not far from me. There's simply no way that those two patterns of thought can be equated.

So there's something tremendously precious here. The great thing about our people of all kinds is that they accept it. I think they feel it would be great if in the outer world this kind of normal acceptance of each other were the case, instead of the distance that until recently characterized the relationships of Christian and Jewish people.

Q: Very interesting.

You mentioned the benefit put on by the Navy Relief Society. What was the role of the chaplain with the Relief Society at Quonset?

Capt. J.: Frank O'Leary, as the senior chaplain, was the executive secretary - wait a minute, the executive vice president. By regulation, as I remember, he couldn't be the executive secretary. That job was held by a civilian social worker, Emily Farrell. She did much of the interviewing, but the chaplains did a great deal. Many men would come to us who didn't want to talk to a civilian. They needed money, they needed family help, they needed referral to a social agency. They knew Frank and they knew me and they would come to us. We could often then get them over to Emily, who had expertise in this that we didn't have on hard questions, and they would go. But they wouldn't come to her often for the initial thing.

I was ordered to Newfoundland during that year to help organize a Navy Relief auxiliary there. The chapter would be at Quonset Point, but our auxiliary would be up in Newfoundland.

Q: In Halifax?

Capt. J.: No, at the Naval Air Station up there. I forget where it was now.

Q: Argentina?

Capt. J.: Yes. I don't know what has happened to the Auxiliary since. It meant that instead of having Navy Relief problems referred from Argentina to Quonset Point there was an agency right at hand that could do the work. It was financed from our office and the books were kept at our office, that kind of thing. They reported to us. It seemed to be a good arrangement.

Q: Did you have the same feeling that Roland seemed to have about the Navy Relief and the role of the chaplain? He resented the role of the chaplain.

Capt. J.: Yes. Let me distinguish, if I may. I didn't have a resentment toward what I did at Quonset Point. I think that many men might have refused to come in to Navy Relief if in some sense the chaplain had not been there to be of help, to cooperate and to lead them sometimes.

Now, there's another aspect of things where I think the Navy Relief Society and the personnel people in the Navy have not been honest. It is this. Chaplains have been assigned in the past - whether this is true now, I can't tell you - to duty in places where their entire performance of duty was for the Navy Relief Society. There was a time when some of this could have been understood. In 1937, let us say, there were few chaplains and the Navy Relief Society was a small struggling organization - it was a matter of getting a few bucks for a sailor making $21 a month. During World War II, the Navy Relief Society became an immensely wealthy organization. Vast amounts of money were raised. They were gathered in many ways, through boxing matches and shows and other athletic events, by the annual drive from a vast Navy and Marine

Corps by appeal to civilian resources. When the war ended, here was this huge amount of money, and the armed forces were pared down to roughly the size we have now, maybe a little smaller.

I got involved professionally in this because I was ordered to duty in Washington. In the course of that duty I prepared an instruction requiring a change in policy on the part of the Navy with regard to chaplains and the Navy Relief Society. It defined a carefully limited relationship between the two. I was promised that it would be signed, but at the last moment Vincent Murphy, a retired vice admiral, who was then the president of the Navy Relief Society, got in touch with the Chief of Naval Personnel and pulled the rug out from under. CNP refused to sign it.

The burden of this, very simply, was that now the Navy had become a big boy, no longer the 100,000 men of 1936, the Marine Corps no longer the 19,000 of the mid-thirties. The Navy was big. The Navy Relief Society now handled a large capital fund. The time had come to professionalize Navy Relief services, to see that sailors and Marines got the very best professional service that could be provided to them in many fields, social work, psychiatric social work, and so on. But the Navy Relief Society, still run by naval officers, thought of things as they were in the thirties, saw the Society as a personal domain, and felt that saving a nickel here and a nickel there was the essence of good management. There were, so to speak, battleship admirals in the age of the carriers. Well, the essence of good management was to provide the best possible services, and this they did not accomplish.

These services could easily have been made available by the income of the Society. It would have been a rare year when the Society would have run into a deficit, and that would have been a year such as, let us say, when they had an earthquake in Alaska or something of that magnitude. But we would then have had professional social services working with other professional services in the Navy. In other fields than the Navy we find professional services developing during that period that were essentially needed. The Navy internally saw their necessity. We saw the development of the Medical Service Corps, personnel management, food services and so on. Navy Relief was one instance where there was a refusal to do it.

By the same token, from the standpoint of personnel administration in the Navy, every billet has to be justified, in terms of a particular job description. There's no legal way to write a billet description that has a chaplain working 100 per cent of his time for the Navy Relief Society. It's against the law. The Navy Relief Society is a private organization.

This sounds as if I'm hostile to the Society. I'm not. I'm hostile, however, to the deception that is practiced, or was practiced then. I certainly am hostile to clergy being used for purposes for which their churches did not endorse them, being used full time by a private agency, being taken out of the ministry of religion. I'm for what the Navy Relief Society does. I'm for what I did in Quonset Point. I have no apologies for it. I would go to my church tomorrow and say that this was an important part of my ministry. But I'm against the basic fraud that was perpetrated in the past by misuse of Navy chaplains. The Navy Relief Society refused to come into the twentieth century and to become the kind of professional organization that the Navy in every other respect has found necessary. I resent that almost as much as its prostitution of the Navy chaplaincy.

Q: I am glad you brought in that discussion of the Navy Relief Society.

Capt. J.: Well, I don't know if things have changed and, if they have, I'm a great believer in it. There's no other organization that does as much for the bluejacket.

Q: What about the assistance rendered by the American Red Cross?

Capt. J.: Priceless. Here, again, is a matter on which I have very strong feelings. I heard routine criticism and bad-mouthing of the Red Cross while I was in the service, for many years and in many places. This generally is uniformed, ignorant criticism by people who don't know what the Red Cross does.

I've had Red Cross men go with our divisions into combat and serve men there willingly, not having any official standing in the event they were taken POW, for example. They were simply members of the Red Cross and they hoped for the best, just as chaplains hope for the best. What the Red Cross does for men routinely every day in the service in the way of verifying emergency-leave situations, providing emergency assistance in terms of money, sometimes housing, food, other things - it's very hard for me to accept anybody criticizing it. Because the privacy of the recipient is respected, a great deal of what the Red Cross does is not noticed. The only way people sometimes learn about it is when they come to a chaplain and say "I need help. I'm behind in my furniture payments." And we give a buzz to the Red Cross. They say, "How about coming over and Mrs. Smith will talk to you," and it's taken care of.

So I think Red Cross from the standpoint of the service is often a very maligned organization and deserves better from servicemen than I think it receives.

Q: That sort of criticism is always based on something very specific, a minor case that didn't materialize, perhaps.

Capt. J.: Very often. Sometimes it is based, too, on mistakes made by Red Cross men. But if the Chaplain Corps were to be judged by the mistakes we make, God bless us, we'd be dead. You have to judge the Red Cross as you judge anybody else, by the totality of their function. The closer you find a commanding officer to the needs of his men and the chaplain to the needs of his men, the more you will find those people depending on the Red Cross and believing in the Red Cross. It's people who don't know, I think, who criticize the Red Cross.

Some of this may date back as far as World War I and at my age I can't speak with firsthand knowledge there. But I've heard that kind of criticism. The Salvation Army is spoken of well but no one much asking the question, "What were they allowed to do by the military commands?" I don't know the orders but I strongly suspect they were not allowed to go on the front lines.

Q: Well, Sir, after your Quonset Point service, you left in August of 1949 and went back to the Marines, to the Second Marine Division, in Lejeune.

Capt. J.: Yes.

Q: And you smiled?

Capt. J.: I was very happy. I had wanted to go back to the Marines. I couldn't complain against duty in the cruiser and being sent to Harvard and because I had to finish off a two-year cruise ashore. I couldn't complain against going to Quonset Point. But I always wanted to go back to the Marines and now I was being sent. As I mentioned to you before, I had been at Lejeune very early in the game. I joined up and was assigned as regimental chaplain to the Second Marines.

We had a half-size regiment, 1,500 men, two rifle companies to a battalion, two battalions to the regiment. There were some attached artillery, the Tenth Marines, engineers, and so on. Each regiment in our turn had a battalion that went to the Med. A battalion from the Second Marine Division was always on duty in the Mediterranean.

Q: With the Sixth Fleet?

Capt. J.: Yes. I didn't go out there. It occurred to me that the chaplain should participate in the training of the Marines, specially from the standpoint of offering something in the way of ethical instruction. I went to see my colonel, who was a young colonel then and became a young brigadier general, by the name of Randall Victory, and I said to him, "I want into your training schedule." He said, "What do you want to do?" and I told him. This is a great thing about the Marines. You can do something like this and they will listen to you. He said, sure, "We're not getting much mileage out of you. You could just sit in your office while I go out among the troops. Here we've got a man who is a specialist in his field; we should be using you, and we'd get more mileage out of you." It was that simple to him.

So I began to give what then was called - the Army had them doing it before us - character guidance, which later got called character education, moral leadership and other titles, going to the troops and conducting discussions with them on ethical questions, in the field for the most part. Not in barracks, unless it was really bad weather in the winter or something. The troops were willing to talk. I mentioned to you before that if you have served with the Marines before and especially if you've had combat experience, the senior NCOs say to the people, "The chaplain's coming, now listen to this guy. He's been with us and he generally knows what he's talking about." Well, this sets everything up.

I'd played some baseball in my younger years. We started a divisional baseball league. The regiments had teams, special troops and so on. So I was invited with Frank Tatum, CO of H & S Company, to coach the regimental baseball team. We had a very knowledgeable regimental 1 officer by the name of Bill Reaves. Frank was an old enlisted man. He and I talked about the team and finally said to each other, "Let's go and see Bill Reaves."

We said to Bill, "We're going to be in this league and we need some ball players and we'd appreciate some cooperation from 1 section."

Bill had been in the Marine Corps then twenty years or more, so he euchered around. We pretty soon got some transfers into the regiment and they were pretty good ball players.

Q: Proselyting!

Capt. J.: Well, yes. Do you want to play ball? We need ball players. We started to run away with this thing. We cornered the talent. In the meantime, there was a base team. This was what was called the big team. It played minor league ball clubs and college ball clubs and traveling Cuban Giants, and at other military bases. It was coached by a great Marine named Mo Zorn, later company commander in the Seventh Marines. He was then a company commander, I guess, in the Sixth Marines.

Anyway, Mo was having an awfully bad year. He should have stood in bed. His people couldn't win for losing and they looked awful. After work the guys would go over to the bar in the O Club and start to talk. Then there would be talk about Zorn's club. Someone would say, "They've got to get rid of the manager, you know, he's no damned good."

Then, as we started to win, Second Marine officers would go out and they'd see Mo and they'd say, "Look we've got a ball club. We'll take you any day of the week. Zorn was saying forget it, but finally the thing got to the point where money started to be put up and Zorn agreed to a ball game. Well, it was really the biggest thing in the Division at that moment. Everybody was excused to go to the ball game.

Q: More entertaining than ethics!

Capt. J.: Money being handed around like mad. Well, to make a long story short, we beat them quite handily. I forget, but 7 to 2 or something. And that night was a big night at the Club. The Second Marines were riding high, collecting free drinks from the losers.

Next morning I went in to talk with Frank and savor our victory. I tell you he looked as if he'd been harpooned. He said:

"Bill Reaves just came down to see me. Everyone of our ball players has been transferred to the base."

Our general had two hats. He was the base commander and he was also the division commander. From the base-commander hat he ordered the division commander to transfer our ball players to the base. As a result Mo Zorn had himself a ball club —

Q: By fiat!

Capt. J.: Yes, just like that! We had a couple of ball games left and started to scramble for some bodies. Before we could do anything we got orders, duty beyond the seas, Korea.

Q: You were saved by a war!

Capt. J.: Oh, a lot of boys who played in that league never lived beyond it. It was the last fun thing they ever did.

Q: You started to tell me about the moral leadership training you introduced there, and you put emphasis on discussion.

Capt. J.: Yes. A great deal of Marine, and I suppose Army and Navy training then, was many years behind the times in terms of communications. Some things were great. These had come out of the war, when training devices and aids of various sorts had been prepared for the Navy by professionals and had been executed by professionals. But some of the other things, how to field-strip an M-1, these came from Caesar's Gallic wars, and maybe some of them couldn't be changed. But there was other instructing that was simply straight lecture given by people incompetent to hold a decent conversation, to say nothing of lecturing.

Q: Learning by rote!

Capt. J.: Exactly. Learning by rote the whole thing. It didn't seem to me that this was going to do any good. It seemed to me that the only thing that was going to make any impact on the minds of these kids was something in which they participated.

My experience tended to ratify this. I remember talking about the question of discipline. My point is the obvious one, whereas discipline is a voluntary discipleship, whence the word comes. It is voluntary choice to follow a person or way of life which becomes guiding and dominating in the life of a man. This was my burden.

We talked about it. Finally, one old master sergeant, with whom I'd served before, said, more or less, "Chaplain, I don't like to disagree with you, but I've got to be fair to these Marines and I've got to tell you where I don't see it the way you do." I said, "OK, fine, Sergeant." He said, "Take my boy. I caught him smoking a cigarette when I'd told him not to. I didn't give him any of this stuff of be a disciple and follow me - because I smoked cigarettes, too - I did something that works. I took him out behind the barn with a strap and I learned him - whack, whack-" And he settled back in comfortable certainty as only a Marine sergeant can. There was a silence. Everybody cogitated on how he took him out and "learned" him. Then a bright little sergeant said:

"Now, Sarge, I want to ask you a question. I want to know what you learned him. Did you learn him not to smoke cigarettes, or did you learn him not to get caught smoking cigarettes?"

I was home safe. The Marines took this. All at once, there was all the difference in the world. They knew very well the common thing that it's good if you don't get caught, but when somebody asserts it as a teaching device they aren't going to buy that.

In the short run a particular discussion may abort. In the long run if the people are really free and easy and feel that their participation is respected and welcomed, I think you end up having somebody most of the time hitting the center of the target and saying, "Wait a minute."

Q: And that's the teaching element?

Capt. J.: Oh, yes, and obviously that's much more powerful teaching than if I had said, "Well, look, Sarge, let me tell you something now." They'd just say the chaplain's sounding off again.

Q: Yes. He's preaching.

Capt. J.: He's preaching, but when another Marine said it they thought this was a valid question. He saw it was. It started him thinking. He hadn't thought of that. And he wasn't responding to me, he was responding to a peer. Somewhere in there, I think, is where we have something to give, if we can learn restraint. I suppose we're so expert in pontificating -

Q: We jump in!

Capt. J.: I think sometimes we do.

Q: But in that case you did not. This was the genesis of the discussion group?

Capt. J.: I wouldn't say so. But it was with me.

Q: That's what I mean.

Capt. J.: Yes. This was about October, 1949. I suspect that

probably there were other chaplains in the Navy doing something comparable at the same time. I don't know this.

Q: If so, it wasn't by direction, they simply discovered this on their own?

Capt. J.: Yes, it was not by any central direction from on high. I realized if I was going to do this that it couldn't be an individual solo effort on my part. I was asking the colonel that I wanted to get in on his training schedules. This had to be formally an assignment to me that appeared in the training schedule in writing. The whole regiment would see that the colonel had said this was going to happen. Once they see that, there's no question about whether it should happen or not. It's going to happen. And that's one of the advantages of being in the military service.

I'd like to say one other thing. It's an awfully easy thing to blow, so that after two weeks it's entirely conceivable that a company commander would get in touch with the commanding officer and say, "Hey, look, get this padre off us. He's riding us to death. This stuff is deadly." And pretty soon the order is quietly cancelled; there's no big todo about it and the guy is out with his pieties again.

Q: But that did not happen in your case?

Capt. J.: It didn't happen in my case.

Q: Tell me how you conducted it.

Capt. J.: It was pretty simple. First I made known in advance what we were going to talk about.

Q: How did you do that? Posted it?

Capt. J.: Oh, no, no. You could post it. I had it read in the orders of the day, "This morning's discussion will be on the subject of umpty-ump," and in other ways. Often I would invite a specialist in.

For example, I got involved in questions of sex and I found a doctor who was literate. This doctor was literate not only in understanding the physical aspects of sex but the psychological and the moral aspects. So when it came time, on this I'd say to the Marines, "Well, here's the subject, on which I have some ideas, but on the other hand we've got a professional here. You can talk to him." And they'd talk with the doctor in the same way.

Q: You used other experts in addition to the doctor on sex?

Capt. J.: Yes. In a place as large as Camp Lejeune there were an awful lot of people who had expertise in an awful lot of areas, if we could find out who they were.

Q: You mean people on station?

Capt. J.: On station and sometimes they were enlisted people, sometimes officers, sometimes other people.

A byproduct, though, of this experience, in the Second Marines anyway, was to me even more interesting than the discussions we had. One of the important realities in Marine social life is barracks conversation. It's a tremendously important factor in peer influence. I was told that some of the interesting discussions that we held began to preempt barracks conversation. People unwilling to talk in the discussion groups -

Q: That's natural!

Capt. J.: Natural - became willing to ask questions and to talk, hold opinions in the barracks. Sometimes they would have really good bull sessions with the happy option of not having the chaplain there.

Q: When did these take place, generally speaking? At the end of the day?

Capt. J.: It took place at many different times. I got reports about them from enlisted men who were favorably inclined toward this activity, who felt that something along this line should be done with their buddies, who generally were sympathetic to my point of view. So I found out really almost without trying a great deal about barracks discussions that took place as a consequence. I think I can fairly say that to the extent we had impact it wasn't limited to what happened in the training schedule. If we really talked about something useful, something that stuck in their minds, it simply spread through the regiment. A lot of people talked about it. I wouldn't say at all that a lot of people were converted to anything in particular. I would say, though, that certain points of view that had not been prominent or even noticeable before were beginning to get heard, and they were getting heard from Marines to Marines not from me to them.

Q: How large a group would you have as a discussion group?

Capt. J.: I'd have a fixed group at a time. It would depend. I'd normally have a platoon, which would be about forty-two men, which is a little large.

Q: Too large for the shy ones to speak up?

Capt. J.: Oh, sure, and that you'd sort of expect. You'd hope that for the shy ones there'd be something interesting enough to keep their attention and to rub off on them. Later, however, as I say, some of these people would talk in the barracks who wouldn't talk in the group, and there would be a concentration, for a time, anyway, on some of these subjects, for the moment putting to one side the favorite subjects of barracks conversation.

Q: Did you attempt to incorporate your experiences in developing this series? Did you attempt to do that in some sort of a manual?

Capt. J.: No, I did not. There are a number of reasons for it. The chief probably was that at the time when we were ordered overseas I still had no great confidence in the content of what we were doing. My intentions were good but I felt that something much better could be done than what I was doing. I had begun to develop

G. Jones #2 - 156

confidence in our method, in the discussion method. It didn't seem to me I had anything that would approach, however, the preparation of a manual.

Q: If you'd been there longer this would probably have evolved, but you were only there a year, were you not?

Capt. J.: I was only there a year. Whether it would after another year, which would have been my tour, I don't know.

Q: I read your article on citizenship education in the armed forces and printed in the <u>Junior College Journal</u> for September 1952. You referred to your tour of duty in Parris Island and were supporting generally the idea of citizen education as a very valuable development in the military.

Capt. J.: Yes. By the time I had gone to Parris Island a number of changes had taken place. The most important was that I had been in the office of the Chief of Chaplains in 1951 and had been urging that this program be given formal authorization within the naval service. A lot of things had taken place since I'd left Camp Lejeune. Other chaplains were by this time involved, maybe had been before I had been. I wanted the chief to sponsor a program formally, to get money, to get training for people to run it, to get time in training schedules, to use it - all of these things. Well, there was very little response in the office of the Chief of Chaplains. This was one of a number of complaints that I had. I felt we were just spinning wheels and I wanted to get out of there and go some place else. So I ended up going to Parris Island.

Other people before me had inaugurated a program at Parris Island. It was not a very good one, but they had time in the training schedule. The question was whether we were going to use it well enough. We began to develop some materials that we hoped would improve on what they were using. We got more time in the training schedule for recruits. We also got time in the training schedule of permanent personnel, the enlisted personnel. I have some place here copies of lectures that I gave to all of the officers at Parris Island in connection with this. I was strongly supported by the commanding general, whom you may know, Merwin Silverthorne, a lieutenant general, former assistant commandant of the Marine Corps. So we were instructing basically on every level, if you count what I was doing with the officers as being instruction for the people authorizing the program in various commands so that they would know what they were doing.

At this point, our stress was largely, I would say, in the area of citizenship education.

Q: It had grown into a much larger area rather than i?

Capt. J.: No. At this point I would say it had compressed into a smaller subject area which had become more broadly executed.

Q: I see.

Capt. J.: This was what the Marines down there were willing to buy at the time, citizenship education. Moral or character education they weren't ready for. They didn't want to talk this too much. This was not Camp Lejeune of two years before but a recruit training depot; they were talking about making the Marine a good citizen first of the Marine Corps. This they could accept. They could accept the notion, for example, that competence in one's job is a moral category. For one to clean a rifle well is a moral achievement as well as a mechanical accomplishment. If he cleans it badly, it's not only lousy mechanics - if he intends to clean it badly, it's lousy morals, too. We were talking at this level of morality, pragmatic, not the highest by any means. But this is where we had to begin.

We moved from this into other echelons. We eventually had somebody teaching the women Marines, who also were trained down there, and were able to raise the level of the indoctrination. As I remember the <u>Junior College Journal</u> thing was a request to me. Somebody had heard that we were doing something in citizenship education and I tried to describe it.

Q: I gathered from the article that that probably was the case. I take it that the new recruits were at Parris Island but the men at LeJeune were -

Capt. J.: Not recruits. They were in the FMF. I was in the FMF, in the Second Marine Division. This doesn't involve at all what was happening to permanently based personnel there, who were attached to the Marine Corps base at Camp Lejeune. Many of these men were men who had combat experience, some of them were not.

Some of them were men fresh from boot camp.

Q: That was an interesting experience for you to be involved in at Lejeune. I mean the additional effort in that educational area.

Capt. J.: It was indeed.

Q: And it was more or less innovative for the Marine Corps as a whole, wasn't it?

Capt. J.: I don't know how much because, as I say, I don't know to what extent other chaplains at that time were doing this kind of thing.

Q: Going back previous to that time, when you were at the Williamsburg school, was there any thought of this sort of thing developing among chaplains in the various branches of the service?

Capt. J.: Not to my knowledge. So far as I can remember, the concept began in the U.S. Army, with the Army Chaplain Corps. and it was strongly encouraged by the Army chief of staff about vintage 1946, 1947. Lawton Collins, perhaps. I couldn't say, but it seems to me it was about of his vintage and, having that kind of command support, it became an Army-wide program. There wasn't anybody else in the Army qualified to offer this kind of thing. The Army felt it ought to be offered, so almost in a sense by default the chaplains ended up doing it. Their materials of that vintage were very, very poor.

Q: Was there any relationship between the origins and development of that sort of thing in the Army with what was going on in the civilian population? I mean was there, as one casts his mind back, beginning to be a breakdown in moral standards in the civilian world?

Capt. J.: I don't know. That's a question on which I'm sure you could get opinions.

On the question of character education, however, which is a separate question, there were things happening in the civilian world. Some universities, Columbia in particular, were beginning to do studies in this field. Some school systems were beginning to make experiments. In due course we found work being done especially in the Middle West having to do with moral education. That effort has continued on a small scale, so far as I know, ever since. Now we have at Harvard, for example, a man who is probably the world's greatest expert in this field. He doesn't have a lot of programatic work being done over the country at which he can look, but he is a man who is a professional in the area of character education.

Another man with whom I had worked here at this school has been in this area, too. He is a Jesuit by the name of Jim di Giacomo. Jim is an adjunct professor at Fordham and he teaches at Brooklyn Prep. A few years ago I was interested in doing away with required chapel here in the school, which I was convinced was a very bad thing. I had from my own observation come to the conclusion that required religion was very damaging to young people.

One of the reasons was that, in my opinion, there was among adolescents an underlying subliminal fear of the God concept. I didn't have any clinical evidence to support that view. Then I found that work had been done in this field by Jim di Giacomo. He strongly defended that view on the basis of hiw own clinical findings. I got in touch with him. I had him up here at the school telling the people we're doing damage to these kids by making them go to church. The official representative of God, so to speak, appeared in cassock and surplice and was seen by them as a threat against whom they could not defend themselves. A highly threatening situation to teenagers. In dealing with di Giacomo I found that some of the basic concepts attending character education had the same kind of clinical support.

We were very interested in separating character education from any aspect of enforced religion. This was very hard for the chaplains, Catholic chaplains in particular, who found themselves having to fall back on natural theology and on an ethic that had theistic support, and found themselves simply unable to copy or really honestly to present another ethic.

We were interested in presenting an ethic that was situational, that arose out of the common necessities of life, to which men had to respond and to which they could respond ethically or unethically but without an authoritarian base, especially without a particular theological base, and yet one that was consistent with the Hebraic ethic though not consistent nor inconsistent with Christian ethics. Inconsistent in the sense that the Christian ethic is not an ethic of law. We were talking an ethic of law in a limited sense, so we couldn't cope with an ethic of grace.

I had some interesting talks about this with Jim Gustafson, who was at first very much opposed to the effort we were making and felt it was a waste of time. Gardually, as time passed, I think he changed to a degree. He felt that the ethical demands of different situations sometimes called for different solutions, for the possible solution and not the absolute solution.

Q: Well, shall we go to Korea?

Capt. J.: Yes, all right.

Q: In August of 1950 you went with the First Marine Division.

Capt. J.: Yes. I was with the Second Division, as you know, in Camp Lejeune. We were ordered in July to Camp Pendleton to help to constitute the new First Marine Division, the union of the then First Marine Division at Pendleton and the Second Marine Division, both of which were very much under-strength, of isolated Marine units from various commands, and of the raiding of Marine barracks all over the country, all over the world, for veteran Marines, raiding ships' detachments for veteran Marines, grabbing for combat veteran Marines any place we could get them.

Q: This was because of the suddenness of the involvement?

Capt. J.: Yes.

Q: And the state of our armed forces?

Capt. J.: Yes. The state of our armed forces. Louis Johnson, in effect, had wrecked them, if I may speak unpolitically! These were good Marines but there were too few. General MacArthur had asked for a division and the government had said there would be a division, and so he got a division.

When we got to Pendleton a very complex system was set up of deciding who could go and who could not go. I forget the criteria that were established. We called in reserve units, too. If one was a reserve he had to have belonged for so long a time and gone to so many drills and so on. If one were a regular he would have had to have met certain criteria. Many, many men were turned down. Many other men who, under other circumstances, would not have been taken - married men who had fought four years in the Second World War, for example - were taken. Those men would not have been taken under other circumstances, but there was a time factor and they were taken.

When we arrived we found that Colonel Puller, Lewis Puller, was going to be our regimental commander. He'd been on duty at Pearl Harbor. When Korea broke out he sent a dispatch to the commandant asking for command of a regiment. He'd already commanded a regiment. The commandant, I think, was not inclined, but Puller bombarded him with this and promised to pay his own fare back and that of his family, and he did. He paid for his family to go to Saluda, Virginia, and he himself ended up at Pendleton at his own expense and he took command.

I had known his brother Sammy. I had heard all the sea stories

G. Jones #2 - 164

about Lewis Puller in between wars, but I didn't know him. I found to my happiness that he was a great regimental commander and a good Christian man. He has his limitations, as all of us do, but they were in a context that I felt I could understand and sympathize with. I felt he was very much sinned against by the press. He was a man who, by the nature of the case, attracted comment as sugar attracts flies, and a great deal of the comment was uninformed. They didn't understand the Marines.

When I went to see him and introduce myself, he knew my name. He said, "Well, what's your idea of being a chaplain in this outfit?" A good question, right?

Q: Much to the point.

Capt. J.: It was the point, wasn't it?

I said, "Serving the troops wherever they are." He said, "You do that, and you tell me what you want me to do to help you. I'll never get in your way." And I found this was true. I could go any place I wanted in the regiment at any time. I could use his name to support what I wanted done. Amazing man. But in a couple of days when I saw these great varieties of personnel coming in, in a hurry, unprepared, especially the reserves, I went to him and I said, "We're going to be in combat before very long. I checked with an insurance man in San Diego and no war clause has yet been put into insurance. I'd like to invite as many insurance men as I can from San Diego to come up and sell insurance to the First Marines."

He said, "OK, what do you need?"

I said, "I need a huge tent, the biggest tent I can get, many tables, long lines of tables, and then I'd like to have the regiment mustered, have it explained to them what's going to happen, and have them marched through and those who want can buy insurance, now."

He said, "It will be done. The only thing that will have priority is the rifle range." They put up these huge tents, set up these long lines of tables. I don't know how many insurance men we got from San Diego, twenty maybe, in that vicinity, set them up, and brought these kids through. It was one of the most beautiful and one of the most pathetic experiences I ever had in my life. The kids did buy insurance. I don't know how much. God knows how much. The war clause was going to be invoked in a matter of three or four days. Marines came in -

Q: I was wondering about the insurance companies, why they would sell insurance under those circumstances?

Capt. J.: I think the insurance companies might not have been willing to. I think the insurance agents were. That may be a little too crass an explanation. I talked first with an ex-Marine named Rocky Pharr, and he recruited the agents. A few of the men were veteran Marines whose wife was the Marine Corps, had no home, no family. They're going to get shot at again, these men, and they figured they might as well get some insurance. They were not going to be able to spend their money, anyway.

Q: Was there in existence no government insurance?

Capt. J.: Oh, there was then government insurance. This was private insurance.

Q: Supplementary?

Capt. J.: Supplementary, yes, to whatever they had. There were kids who wanted to get insurance but had no one to leave it to. I'd never known before for how many people the Marine Corps is home, their only home. I tell you, you hear a few things like this and it brings tears to your eyes. You figure from how far behind some people have to come and what great people they end up being. It's awfully easy to pass judgment.

Anyway, we sold insurance. Chesty was very pleased. Not least because he felt the insurance companies were getting taken! He was sort of pleased at that. Well, be that as it may.

In thirty days some of those beneficiaries began collecting.

I had a curious experience there. I had learned before I left Lejeune that I was going to be ordered into the Chief of Chaplains' office to relieve Harris Howe, who was a very dear friend and is a very dear friend of mine. Big, brash, aggressive, loud guy. He'd been a Baptist and has become an Episcopalian since. Harris told me I was to come in and relieve him as the personnel officer, the detail officer. I wasn't too happy about this but there wasn't much I could do.

Well, our move to Pendleton caught Harris by surprise. He wasn't expecting me to go. He heard I had gone after a few days, so he sent a dispatch out detaching me.

Q: As of now?

Capt. J.: As of now, return to Lejeune. I'd spend probably six weeks or two months there and then relieve him in Washington. The first I heard about this was a call to go up and see the colonel. He said, "Say, I've got this set of orders for you. Do you want to go?" I said, "Of course, not." Now here's the difference in the mentality of the Marine Corps and the Navy. A Marine commander going into battle gets whoever he wants from wherever. He gets whatever the Marine Corps can give him, no matter from where. In the Navy you make do with what you have.

Chesty Puller talked like a Marine and his thinking was very simple. I'll send a dispatch saying I need this guy, and he did. This got to Harris Howe's desk in the Chaplains' Division and it infuriated him. This damned Jones is pulling strings, he thought, he's trying to stay there, he's upsetting my plan! So he went up with a dispatch for the signature of the Chief of Personnel saying "Detach immediately."

Q: Who was the chief?

Capt. J.: I think it was Admiral Roper, but I'm not sure - John Roper. Anyway, Roper didn't know so he put his John Hancock on it. Well, here comes a dispatch detaching me again. Then Chesty got in the act. He called me in and we talked. He had some choice opinions about the Chief of Naval Personnel and various other people in Washington. He said, "I am going to prepare a dispatch and this is going to be for General Smith personally to send to the commandant of the Marine Corps. We're not going to go for that damned Navy nonsense."

Q: Marine Corps chaplains!

Capt. J.: Well, I said, "Aye, aye, Sir." So he did. He prepared a hot one and General Smith tempered it. General Smith was a very gentle person. I don't know if you know him?

Q: No.

Capt. J.: Well, he's one of God's elect, a very devout man, a Christian Scientist, a very gentle person. So he gentled Chesty's dispatch, sent it to the commandant, who was General Cates, whom Chesty and I both knew, said, "Tell the Chief of Naval Personnel forget it. Cancel this order. I want Jones to say," signed O.P. Smith. In the Marine Corps that's the end of the argument. The commandant is not about to say to a general, a major general in the field, you can't have this major or this lieutenant colonel. So the commandant faithfully sent it down to the Chief of Naval Personnel and Camp Lejeune was an info adder. You know how bureaucracy works.

Q: Yes, I do.

Capt. J.: Well, old Harris really blew his stack this time. I had not only gone over the head of Harris Howe but also over the head of the Chief of Naval Personnel. Now the Commandant had come in and the Marines were telling Harris how to run the Navy. This had to stop. So he sent a real hot message: "Unless," the dispatch read,

"Jones is aboard ship en route, send him back immediately." This thing came in and I was in my tent. It was early evening. The colonel's jeep pulled up. The old man was in the jeep and his bodyguard, a man by the name of Jones. Now Jones - what is this family of Neanderthals that appeared on TV, do you remember? - the Flintstones, Jones looked like a Flintstone. He would fight anybody any time. He was a dead shot and he walked around Chesty Puller the way the Secret Service walks around the president. He was looking at everybody. He was suspicious of everybody!

I thought, "My God, what's happened now? He's got Jones with him."

The old man took his pipe out of his mouth and said, "This blankety blank thing just came. Unless you're aboard ship, you've got to go back." I said, "Aye, aye, Sir."

"Well," he said, "how long will it take you to get aboard ship?"

I said, "Right now, Sir."

"You've got your 782 gear packed?"

"Yes, Sir, I have."

"Jones, you drive him down to San Diego and get him on a ship."

Q: Any ship!

Capt. J.: Jones did. He drove me down to San Diego and I got aboard ship. Then the old man sent a dispatch saying, "Chaplain Jones already aboard ship." I waited there three days for other people to get loaded up. This didn't suit Harris Howe, He didn't know what had happened, but he figured he'd been had by somebody. His own detachment from the bureau was going to be affected, all that kind of thing.

Q: You were kidnapped!

Capt. J.: Well, pleasantly kidnapped, but in the Navy it never would have happened.

Q: So you did get under way?

Capt. J.: Yes, we did. We went to Kobe. We'd been briefed during the voyage about landing on the 15th of September at Inchon. We learned where we were going, about the sea wall, and about Wolmi-Do. The Fifth Marines were going to take that. And about naval gunfire and how the fleet would come in to land the Fifth Marines, then go back out and wait for high tide and so on.

Q: All that was pretty formidable information, wasn't it?

Capt. J.: It was at the time. The tide rise was 29 feet, and the Navy was saying this is a hazardous thing. General MacArthur was saying no problem at all. Admiral Doyle was the task force commander. He was an experienced sailor and he was saying, "I don't want any part of this."

Q: Was that Arty Doyle?

Capt. J.: I forget his first name. Could be, but I don't know.
MacArthur then was coming with this bit about "I have complete

faith in the Navy and the Marine Corps." If there's anything that disarms you completely it's an expression of complete faith in you. Anyway the decision was made. We were going to land.

When we went to Kobe to transship and combat load some of the ships, this typhoon hit us. We were torn away from the pier. Several other ships were adrift in the harbor. It was a very nasty thing. We didn't have steam up. It took a while to do that. Fortunately, there was no really serious collision though there could have been. But these transport skippers were very good, very capable, stayed out of each others' way until they got steam up and fought the thing out.

We went then from Kobe through bad seas to the Inchon landing and ran into all the things they'd predicted. It was an easy landing, not many casualties. They had to blow up the sea wall to bring in reinforcements and supplies and I lost the one important thing any chaplain has - my communion kit. They blew up the sea wall too soon. Huge chunks of concrete, ranging from the size of that TV set to the size of this room, started to come down. We lost some people, and one of those things landed on my communion set. So in the very first half-hour on the beach, there I was. We went through the city without much opposition. We stopped outside. It had been raining and by this time there was a heavy storm. Our regiment was deployed on either side of the main road to Seoul. The Fifth Marines were on our left.

We had three chaplains in our regiment, great guys. There was a boy by the name of Jim Lewis with the Third Battalion, who is now no longer in the Navy. A Catholic chaplain, Kevin Keaney, was with the Second Battalion, and I was with the First Battalion. The First Battalion was on the line that night, sitting in the ditch of the road, and the ditch was maybe eight or nine feet below the road. We decided to just sit there and sleep. We had our ponchos on.

The night passed, and the run continued heavy. The water coming down the ditch started to rise and by the time we got in the morning water was running over our knees. We were too pooped to move. Also we didn't want to move for fear some untrained Marine some place would unload at us. So we were cold and miserable in the morning. But the operation from there on, I think, was quite routine. Outside of Yong Dong Po we had to assault two hills and I banged a knee in the process. We had to assault these hills directly. We lay down heavy mortar fire. When I saw the assault start up one of the hills, I left the one I was on and ran down to get behind the assault to find casualties. I fell and got up limping badly. Later I got a corpsman who tied my knee up. We lost several killed attacking Hill 85 and I wandered around trying to help these people.

One of our companies, Able Company, then went ahead of us into Yong Dong Po. That is a city across the Han from Seoul. Bob Barrow, who's now a three-star general in headquarters, was a captain then, found an opening and knifed right on into the center of the city. He found a railroad passing through and dug the company in on both banks of the railroad. Then, of course, the North Koreans found out that he was there and began to attack.

But he was very securely sited and he had machine guns on either flank and cut these people down. He ended up holding out. I'll never forget one thing that happened, though. The North Koreans were regrouping behind some of the buildings in the city for another assault. They were being harangued by an officer, who was building them up to blood pitch. The Marines could hear this but they didn't know what he was saying. Barrow called down to the end of the line saying, "Can anybody see this character? What's he doing?"

Nobody could, so a Marine at the end of the line slithered down the bank and on his belly went across, still in the darkness, until he got into visual range of this man. There he was standing on a kind of rostrum making a speech to his troops. So the Marine very deliberately zeroed in, shot him, and killed him. Then he got back to his position.

Barrow heard the shot and called back, "What the hell happened?" The boy who had shot him said, "Captain, that poor bastard just talked himself to death."

Well, we took Yong Dong Po, crossed the river, went through Soeul, a very destructive fight going through the city. The Seventh Marines came in about that time, about ten days after we'd been ashore, went in on our left flank. In the middle of the city some of the troops came up from the perimeter down around Pusan, the Seventh Army Division, and there was a failure in liaison. Suddenly we came under heavy artillery fire. The Seventh Division was on what was called South Mountain, looking down into the city and apparently got confused. So we were under heavy fire for a while from them. The Seventh Marines on our left flank continued and we worked through the city. There was a kind of competition about raising American flags in places. MacArthur announced the city had been secured about four days before it was because there was some magical date in his mind, I forget what it was now, that was important for psychological reasons.

Q: The 15th itself was a magical date, wasn't it?

Capt. J.: I guess it was. Well, the 15th was determined really by the tide. I don't know whether other factors had come in. We ended up outside the city, in defensive positions, waiting for the Army to come up from the south. While we were there, I saw something that I found very hard to believe.

I'd seen a lot of corpses in the city. These were described to me as having been killed by the enemy. But then there came some reason to believe that this was not entirely the case. There had been a Captain Kim, South Korean Army, who had shared a foxhole with me two or three nights. One day he disappeared and didn't return. In due course, we found to our surprise that he was a North Korean officer and he'd been caught and executed.

Q: And he'd been sharing your foxhole?

Capt. J.: Yes, and of course accepted. I don't think there was any danger to me at all from this.

Q: No, but was he trying to gain some intelligence?

Capt. J.: Oh, he was trying to gain intelligence, and I think he shared my foxhole only through accident, not through any thought that I knew anything that would help him.

Q: He spoke English, did he?

Capt. J.: He spoke English very well, yes.

When we got to the outskirts of Seoul and were waiting for the troops from the south, one afternoon our battalion commander went off to a conference. He is a very unusual man, Jack Hawkins, a retired colonel now. He had been captured when he was with the Fourth Marines in Corregidor. After a year as a POW, he escaped from Cabanatuan with eight or nine officers and went up into the hills and for another year conducted guerrilla warfare against the Japanese.

Q: In Luzon somewhere?

Capt. J.: In Mindanao, before he was evacuated. A very cool customer and a very fine officer.

Anyhow, I was up on the hill this day at a machine-gun position with a master sergeant, Barber, who was a very good friend of mine. We saw this long procession of people coming toward our line. I said to Barber, "What the devil is happening here?" And he said, "I don't know." So I said, "I'll go down and see." I went down and found that this was a group of people escorted by South Korean officers and men, about 100 people, civilians all, who were being taken up there. They were carrying shovels and picks to dig their own graves and be executed. These were people who were alleged to have supported the enemy in the city. This was civil war, which is very unlike any other war. There were kids there, some eight years old, who were going to be shot because they had carried messages for the North Koreans for a stick of gum, pregnant women to be shot, old ones ignorant about any issues.

When they saw me come down they stopped. They probably thought I was a Marine line officer. Anyway, they soon saw the cross and knew I was a chaplain. So I said to them, "You cannot advance any farther until the Marine commanding officer comes down and authorizes it. You must stay here." The captain, who was the officer in charge, said, "I operate under my own orders and we are planning to execute these people." I pointed out our machine gun position and said, "Do not move, it is very dangerous if you do."

Finally, they settled down. Everybody sat down and waited. Hawkins came back in due course. He went down and verified the allegations we had made to him and took these people away from the South Koreans, at some risk to him, and got them safe some place. I don't know where he got them.

This kind of thing was happening all over the front during this period. I'm sure this was not the only group to whom this was happening.

Q: This was responsible for some of the bodies that were seen in the city?

Capt. J.: Without a doubt. Without a doubt, too, however, some were the responsibility of the North Koreans. Everybody was killing everybody.

As we were moving down the streets, you could tell when we were going to move by hearing the Marines yell, "Fire in the hole." They had come to a new obstruction in the street, they had mined it, and now they were getting away from it so they could blow it up and then advance through it.

A curious thing that I remember in the city - a couple of curious things. One day I recalled that it was Sunday. So I passed the word that I'd be celebrating Holy Communion behind a certain building, out of the line of fire. The fire was coming down the streets.

Q: You'd acquired a kit in the meantime, had you?

Capt. J.: Oh, I got one from the Division chaplain right away. I called him or got in touch with him some way.

I began to celebrate Holy Communion on the back of a jeep. I was simply in my fatigues and a stole and I had a chalice. The Marines started to gather, and out of the holes of the buildings came Koreans, Korean Christians. They understood what was happening. I celebrated Holy Communion and they received. How many there were I don't know but I'll give you a guess. I would say that maybe that particular time there were twenty-five Marines and I would guess more than twice as many Koreans. They didn't know me, I didn't know them, but they knew what was happening, they attended to receive, then disappeared.

I'll never forget something else that happened with Chesty Puller. He was a devout Episcopalian. His personal life could stand muster with anybody's. He had a little trouble with language.

Q: Between strong language and mild language!

Capt. J.: Yes! One day when we were going through Seoul we were having a narrow.

Q: What do you mean a "a narrow"?

Capt. J.: We were having bad trouble. We were under attack, very heavy attack, and this was coming successively from our left down the line. Nobody was running around. Everybody was standing by to repel boarders. I remembered that the next day was Sunday. I called the division chaplain and said, "Look, I'm not going to be able to go back to the regimental CP for a service tomorrow. Can you send somebody up from the rear echelon who will take my place?" He said sure, so I went back and forgot about it.

A day or two later, things had quieted down and I went back to the regiment to see how things were and to get a word or two as to what was happening that I could pass among the troops. I ran into Colonel Puller, sitting on a curbstone, so I pulled up alongside and sat down with him. We started to talk. He wanted to know about things, casualties, who was doing what, the kind of things he'd want to know, and then he said:

"I want to ask you something. We had a chaplain come up from the division to celebrate Communion. It was the God-damnedest thing

I ever saw in my life. This fellow came out and he had these little glasses and he had little pieces of bread passed out. Just a hell of a thing."

Q: Grape juice, too, didn't he?

Capt. J.: I don't remember. I said, "Colonel, were you able to receive?" and he said yes. I said, "Well, I don't think we ought to talk about it like that." He said, "I'm way out of line." I think that takes a big man. There were many fine things about that man. I am grieved at how greatly he's misunderstood, or was misunderstood, by many people.

Q: Did you have contact with Krulak?

Capt. J.: No. I knew Krulak from other places in the South Pacific. He commanded a paratroop battalion, I think. I'm trying to remember now.

Q: He was also involved, I think, with torpedo boats, wasn't he?

Capt. J.: This I don't know. I know that when the people I was with landed at Bougainville our intelligence was tricky. We didn't know things that we would like to have known. It was decided to make a diversion at Choiseul, which was another island over alongside. So Krulak and this battalion of raiders - I think they were raiders - were landed at Choiseul. He was simply supposed to make all kinds of noise and diversion, not worry about winning any battles and then get off the place. He conducted a classic operation, still taught in war colleges: how to take a battalion on a diversionary operation. They didn't fight any major battles but he won everything they fought. I think he lost scarcely a man. He was very conservative with life, as Evans Carlson was. They got off Choiseul having served the purpose. The Japanese who had been down around Kahili, in the south of Bougainville, moved promptly over to the eastern shore of the island opposite from our landing, getting ready to transfer over to Choiseul. Of course, we had landed on the western shore, and that did the trick. Then the New Zealanders came up, landed and took the southern part of the Treasury Islands.

Q: Did you by any chance witness that famous ride by MacArthur and Struble as they were going up almost into the enemy lines after Inchon?

Capt. J.: No, I didn't. I saw nothing of General MacArthur. I did see Colonel Puller after the return of the South Korean government to Syngman Rhee, which he had attended and which was cut short, I think, by a little artillery fire. Puller's opinion of that exercise could never appear in print! He didn't have a high opinion of MacArthur to begin with. In any case, this particular exercise lowered it. He felt that O. P. Smith was much more of a soldier than MacArthur was. He felt basically MacArthur was a Hollywood actor and that he was all for the purple prose. This was not having been entirely fair.

Q: As a chaplain right with the Marines when they were being fired upon and so forth, did you have any armament yourself at that point?

Capt. J.: Yes, I did. Wait a minute, at that point I don't know that I did. I didn't. Later on I did and it came to me in a curious fashion. There was a North Korean captain whose body was found - and he had a .763 Austrian or Spanish automatic that fired a 32 caliber. Somehow, I was there and somebody said to me, well, it's all yours, if you want it.

After that, something happened that suggested to our people that I should carry arms. In World War II when I was with the Third Marines I was ordered to carry arms and used them. I started carrying a carbine, a very impractical thing for a chaplain for lots of reasons. A seabee saw it and wanted it and he had an old Colt police special, .45 revolver. He said, "I'll trade you even," and so we did. We were in the jungle moving behind the lines and ran into an ambush with this boy Clem Bolton I mentioned to you. We had to shoot our way out of it. That Colt thing fired a big .45-caliber slug. You could almost hear it going through.

Q: Like a cannon ball!

Capt. J.: Almost. I still have both of them some place.

Q: What was the policy in the Chaplain Corps?

Capt. J.: The policy of the Chaplain Corps was very clear. One should never bear arms.

Q: But when you're subject to snipers and their actions?

Capt. J.: That's all right but it isn't so much snipers. The Marines in the field had the experience that when they went by the Geneva Convention, when corpsmen and chaplains and doctors wore the arm band, they were systematically picked up and shot. So the Marines forbade the arm band. Then they found that corpsmen were specially selected to be shot and, at that point, the question of arming the noncombatants came up. Neither the Japanese nor the North Koreans had signed the Geneva Convention and they could honestly say it wasn't binding on them. What was the best thing to do in the circumstances? I'm not sure. At the time I felt, and I guess probably I'd still feel it, that given those circumstances, if I were in a situation - and I had been in Bougainville and in Guadalcanal - where I might have to protect wounded, I would have used a weapon.

Q: As you pointed out, you had to protect yourself, you had to shoot your way out.

Capt. J.: And this was no problem at all!

Q: Without a gun, you would have been dead?

Capt. J.: I had Clem Bolton and he was pretty good, but one rifle was not very much. When you have two men who can separate their fire at different targets, your chances are much better.

Q: Is it not all right to say that if every nation involved observed the convention scrupulously, then the regulation of the Chaplain Corps would be correct? But otherwise -

Capt. J.: I think the regulation is correct as it is. I think we have to assume that people will obey the convention until we find out differently. The thing that I think sometimes we forget is that with some radical exceptions such as Malmedy, the Germans observed the convention scrupulously. There was no problem with them about having to arm chaplains or doctors. Chaplains were killed and corpsmen were killed in the normal course of event. That's a risk you take. But the question of being singled out because of your occupation is something else, and this is what we were dealing with with the Japanese and also with the North Koreans.

Q: Different somewhat from the West European attitude?

Capt. J.: Very different, but having no tradition like the West European tradition of clergy who are neutral in a fundamental way.

Q: You traveled around in various parts of Korea by LST?

Capt. J.: Yes. We went round from Inchon round the southern end of the peninsula to Wonsan. Landed at Wonsan, an administrative landing.

Q: Was there any danger from mines?

Capt. J.: There was danger from mines. As a matter of fact, we were delayed five or six days while mines were swept at the entrance to Wonsan Harbor. We cruised back and forth until the minesweeping had been completed. Went in to Wonsan, an administrative landing. It was an easy landing, no problem. The division then was deployed in a semicircle round Wonsan.

The 1st Battalion, First Marines, was sent to a place called Kojo, about 35 miles south of Wonsan, to be a buffer against enemy forces coming up from the south. These were, generally speaking, fairly well disorganized by this time.

Some of them weren't, and it was our bad luck that coming up the costal road the opposite side of the peninsula from Seoul was a division that was known as the Diamond Hill Gang. That's what they were called, but it was a complete North Korean division. They hadn't taken bad losses in the south and they had something in the vicinity of 9,000 men. Our people were deployed along a ridge that ran athwartships of the peninsula about 700 yards, then there was a road near the beach, and on the beach there was a large hill. And then in advance of us about 400 yards on another eminence we placed one company of Marines. So we had two companies on the ridge, we had one company forward, and we had a weapons company behind the ridge, mortars and so on.

We went down by train. Our mission was to protect an ammunition depot. We relieved some South Korean troops. They removed all the ammunition and there was no mission left for us, in effect. Anyway, we deployed and took these positions and that night we were hit by this NK division. We then had about 750 men. We'd been promised a destroyer and a battery of artillery and neither of them arrived. These people hit us hard. They hit Noren's company in advance, and they took heavy casualties. They had to evacuate from the eminence that they had and take lower ground, dig in again.

The companies on the ridge were attacked frontally and on the flank very heavily, and they stood. We took heavy casualties there and dished out a lot of casualties, too. The question was whether we would hold on the ridge and we did.

Then we lost communication with Noren's company, didn't know what was happening. After the assault, he reassembled what was left, still near 400 yards to our front. We reestablished communication, found out what had happened, and ordered them to stay there during the night and to attempt to come back in the morning. And he did. Noren came back in the morning.

I had a very interesting personal experience. When I was on Bougainville with the Third Marines of the Third Marine Division, one of our patrols was out in front of the lines. I had gone out to meet them coming in, because I had heard that they had been hit by the Japanese and had taken quite a number of casualties. One of the Marines in the patrol came in, talked with me and asked me to pray with him, which I did. He was a boy by the name of Salisbury. When I went down the front of this ridge at Kojo in the morning with some other people to meet this company coming in, they were carrying their dead and wounded. One of the Marines stopped, a master sergeant, and he said, "Last night when we were hit I was wondering if I'd ever get out and I remembered that you were up here on the ridge. I remembered that other time in Bougainville when you met us and I said to myself I'm going to make it. I almost saw in my mind's eye that you'd be there."

It was the same boy. Salisbury had been in the Marines then

about twelve years.

Q: How moving!

Capt. J.: It was a one-in-a-million kind of experience. He remembered how I met them the other time. Then he was a PFC, scared to death, as any good man would have been. He'd been brought up in a devout home and when he got in he wanted to give thanks and there I was.

Q: Did you have anything to do with any of the Marine flyers?

Capt. J.: No. In Korea I had nothing to do with them. I went by Kimpo a couple of times, from which they operated. The only flyer that I knew at all was a great boy we had with our regiment who was an observation pilot. He flew an OY, which is a high-wing, single-engine monoplane.

Q: Slow?

Capt. J.: Slow, slow, slow, and slower. His name was Jim Mariedes and, in my book, he deserves whatever high decoration anybody can give him. When we needed artillery fire, he took all kinds of risks to give us a fighting chance.

Anyway, we had been surrounded in Kojo and it began to look bad. We managed to get a man back up to Wonsan, a young lieutenant by the name of Gardner. He and his wife had spent their last night in our house at Camp Lejeune before we left. A beautiful boy. He got back up to Chesty and he told him the position. So Chesty routed out the Navy and got us that destroyer that should have been there before. Then he routed out the Tenth Marines and sent down a battery of 75s. These would have made a tremendous difference the night that Wesley Noren was all chewed up. Then he sent down our Second Battalion to help us out.

All this movement on the railroad, of course, didn't escape the attention of the North Koreans. They saw all this happening and so they attacked us again in the morning, and I had a bad time. Everybody did, but I had a bad time because it looked as if things were quiet. We moved off the ridge onto this hill that was literally on the beach. I'd say the hill was 400-feet high, maybe and conical. We dug a perimeter around it, about a third of the way up, good field of fire, and we got a company on top. Able company was on top, Bob Barrow's company. I held service, celebrated Communion, went around giving Communion to men in the holes.

Then the phone rang. The Marines on top, Jack Swords' platoon of Bob Barrows' Able Company, wanted me to come up and serve Communion. So I started up. Well, the North Koreans were on the ridge across the road from us. I'd no sooner started to go up than there came this bang right by me. It was obvious that a sniper had me zeroed in. I ran and got behind a rock, waited, Then when I thought it was safe I ran up again, got behind something else, and he was right on. That guy chased me all the way up the hill.

Q: From rock to rock!

Capt. J.: Well, it was rock or whatever. I was angry. These Marines at the top of the hill had seen me and encouraged me in macabre Marine humor, "They've got the old chaplain running! Got him going! Come on, padre!" I heard some of that and I was not happy. When I arrived at the top Jack Swords saw me and said, "You're in no mood to celebrate the Communion. Sit down." He was right.

My orders came by dispatch, and I was flown out of there by helicopter.

Q: That, too, was hazardous, wasn't it, flying in a helicopter out of there?

Capt. J.: It needn't have been but it was. We still had road blocks all round Wonsan and this pilot had been flying out our dead. First he flew out our wounded, then he flew out our dead. Then there was only one dead remaining and I had orders, and somebody had told him. So he said to me OK, and we were flying the body back and flying me.

He asked me, "Do you like ducks?" Well, I didn't know what he was talking about, so he swooped down and there were some lakes in the vicinity and thousands and thousands of ducks there. With the noise of the helicopter, these things came zooming up and he had to pull right up, almost vertically, to get away from them or we would have been caught in them.

Q: Didn't he expect that?

Capt. J.: No, because he was one of these funny people. Anyway, we'd no sooner got above this when he said, "I'll show you where the Third Battalion is. They've got a road block at Amnion." So we went right down on the North Korean line and here these guys were standing up and firing at us. We were at 150 feet, maybe. And there was the Third Battalion, sure enough, down there.

Then in Wonsan we had a beautiful boy, a Catholic chaplain, now dead, died too young, by the name of Pat Killeen. His brother, Jim, is now a bishop and is the military ordinary for the Roman Catholic Church. Pat was with one of the rear-echelon outfits, I don't know which, when I had to report in to division headquarters in Wonsan to take off for the States. The division chaplain said to me, "Look, you'd better stay here overnight. There's nothing out now and we'll get you on something in the morning." I said OK. We were sitting there talking and things were quiet, and they wanted to know about our trouble down south. I was talking about that. Then Pat Killeen spotted this little weapon I had and he said to me, "Hey, may I have a look at it?" I said sure, so I took it out, cleared the chamber, automatically almost - there wasn't anything in the chamber, but I cleared it out and handed it to him. He looked around and played around with it a little bit, cleared the chamber again, and got a cartridge in it, and all at once, right by my ear and Bob Schwyhart's, who was the division chaplain, bang went this cartridge. He had fired the thing unwittingly. It went by me a foot and a half maybe and it ended up right in a Marine folding cot where, just a minute before, one of the other chaplains had been lying down with his head on the pillow.

Of course, that shook us all up. What shook us up more was that this was a quiet area and nobody was supposed to be firing, and all at once here's the sound of a report. I tell you all hell broke loose. Everybody was trying to find out who did it.

Q: North Koreans in our midst!

Capt. J.: Or whatever.

I flew back to the States.

Q: Who came for your relief?

Capt. J.: There was already a chaplain in the division who was ready to come. He wasn't slated for this but when I left he was ordered in, a fellow by the name of Bill Lyons, a very fine guy. He didn't stay in the Navy much longer, after Korea. He left and I don't know what's happened to him since, but he was a real fine type. From everything I heard from the guys afterwards, he did a really good job, was a good chaplain.

This is a story that it seems to me, Jack, is more important than any story I have told you. It's not my story, although I was involved. It's the story of a Navy wife and it's a story about what happens with Marines when a lot of us, say, like the Second Marine Division, get orders to proceed immediately, within twenty-four hours, for duty beyond the seas. Let Ruthie describe briefly what happened to us at LeJeune when that happened to the Second Division.

Q: This story is being told by Ruth Jones.

Mrs. J.: When we got the orders the flyers at Cherry Point Marine Corps Air Station sent word over that they would be willing to drive any wife to any part of the country if she wasn't able to drive, if she was pregnant or what not. Then they would fly from the nearest facility back to Cherry Point.

The wives who had no children volunteered to babysit for those of us who had children while we made arrangements for packing and shipping our furniture. It was a tremendous experience. It was one big family.

Q: How many women were involved in this?

Mrs. J.: Thousands.

Capt. J.: Yes, I would think. Many, many hundreds, anyway. This was a whole community. It wasn't a few people here and there saying this. This was all of Cherry Point.

Q: Breaking up at one point?

Capt. J.: Yes, indeed.

Mrs. J.: The only people who were staying were the base people. All the division people were going out. Unfortunately, the children had a rough time because the base children were saying to the division children, "Oh, your daddy's going off to war. He's going to get killed." That was the only bad part of it.

G. Jones #2 - 192

Capt. J.: And you understood. That happened with our kids. Before I left, Ruthie went upstairs, heard some noise, and found our oldest little one sobbing. She was about eight then. Because some kids had told her that and she wasn't about to let me hear it.

Q: She heard her daddy was going to get killed?

Mrs. J.: Yes.

Q: So this was a great effort at cooperation?

Mrs. J.: Yes. There was one wife who had seven children and she was about eight months pregnant, and she had to go to Texas, and one of the Marine flyers drove her and her kids to Texas and then flew back. It was just amazing.

Capt. J.: Handled the housing.

Mrs. J.: Also they closed all the housing down. Any new people coming aboard the base were not allowed to move into housing because the housing was frozen as of that date. Glyn's best friend, Bob Cole, was ordered down as the division chaplain and he arrived -

Capt. J.: Of the new Second Marine Division.

Mrs. J.: Yes. Glyn left at 6:30 in the morning and Bob and Betty arrived at 6:30 at night with four children, no place to stay. So they moved in with me and stayed a month. We had a month's time. I stayed the month because, meanwhile, I was getting word from the division adjutant that Glyn was coming back - you know, the orders that were sent out. So every day he would come and say he's coming back. Then the next day he'd say no, he's not coming back. This went on for a week!

Q: And how did you feel about this?

Mrs. J.: Oh, I was up one day and down the next, and knowing that he wouldn't want to come back. I cancelled my moving date and everything, but that was all right because Bob and Betty could stay with me.

Then, finally, one day the Catholic chaplain came in, Frank O'Leary, and he looked so drawn. He didn't want to let me know. And I said, OK, Frank, he's not coming back?" And he said no! Then I packed.

Capt. J.: That was Francis Timothy, the same one who'd been with us at Quonset.

Q: By that time, I suppose, most of the women had gone?

Mrs. J.: A lot of them had.

Q: And the housing was still frozen?

Mrs. J.: Yes. It was frozen for a whole month.

Q: Even though some of the houses were vacant?

Mrs. J.: Right, yes.

Capt. J.: The amazing thing and we remember it to this day, was that this wasn't surprising to us then.

Q: You mean your sense of cooperation?

Capt. J.: Yes. I think it didn't dawn on us until after. All at once, we had seen something extraordinary. The feeling was then, I suppose, that if the same thing had happened in reverse, we would have gone to Cherry Point and done what we could.

Q: It's interesting to speculate under what circumstances something like that might occur in civilian society?

Capt. J.: Civilian society is capable of a great deal, as you know, of self-sacrifice, of cooperation.

Q: In the case of a sudden act of nature, so to speak.

Capt. J.: Yes, indeed. I think one of the things that - something very elemental that was taking place at Cherry Point and Camp Lejeune was that an awful lot of these wives were wives who had sweated out combat before.

Mrs. J.: Yes.

Capt. J.: An awful lot of those men who were leaving were going back again. Their wives knew the name of the game -

Mrs. J.: It's a lot harder the second time.

Q: I would think so because it wasn't so unknown, was it?

Mrs. J.: No. The first time I was young and very immature, just married, and I didn't realize what was going on. Then, when I found out what he did in World War II, I worried more, knowing he was going out again.

Capt. J.: A lot of families, I think, felt that way.

Mrs. J.: Oh, yes.

Capt. J.: There was no disillusion at all, no false expectations. They were facing things directly, and the other wives whose husbands also had gone through this, and the husbands, too, were charging in. An amazing spectacle!

Q: And it bespeaks the character of service people.

Capt. J.: Oh, it does.

Q: How they grow in the service.

Capt. J.: Yes, of course, and I'm sure that this is true of all the services, but it happened to us with the Marine Corps.

Mrs. J.: It happened with the Navy, too, not as much, but Harris Howe said so.

Capt. J.: Well, in individual cases, certainly.

Mrs. J.: When Glyn was evacuated from London.

Capt. J.: The same Harris who got mad because he wanted me to come back from Pendleton to Lejeune.

Mrs. J.: Harris retired now. He met me at the plane in San Diego. He said, "Ruthie, I have an apartment for you. It's all furnished. There's food in the refrigerator. The beds are made. There are bandages in the medicine chest. Here are the keys to my second car. You keep it as long as you want. There's a shopping center on one side of the apartment, an elementary school on the other, and it's very convenient to get to the Naval Hospital."

Capt. J.: We were shipmates, ok. It does happen millions of times in the Navy.

The thing about Camp Lejeune, I think, was the magnitude of everybody doing it and the non-drama of it.

Q: It was done in a methodical way?

Capt. J.: Methodical, willing.

Mrs. J.: And just like this.

Capt. J.: No drama, no heroics, no nothing. The Marines said we'll drive you any place. Well, how are you going to get back home? Oh, one of the pilots is going to fly up and pick me up. That's what they did. It's the kind of thing you'd like to have all the American people know about.

Interview No. 3 with Captain Glyn Jones, CHC, U.S.N. (Retired)

Place: U.S. Naval Institute, Annapolis, Maryland
Date: Thursday morning, 31 March 1977
Subject: Biography
By: John T. Mason, Jr.

Q: Well, I'd delighted to welcome you on board here, Glyn. Last time, as you recall, you completed your story of combat in Korea. You went out there in August of 1950 with the First Marine Division and you returned to Washington in December. It was a quick trip.

Capt. J.: Yes, but it was a sharp one.

Q: I wonder if, before you come back to Washington and the Bureau of Personnel, you would tell me in summary form about the chaplain in combat. You have a little paper over there, which is most intriguing, about the chaplain in combat, a sort of a summary of some of the things you learned personally. You had been in combat in Korea, you'd been down in the Solomon Islands, where the struggle was fiercest, on both occasions. So I wonder if you'd tell me in summary form something about that?

Capt. J.: It's hard to know where to begin. Perhaps the place to start is with his calling as a clergyman. It seems to me that this is the center of everything pertaining to the chaplain's work in combat. It is unquestioned in combat that the chaplain is first, foremost, and all the time a minister of religion. Once that is clear, then the question becomes one of tactics, how best to apply the ministry, how to reach men who need you, how to make yourself available in various circumstances, how to travel, when not to travel, establishing your priorities of ministry - all of these things, I think, become what you might call the professional aspect of ministering in combat.

Q: And all under duress?

Capt. J.: Yes. You're under a strain all the time. The thing that really bothers you the most, I think, is that you never get the whole job done. There's no way in a Marine Regiment, which normally now has three chaplains, for a chaplain to be every place where he's needed. There are men who get hit and aren't picked up for a long time because no one knows they're hit. There are men who die, perhaps in sight of you, and you can't reach them. This kind of thing gets very frustrating.

So it seems to me that, once his own calling is clear in his mind, the chaplain's job is to learn the skills by which he can function in the field. These are not complex but combat is the wrong place to learn them. He has to learn how to travel, he has to learn to move in different kinds of terrain, how to read a compass, to recognize various kinds of fire both from his side and from the enemy, to understand how to reach various positions from the place where he is. Above all, I think, he must understand the importance of not exposing himself unnecessarily.

Q: And yet, to a certain degree, he must share the dangers of the men, must he not?

Capt. J.: I don't see how we can minister otherwise. Yet he has to be as canny with regard to preserving his life as any of the men must be. This, in the Marine Corps, and I'm sure in the Army, is carefully taught to the men. They're not recklessly to risk themselves. They are to behave in combat in terms of calculated probabilities, always trying to get the job done with the least expenditure of life. I think the chaplain has to do this. He must especially because when the chaplains are wounded or killed it has a most depressing effect on the men.

I remember in the Solomons visiting an Army outfit of the 43rd National Guard Division whose chaplain, Neil Doyle, had been killed. In walking around among the men I found that their response unvaryingly was one of depression, worse depression than I think they might have felt otherwise.

Q: So the chaplain can't exercise any degree of fatalism in his ministrations?

Capt. J.: I don't think so, not and be true to his own calling. I think he can exercise all dimensions of faith, but merely to walk around unwitting, uncaring with regard to the possibility of his own death or his own being wounded, I think is irresponsible. He's needed too much to take that kind of an attitude.

Q: You mention in your little paper the fact that for the combat Marine or soldier his horizons sort of shrink —

Capt. J.: They do.

Q: — and there is an immediacy to his horizon. Does this affect the chaplain also?

Capt. J.: It can. I think to some extent it does. However, the chaplain who is involved in his calling possesses a certain number of protections against this happening. The most important of them is his own devotional life. If he is regular in pursuit of his devotional disciplines, he finds that by the nature of the case, again and again, every day, they restore perspectives. In one way, this is one of the most important things the chaplain has to give to troops. He is either drinking from a well of living water or he's just another guy, and if he is drinking from a well of living water it is precisely this restoration of perspective, of the large picture, that is one of the valuable ministries he brings to people.

Q: That's a very interesting observation. You also say that the men are heavily afflicted with a sense of guilt as they confront death in battle.

Capt. J.: I don't know that it is so much when they confront death. They are afflicted with a sense of guilt when they kill, to a degree. A great deal of that is rationalizing. They don't kill on their own authority, they have been trained to do this. If the cause is just, as they understand it, there is reason for it. The strongest feeling of guilt, I think, comes after combat, and it is guilt because they survived, not guilt over what they have done, guilt because they have survived.

Q: And some of their comrades have not.

Capt. J.: Some of their comrades have not. And there's the never-ending question "why he and not I." Why was I spared and this man, who, perhaps, was a better man than I, was not spared? Here, an experienced chaplain will find a great deal to do with his troops in facing this question. Often men are not themselves aware of it. They feel this way, but they are not aware of what it is they feel.

Q: How effective can a chaplain be in erasing some of this feeling of guilt?

Capt. J.: Oh, I think very effective, and not only the chaplain, I think Marine Officers and non-commissioned officers can be. Once they understand what is happening in their daily relations with troops, they can relate to men in such a way as to dispel a great deal of it. One thing that helps, of course, is to bring it out into the open so that men become aware that they have this feeling and what the feeling is. Once it's out in the open, it can be talked about, and once it's talked about, ventilated, I think a great deal of it disappears.

Q: You also talk about the development of a very-deep-seated sense of communion in battle?

Capt. J.: Yes. It's a contradiction that something as terrible as war can produce something as beautiful as the friendships that I have seen created among men at war. In battle, especially, you find men who before may have been vociferous and loud and aggressive becoming suddenly tender and compassionate, caring for each other. You see other extremes. Men can be wrought up in the passion of battle to such a degree that they will kill anything in sight, trees, animals. They become that destructive. And yet, at the same time, there comes this other dimension of caring. You find it extended not only to your own comrades but to prisoners of war. Once the passion of the moment has died, no one is as generous to the enemy and to prisoners and to his wounded as the Marine.

Q: I would take it that no matter how often you shared combat experience with men, it's a learning process for you?

Capt. J.: Oh, indeed. One learns many, many things. You learn a great deal about how other human beings behave under stress. You see whole layers of yourself laid bare. When you look at yourself in the circumstances, it is almost to see yourself peeled away the way one peels an onion. You find ever-new dimensions of yourself, some of which you'd been aware of and didn't want necessarily to look at, but others - quite amazing. You find possibilities in yourself that had never been summoned before, but came to the top under this kind of pressure.

Q: What does this do to the doctrine of man as a theologian studies it?

Capt. J.: I think I would have to say - and this, you understand, is a personal view - that the experience of combat confirms profoundly the classic Christian doctrine of man. Nowhere else do you see as vividly the acting-out of man, the sinner, the terrible dimensions of mob activity, of violence, that are locked up in the human personality. And yet, as I said a moment ago, by the same token you see possibilities burgeoning all about you. The man who, in barracks, was a chronic minor offender becomes a bigger, better, more caring person right before your eyes. As Niebuhr says in the Nature and Destiny of Man, there are both the predicament and the possibility of man, both of which are central to Christian understanding.

Q: And, having seen it under those circumstances as clearly as you see it under those circumstances, can you take it out of that experience, out of that context, and enrich your ministry henceforth? Were you able to do that?

Capt. J.: It's rash for a man to evaluate his own ministry. Having said this, I imagine that I would have been a far worse minister in the intervening years without that experience, not that I've been a very good one. But I think there's no way in which I can look at a youngster in my school without understanding his potential as a human being in a Christian sense, both for evil and for good.

Before I came to this job as a prep school chaplain I was offered an administrative job in my denomination. It was very attractive. I finally decided to come to the school. A couple of years later, the man who offered me the job came up to preach for me. He looked around and he said:

"How does it feel not to be where the action is?"
The action for him, you see, was that denominational headquarters. And, of course, my response had to be:

"I'm on the front line. This is really where the action is, for we are deciding the destiny of some hundreds of young people and trying to give them insight into things." And for that task I think that my experience of learning about men in combat has been tremendously useful.

Q: As you survey the scene of your fellow chaplains who also experienced combat and were exposed to this deep-seated lesson as to the nature of man, what has been the result with some of them?

Capt. J.: So far as I understand them, it seems to me it has been very similar to my experience. I think they have come out of combat not with a new understanding of man but with confirmation of a very ancient understanding of man. I think, too, that many of us have come out more compassionate people than we were before, less censorious. We have experienced our own human limitations, we have seen the most terrible expression of them in others. I think we have a sense of relatedness to human beings that maybe we would not have had before.

Martin Buber says that love is responsibility for another. I think that in this sense we chaplains have become lovers beyond what we would have been otherwise.

Q: Tell me about your journey back from Korea. As I say, it was a short trip, but it was a violent one!

Capt. J.: Yes, while it lasted. The journey back was I think very conventional. I flew back. Harris Howe made sure I got home in a hurry, and I reported sometime in January, it seems to me, for duty in BuPers as the detail officer of the Chaplain Corps.

Q: This was a much more relaxed assignment at that point, was it not?

Capt. J.: Yes, certainly in the sense that it had nothing like the stress of battle. It was a very tense kind of assignment, of course, in another sense. The Navy and the Marine Corps were gearing up, adding personnel, and we had to find chaplains, set up the chaplains school again, and start to order chaplains to active duty. We were having to recall reserves. This was an action that our chief did not want to take and delayed perhaps too long in taking, but which obviously had to be done. In the Marine Corps the recall of some of the reserves caused a great deal of bitterness. Those who were most ready in the Marine Corps were often men who had done four years of service in World War II, with all the hazards involved in that, who had remained in the Marine Corps Reserve and who now were being called ahead of other people with less experience. We were having to do the same thing. So we had some problems.

Q: And in that seat that you occupied you were a kind of Jehovah-like figure, were you not, in terms of the destiny of the man and the development of his career?

Capt. J.: Yes, I was and this posed problems, personal problems for me. I felt immediately the temptation to play God, inherent in that kind of a job. I had to remind myself of a couple of things that were very important. One was that the men whose orders I wrote were men who themselves were called.

Q: In a similar sense to a mission?

Capt. J.: Yes, called to a mission. I believed that in some sense - and I still do - that a set of orders from the Navy to a minister or a priest is merely another call, an extension of his basic call to the ministry. I hoped that most of the chaplains could take that view. I must say, to my great satisfaction, almost all of them did. I had much less hassle in the way of requests for special treatment, requests to have orders changed or cancelled than my opposite numbers in the line and in other areas. My big problem was to try to satisfy every chaplain in terms of his being sent into combat. I always had more volunteers stacked up on my desk for duty with the First Marine Division, for example, than I was ever able to send.

Q: That was his overriding mission as a chaplain in the service, to see combat?

Capt. J.: They felt that, if they were needed for combat, they should make it known. I think that many were disappointed when they couldn't be sent, let's say, to the First Marine Division but, like good soldiers, they went where they were sent.

I was not long in the job, about a year, but at the end of the year I still had more letters volunteering for duty with the division than there were billets to fill, so there was never a problem there.

Q: In that job, you had to be arbitrary in your assignments and yet, in order not to let it overwhelm you, I suppose humility had to enter into the whole thing. This was a call, too?

Capt. J.: I think so. You know the old story about the Franciscans. They allegedly said, "Well, when it comes to scholarship, the Jesuits lead all the rest. When it comes to preaching, the Dominicans are the greatest, but when it comes to humility, we are number one"!

You had to be humble and if you weren't led to humility, in due course you were driven to it. The stakes were very, very high. Any time you wrote a set of orders, you might be sealing the death of the man. This you had to be aware of. I was. I think my predecessors in that job and my successors have become very aware of it if they weren't when they went into the job.

Q: Perhaps I should ask you at this point, one usually associates with a clerical vocation sometimes a feeling of softness that goes with it, a gentleness, which can be fatal if it takes over?

Capt. J.: It can be. Reality is not so. I'm not saying it's necessarily hard. There has to be, I think, especially in the ministry, a certain rocklike quality. I was about to say there has to be a skeleton on which the flesh of life is put and a skeleton can't be made of rubber. It has to be hard enough to hold things together. I think that this is true in the ministry. Unless that character is there, something that is unyielding on certain central issues, then I think the ministry is in trouble. I think that men in the service want that in a chaplain. They may not agree with him but they want to know where to find him. He may stand for things that don't matter greatly to them, but it matters greatly to them that he stands.

It seems to me this may be what you were saying?

Q: Yes. Is this something that you can inculcate into a young neophyte in the Chaplain Corps, or is it something that he has to be born with, too?

Capt. J.: I think it is inculcated but not at the time one enters the chaplaincy. It seems to me that it's a product of a lifetime of educational growth. One's character develops, I believe, in the family, in the church, to a lesser extent in other activities, school, athletics, but a man is moulding himself every day of his growth. At some point he settles for the general outline of his life for the hierarchy of values by which he intends to live. And as these become more stable, then character begins to be sown, it seems to me, and it is this in the chaplain that I think his men most want to see.

I don't think there's anything that we in the Chaplain Corps can do beyond trying to find men of strong character and of strong conviction.

It seems to me there is one thing that does happen in the service. I think the service ministry tends to accentuate both our strengths and our weaknesses. A strong man, I believe, becomes stronger in the Navy and the Marine Corps. Sometimes we have to be careful even about that. We can confuse strength with calcification.

Q: I expect so! Somewhere along the line during that year of duty in Washington, you were wrestling with the subject of rank structure?

Capt. J.: Yes.

Q: What does that imply?

Capt. J.: I believed that with the recall of many reserves who were, many of them, advanced in rank that the rank structure of our corps was sadly out of line. We encountered a conflict between two philosophies. On the one hand there was the philosophy that said that rank does not matter at all and that we, like the doctors, can have all chiefs and no Indians, if we want to. I disagreed with that. The other philosophy was that we should, sofar as circumstances permitted, adhere to a rank structure that was basically like that of the line. If we didn't we would find very senior chaplains going into commands where they were senior to the executive officer, for example, setting up situations that from all standpoints were unhealthy. I lost on that.

Q: How has it evolved to the present?

Capt. J.: I think you'd do better to get an opinion on today's structure from somebody who is on active duty today. I don't feel competent to judge. Generally speaking, however, up to the time of my retirement it seemed to me that we were topheavy in terms of rank. The Navy's policy relating to the line was sometimes applied directly to us and we did not represent the same kind of a problem. We ended up having very few jgs and an awful lot of captains. We ended up, too, having to get some very good people off active duty because of the stress of this situation, sending good people home whom we would have done much better to retain if we could possibly have found a way to do it.

Q: The fact that the Navy's line-officer policies applied sometimes to the chaplains, was this because you were so closely allied with the line officers in terms of BuPers?

Capt. J.: No, I don't think so. I don't think there was any inclination on the part of the policy people in BuPers to put us in a strait jacket. What happened was - and it was at this point that I felt disappointed - that we as an administrative agency having to do with personnel policies did not send forward timely and appropriate information that would enable the policy makers to make a different decision in our case. The feeling was that we'd do better to let things be. The attitude was, Why did we, as clergymen, want to get involved in technical questions of this sort? This, I felt, was abdication of our responsibilities in administering the Chaplain Corps.

Q: In retrospect that year of service in Washington was a very instructive one for you, was it not?

Capt. J.: Oh, I learned a very great deal. I worked with some of the most able and charming men in the Chaplain Corps during that year.

Q: Who was the chief at that point?

Capt. J.: Stan Salisbury, who was a lifelong friend. Stan was a man with whom I disagreed. At that point, I disagreed so strongly that in the end I asked to be detached from the office and sent to other duties. The issues were, first, this question of rank structure, which was a relatively minor one. Secondly, there was the question of the Navy Relief Society. As I mentioned here before, I had prepared an instruction for the signature of the Chief of Naval Personnel redefining the relations between the chaplain and the Navy Relief Society. I had been led to believe that it would go up with a favorable chop from our office, but at the last moment it didn't receive that.

Q: Did it receive a negative one?

Capt. J.: I don't think so. I think it was simply sent up with my chop on it. I had told the Navy Relief Society that I was preparing this. The then-president of the society, Admiral Vincent Murphy, called the Chief of Naval Personnel and objected strongly, so when this hit the Chief's desk he refused to sign it.

Another situation that disturbed me greatly and about which the corps was not going to do anything was here at the academy. Navy Regulations make it very clear that a chaplain is entitled to conduct worship according to the rites of his own church. In the academy the Protestant service on Sunday morning was the service of the Prayer Book. I happen to love the Prayer Book and I use it, but I felt that this was a breach of the law. Duty at the academy, which had been very much a preferred thing through the time of Will Thomas, now became something that good chaplains didn't want. When a good chaplain was sent he always would get into trouble here over that issue. We finally reached the point where our best men refused to go to the Academy.

We had a tremendously fine chaplain by the name of Merle Young who was here during this year that I was in Washington. He came to see me about this matter. He was a Methodist - he loved the Prayer Book, too, but he didn't like the requirement that only the Prayer Book could be used. So we prepared his case. I helped him to write it out and took it to my chief and he refused to act.

Q: What was the Chief's denominational persuasion?

Capt. J.: He was a Presbyterian.

Another issue on which I had strong feelings but which by itself wouldn't have caused me to ask for a transfer had to do with the organizational position of our corps. We were then and we are now a part of the Bureau of Naval Personnel. In this we are treated differently from every professional corps in the Navy. The doctors have their own bureau; JAG is assigned in the executive office of the secretary. I presented to my chief the opinion that we should do whatever was legal and proper to move our assignment out of the Bureau of Naval Personnel to the EXOS level. My argument was very simply that the ministry of religion is not a function of personnel administration and we should not be assigned in position analogous to recruiting and officers' clubs and recreation. He refused to do anything about that.

So, in due course, I felt that my being there was only causing trouble, that under that administration there was little, if any, hope for reforms that I felt necessary to the life of the Chaplain Corps. So I asked to be detached and I was.

Incidentally, a recent Chief of Chaplains raised this issue. After much obfuscating negotiation, the Chief of Chaplains was elevated to an organizational position under the Chief of Naval Operations. I believe he is under the DCNO for Personnel - who is the Chief of Naval Personnel under another hat. In this situation, the ministry of religion becomes not only a function of personnel administration, as in BuPers, but is also a function of the Navy's power to plan and to make war. The Chiefs of Chaplains believe they have taken a forward step. The churches remain blissfully ignorant of the compromised position in which their clergy have been placed. One wonders how this last elevation in the organizational position of the Chief of Chaplains may affect the status of the clergy under the Geneva Convention.

Q: Was the attitude of your chief due to lassitude or was it due to a desire not to get involved, to stir up trouble?

Capt. J.: It's very hard to say. It's especially hard to make that judgment without making invidious judgments about people. I don't know what the motive was. The one thing I strongly believed was that actions that seemed to me obviously necessary were not being taken and were not going to be taken. To someone else with a different doctrine of the ministry these actions might not have seemed nearly as essential as they seemed to me.

Q: That's an interesting way to put it.

Capt. J.: It seems to me at some point that, even in administering an organization like the Chaplain Corps, your basic principles have to be grounded eventually in one or another aspect of the Judeo-Christian faith. My feelings about these matters had to do with my convictions with respect to the doctrine of the ministry.

Q: Were you able to select your next duty?

Glyn Jones #3 - 215

Capt. J.: No. Indeed, my assignment was a very embarrassing one to me. I was ordered to be the senior chaplain at MCRD, Parris Island.

Q: That's the recruit depot?

Capt. J.: Yes. From a personal standpoint, it was an assignment that I would have coveted a few years hence when I was more senior. I was a brand-new commander. This was a captain's billet. It had been for years, was much desired by captains. All at once this brash young commander chaplain from the bureau is sent to Parris Island. The whole Chaplain Corps deduced, of course, that I had written my own orders.

Q: The fair-haired boy!

Capt. J.: Exactly. The truth was that when Stan told me my assignment I complained and made the point that this was a captain's billet. Other men older and senior to me wanted the job and they should have preference. Also, I told him that the appearance of things would be bad both for him and for me. But he insisted, so down I went.

Q: What was his reason for this?

Capt. J.: On the surface, his rationale was that it was a job that I could handle. I had no doubt about that. I'd had more experience with Marines than some of the other chaplains. Since I had come out of combat fairly recently it would be useful in dealing with chaplains in recruit training.

Q: That's a continuing policy, isn't it?

Capt. J.: To a degree, it is now. I didn't necessarily disagree with that reasoning. I merely disagreed with its conclusion that therefore I should be sent to Parris Island. I felt that, in the premises, it would be better if I were sent either to be by myself in a command or to be a junior chaplain under some seniors in a command, but not myself to be in that grade the senior chaplain in one of the two major Marine Corps recruit depots.

Q: How many chaplains would you have under you?

Capt. J.: Thirteen, and thirteen enlisted men.

Q: Give me the scope of the picture down there as you entered it.

Capt. J.: The commanding general down there was Merwin Silverthorne, a lieutenant general who had been assistant commandant of the Marine Corps. He had a command of nine or ten battalions, eight of which were training battalions. I think that the recruit strength as of the time that I reported was in the vicinity of 21,000 men. The chaplains were involved, as you'd expect, in the duty normal to our work. All the chaplains, however, had offices in one building, which was a couple of hundred yards away from the headquarters of the post. If a recruit wanted to see a chaplain, he would have to come up a mile and a half, he would have to walk that distance to see a chaplain, face the hassle of getting permission to see him, and all that sort of thing.

So, shortly after reporting, I went around and called on the various battalion commanders. Almost all of them were old friends, so it was sort of a reunion. I talked to them about the possibility of moving the chaplains into their battalions and disseminating them, so to speak —

Q: Disseminating the holy power!

Capt. J.: Indeed. They were delighted. I went to see the general and asked his permission to do this, we prepared the necessary orders, and the chaplains were disseminated all over the post. Every training battalion had one and we had a couple out at the rifle range where, as you know, there is special training in weapons. I believed that suddenly the chaplains began to be effective. They saw a lot of things that they had never seen before, including some mistreatment of recruits. I had told them in advance that they would see this, that they were to get right to the drill instructors and let them know they'd seen it and to knock it off. If they ran into some persistent offender they were to confront him and say that if it continued they would have to turn him in.

I urged them, on the other hand, to try to cultivate warm and friendly relations with the drill instructors, to go round every day and drink coffee with them, to talk with them, to urge them, before maltreatment became emotionally necessary to them, to see if the chaplain could not help. In due course, the DIs started to see that this was a very logical thing for them to do. Some youngster would become unmanageable or he was unteachable, his attitude was wrong, and rather than hit him over the head, they would bring him to the chaplain. Sometimes the chaplain arranged for the man to have medical treatment, sometimes it involved the necessity for a discharge.

I thought the system of farming out the chaplains was the only system that could be worked in that situation.

Q: Did this add to your own personal obligations and duties? I mean did you stay with these individual chaplains to help them as young fellows to deal with some of the problems that came to them?

Capt. J.: I did a number of things which I think any senior chaplain would do. First, I had every week a training session for chaplains, during which we considered numbers of matters that were important to their functions. Then, I visited them regularly on site, where they were. I also made it known to them that my door was always open, day or night. If they had something they wanted to talk about with me they could do so. Also, I tried sofar as I could to do my part in the workaday ministry. I did quite a lot of counseling, I preached as the other chaplains did - I took my turn, I was assigned by the man who set up the schedule, as they were.

I would say that perhaps my most important counseling was that of the chaplains themselves, who, as they came to know me, began to feel more easy about coming in and discussing personal and professional problems, talking about their hopes in the Chaplain Corps, all the questions that you would think that they would be interested in.

Q: You were there for three years. What sort of turnover was there amoung the juniors there?

Capt. J.: I was there for a little less than two years. A tremendous turnover, for the obvious reason of the ongoing Korean War. We would get chaplains straight from the chaplains' school and give them six months' indoctrination while they worked. This gave them a chance to get to know Marines. Our little training sessions I hoped would be of some help to them. Then, at the end of six months, they'd be ordered to the FMF. By the same token, men returning from the FMF would be sent to us because they had had battle experience with Marines and it was felt that Parris Island would be a good place for them to serve. It seemed to me, generally speaking, that these policies were good.

Q: This is a time when you were closely identified with citizen education. You did talk a little about that last time, but tell me more about it, how it happened to come up in this context.

Capt. J.: I did not bring it up, I found it when I reported to Parris Island. There was throughout the services this movement that's variously called moral guidance, character guidance, character education. In the Marine Corps there was a great interest in it. But the Marine approach to it at that time was cautious.

Glyn Jones #3 - 220

The Marines were doubtful about teaching moral principles qua moral principles, but they did believe strongly in the communication of the principles of good citizenship, beginning with citizenship in the Marine Corps.

And so, at this point, the command wanted to do something about it, the chaplains were available and were willing to help, and the basic job that was done at that time was a series of six presentations on citizenship education. Most of these were given by chaplains. In due course, we tried to persuade the command that this was not really a chaplains' function, it was a command function and that other officers should be made available to give some of these presentations, and they were.

I participated in a number of ways. These presentations were given to drill instructors. We had a drill instructors' school. I spoke every week at the drill instructors' school and got to know them that way. I spoke to the officers, giving the larger picture of the place of this kind of instruction in Marine Corps training.

Q: Did you couch it largely in ethical terms under the aegis of, say, the Fifth Commandment?

Capt. J.: Yes, I did and the six presentations did. The assumption underlying the presentations was that the republican form of government has a moral foundation. Its essence is stated in the Declaration of Independence in the natural law understanding of reality. We felt that this foundation could and should be taught to men so they would understand beyond the working of political processes to the undergirding realities which allowed the processes to function. So while this was citizenship education I think, in a profound sense, it was also moral education.

Q: How fertile was the ground you ploughed?

Capt. J.: Varied. It varied, too, with the capacities of chaplains. Some chaplains were awfully good at this kind of thing, stirred up a great deal of interest, and got considerable responses from these young men. After all, they were a pretty selective group of people, these young recruits, a lot of them were very bright, very responsible. Other chaplains simply put them to sleep!

Q: They lacked teaching ability, I suppose.

Capt. J.: They did. Sometimes they lacked any real feeling of conviction about doing this kind of thing. They did it, it wasn't a bad thing, but they didn't feel strongly that it greatly mattered. And, of course, this was reflected in their presentations. I couldn't blame them for this, you know. We were putting on their shoulders something that was not taught in seminaries, that involved the kind of moral doctrine that to many of them was less than complete, as it was to me essentially. But we were dealing with a lot of kids who weren't Christians or weren't Jews and we had to find some rationale to set forward and to defend moral principle that they could accept.

Q: In retrospect, how did it balance out in terms of the chaplain vis-a-vis the line officer in the presentations from the podium?

Capt. J.: We ended up always having a lot more chaplains. Curiously enough, though, there were some line officers and some senior non-commissioned officers who had strong convictions in these areas. They came in and we did some training, preparing them for giving presentations, and numbers of them did very well. Always, though, the dominant number of instructors were chaplains.

Q: I noted that during this period of time you cited once the Moral Guidance Committee and more or less implied that you had set it up?

Capt. J.: I suggested that it be set up. I had a commanding general who was very interested and immediately thought this was a very good idea.

Q: This was Silverthorne?

Capt. J.: General Silverthorne. We met monthly. There was a little concern at first as to whether we'd have sufficient agenda to justify a meeting. There was always more agenda than we could deal with.

Q: This got down to the nitty gritty specifics of the post, didn't it?

Capt. J.: It did, indeed, yes. We would discuss all kinds of questions - literature that was sold in the PX, excessive drinking, maltreatment of recruits, domestic problems. We'd even get into questions of personnel policy. The Marine Corps at first did as the Chaplain Corps did. They would take men straight out of combat and send them to Parris Island to be drill instructors. Many of these men were not emotionally fit at that point to do this job and we raised the question. In due course, the Marine Corps was to pay badly for this policy. You remember the Ribbon Creek incident?

Q: Yes.

Capt. J.: That happened three years, I think, after I had left.

Q: There have been various incidents.

Capt. J.: There have, yes. The Marine Corps, I think, great as it is in so many ways, has still not really come to grips with the problem of the drill instructor, and especially with the inhuman demands that are made on him. The expectation that he is going to be without flaw and without fault. Then, having tried him beyond what most human beings could stand, to punish him when he breaks. It seems to me the whole system has been a bad system.

You say, what can you do solve it. My feeling at that time was that we should not send to Parris Island Marines straight out of combat. They ought to have some other less strenuous kind of assignment.

Q: A time for emotional adjustment, I suppose?

Capt. J.: Absolutely. Even chaplains fresh out of combat had to be watched for some time before they leveled off.

The other thing that seemed awfully important in the problem of the DI was that he was given, in effect, the final responsibility for running the platoon. The platoon officers were abdicating their jobs. I felt strong that if the platoon officers, and other officers, were on the ball and were doing their jobs, a great deal of tension would be taken off the drill instructors and responsibilities that he had to face would be leveled off all around, so to speak. That didn't happen while I was there. I don't think it had happened by the time of Ribbon Creek, which to me was a perfect illustration of the kind of excess that was often, sometimes routinely, committed by the drill instructors in the absence of proper commissioned officer leadership.

Q: In the nature of a footnote, you might in a sentence or two tell me about Ribbon Creek so that a researcher using this paper would find an answer.

Capt. J.: Ribbon Creek was an incident in which a Marine drill instructor took his platoon off, I believe, from the rifle range, took them into one of the creeks that surround Parris Island, walked them about in the darkness. Suddenly some of the men became panicky and by the time the affair was settled I think some four or five Marine recruits had drowned. The drill instructor was specifically disobeying a written order from the commanding general, but, again, this had often been done and had not been checked by the responsible commissioned officers.

Q: One of the items you had on the agenda for one of these Moral Guidance Committee meetings was the status of men in the company brig. What were some of the problems surrounding this situation?

Capt. J.: The brig is always a problem, even when it is run perfectly! There's no way to run a trouble-free brig, and the brig at Parris Island, I believe, was no worse than most brigs. Here, again, unless there is timely and continuing surveillance by commissioned officers the possibilities for abuse are very great.

I'll never forget an incident involving a Marine who was in the brig at Quonset Point. He was visited by his Marine officer. He was surly and rebellious in talking to the officer. As the officer left, the Marine said to him:

"I'm going to seduce one of these guards tonight." The officer just shoved off. The next morning there was a complaint against the prisoner. He had seduced one of the guards.

We had nothing like that at Parris Island. We did have complaints about the brig. This kind of problem was routine to be on the agenda of the council. The council was made up of representative officers from numerous sources. The recreation officer, for example, was a member, there was a medical officer who belonged, I belonged. The chairman was a colonel on the staff of the general. So there were lots of resources for the agenda.

I don't recall who put that item on it, but I do recall that we promptly looked into the situation in the brig. We found there were some things that needed to be done and they were routinely done by the command.

Q: In looking at the situation as a whole with the Moral Guidance Committee, how were you able to keep the lid, so to speak, on some things? I would imagine that the discussions might get out of control in enthusiasm for doing something.

Capt. J.: I don't recall that that ever happened. The members of the council were mature officers. We didn't have any second lieutenants on the council. The members had broad experience. There was never to my knowledge an item on the agenda which they did not generally understand. We weren't in the business of educating them about the facts of life, so to speak.

I felt the discussions were on a very high level. Even more important, I felt that after we'd had a few meetings the defensive level started to go down markedly. The idea of vested interests, the idea of things that were not discussable, these things went out the window. The general feeling was that we had become persuaded that all of us were interested in the welfare of the men and of the command and that there was nothing that we couldn't discuss if that were the object.

Q: That was a natural development as you became a group.

Capt. J.: I think we did and I think we became a believeable group to the commanding general. I think that when the thing was founded there was a feeling that this was just another do-good operation. General Silverthorne is an avowed Christian and, while he was respected, this was believed to be perhaps as a result of some of his religious eccentricity. But when the work of the council came out again and again as very practical in bringing to light things that should have been brought to light, as always giving people a chance to correct things without making any public charges, then I think trust in the council gradually built. The moral authority of the Council was established.

I think, too, that, as that happened, people who had particular interests were willing to bring them to the council. I remember one of the members of the council was Pauline Beckley, the commander of the women's battalion. Pauline in those days, rightly, I'm sure, was extremely defensive about her prerogatives and about the way in which her girls might be assigned or used in the command.

Q: What was her rank?

Capt. J.: She was a major. In due course, she felt able and willing to bring to the council certain problems that were of a broad scope affecting the women's battalion - all kinds, having to do with men-women relationships and the rest.

I think the council was very useful.

Q: Would you say something about the implementation of decisions arrived at in the council?

Capt. J.: Implementation of the decisions was always a command matter. The council functioned purely as an advisory organization, it had no command authority. Its recommendations were always carefully considered and almost invariably were put into effect by the cognizant agent. A recommendation might be, let us say, to the recruit training battalions, they might be to the women's battalion, might be to the hospital. These remained purely as recommendations, nothing more. On a rare occasion the matter might be of such a character that it would result in the issuance of an order from the commanding general, but not very often.

Q: In the recommendation process from the council, what was the element of time? How long would it take?

Capt. J.: That depended on the problem. There were some problems that needed very little time. All they needed generally was to be pointed out and recognized and somebody would do something about them. Other problems, say the problem of the drill instructors, were perennial. We would have recommendations many times in a year about one or another thing affecting the duty of drill instructors - the conduct of drill instructors or the rules under which they functioned.

One item I remember that was of some importance was the question as to when the red flag would be raised.

Q: The red flag?

Capt. J.: Yes, the red flag to indicate that it was too hot for recruits to be drilled. We lost some rescuits through heat exhaustion, so the medical officer got involved. Well, we got involved first to some extent. The medical officer was very much on the ball and wanted opinions of the line officers and other people who were interested in recruits so that he would make the decision and he did.

Q: That was a fascinating experience, I would say.

Capt. J.: Oh, it was, indeed, a great one because the people were great.

Q: In the record, as you gave it to me, there's some indication that there was a deep-seated and long-drawn-out involvement you had because of a junior chaplain. Do you want to deal with that?

Capt. J.: I'm willing to deal with it as long as no names are named.

Q: All right, because it does show, I think, as one pursues the record, your administrative skill and your diplomacy as well.

Capt. J.: I don't know. The problem was really a very simple one. My obligation was compounded by the fact that I had to write myself the fitness reports of all the chaplains. This was rarely the duty of a chaplain. In the Navy it was never the duty of a chaplain, but, at that time, in the Marine Corps the senior chaplain prepared all fitness reports and forwarded them directly to the bureau -

Glyn Jones #3 - 230

Q: How did that happen to develop?

Capt. J.: I don't quite know. All I know is that when I reported to Parris Island this was the system. I didn't have to show them to the commanding general if I didn't want to, and I think he was rather relieved not to have to prepare them himself. He prepared the report on me and I prepared the reports on the other chaplains.

This particular chaplain was somewhat junior to me. He was a lieutenant commander. He was a Roman Catholic. I knew from my experience in the Bureau that he had been a very difficult person. He had been transferred from a couple of places because of his personal instability and, very uniquely for a Roman Catholic chaplain, he did not get along with chaplains of other faiths. He wasn't liked either by the chaplains of his own faith, so that when I saw his orders coming to us I was afraid that there would be trouble.

When he reported I invited him into my office and I told him quite directly that he had this reputation, that I was aware of it but that I wanted to start from scratch. I didn't want any trouble. I told him that I believed we could get along if he were reasonable. He was the senior of the Catholic chaplains. The others were all very junior and, by the nature of the case, he assumed a dominant role with respect to them.

The duty roster for the coverage of the post during off-duty hours was written by a chaplain who worked with me in the chaplains' center. He was a kind of administrative assistant but also did counseling and other work. During one of our weekly meetings this Catholic chaplain objected to the duty roster, saying that Catholic chaplains were not being fairly treated. I asked him, then, to confer with the chaplain who wrote the rosters and to reach an accommodation. I told him we would do whatever could be done, if this were indeed the case, to correct the matter. But this he didn't do. Instead, he told the young Catholic chaplains not to appear for duty. Of course, this precipitated a confrontation which I had earnestly sought to avoid.

In the course of it he said, in effect, that he did not recognize that I had any authority over the Catholic chaplains with respect to this issue, that he alone had authority over them. Obviously, this was not a position that I could accept. I asked him if he would not come with me and talk to the commanding general. We could set forth our respective positions to the general. He was willing to do this.

Obviously, in the Marine Corps there has to be one boss of the job. We have one commanding general. So, as the general would see it and did see it, we have a senior medical officer. He is the senior. And there's a senior chaplain. He's the senior, too. This chaplain still refused to accept the general's decision and appealed to the military ordinary of the church. The military ordinariate, normally, has no desire to get involved in this kind of thing. So I called him in and I said that if he persisted in this course of action I would have no choice but to give him an unsatisfactory fitness report and to request his detachment. I pleaded with him. I said, "Don't push me into this situation. I don't want to do it because it's personally distasteful for me to do it with any chaplain, but especially with a chaplain of another faith."

Well, he simply refused to give in on any point. So, I prepared a formal letter to him advising him that I was going to send in a report and advising him of his rights, also of his responsibilities within regulations. He was not, for example, entitled in his reply to make any personal comments about the reporting senior. I sent the report to him for him to read and to make his reply. He made his reply, I read it, and it did contain abusive material about me. I called him in and said this was a breach of regulations and I asked him if he would not correct it for his own sake. He refused to change it. In this event, I sent my report and his reply to BuPers via our commanding general, who appended an endorsement wherein he completely defended my course of action, outlined my attempt to accommodate and to reconcile the matter, and also the unmilitary behavior of the other chaplain. He finally pointed out that the chaplain had not only offended in refusing to obey orders but also by breaking regulations in his reply, by forwarding material that was personally abusive with regard to me.

The people in the chaplains' division were very unhappy at this development. I don't know that I blame them, but they were very unhappy, and they felt that I should be put in my place. So the commanding general's request to detach this chaplain was not met. He remained on duty and it was the intention, it turned out,

Glyn Jones #3 - 233

of the division to keep him at Parris Island until he had made his number as commander and to promote him there before detaching him. This, of course, would put me in a very bad light. The promotion came, was forwarded to Parris Island, and the commanding general returned it.

Now, this is a very interesting distinction between the Navy and the Marine Corps. Once you're promoted in the Navy, the promotion comes to you and you have to be promoted. There's nothing anyone can do about it. A commanding general in the Marine Corps, however, may refuse to give a promotion to a man who has disqualified himself in some way, and, using a Marine Corps regulation, our general refused to promote this man on the ground that he was not professionally qualified for promotion.

Q: Did this come as a surprise to headquarters?

Capt. J.: To ours?

Q: Yes.

Capt. J.: It blew them out of their seats. They went, of course, to see the lawyers and the lawyers said this could not apply to a naval officer. In other words, a general may not correctly do this to a naval officer. It became known all over the post, that this had been done. Very regrettable. But, by the same token, it was very clear to the Chaplains' Division that this man was not going to be promoted so long as he was in Parris Island, and they were not about to tangle with a former assistant commandant of the Marine

Corps on that question. So he was then detached.

Q: And during all this long drawn-out process, what about the assignments that the juniors received?

Capt. J.: They performed all their assignments.

Q: They did?

Capt. J.: Yes. I called them in and had to say to them, "I understand that you have been given directions by a senior, but I must tell you these directions are illegal, and if he continues in his course of action he may end up getting a court-martial; he certainly will get an unsatisfactory fitness report." So they started to fly right.

It didn't take them long to discover that they had indeed been misled. Other Catholic chaplains, knowing this man - other Catholic chaplains to whom they spoke - told them that they had been misled, that they were on a path of trouble if they continued to follow this man. So I think they ended up feeling finally that I had tried to be fair and that I had been fair to them in our dealings.

Q: You were talking off tape of the attitude of other Roman Catholic chaplains in that time and later and their reflections on the whole thing.

Capt. J.: Yes. Obviously, it is an extremely unhappy and unfortunate event for a Protestant chaplain to give an unsatisfactory fitness report to a Catholic chaplain. I would have wanted to avoid it in the case of any chaplain. The implications of it, however, in the Chaplain Corps are very considerable. One could readily deduce that the unsat report had been given out of a man's prejudice. It's a measure of the breadth and the tolerance of our Catholic chaplains that during the next couple of years numbers of them spoke to me about this event. Not one was critical. Every one of them had discovered the facts and had said to me that, in the premises, I had made the only decision that was possible. And, so far as I know, to this day I've not heard of any Catholic chaplain feeling that I was motivated by prejudice in taking this action.

Q: That's a very satisfactory feeling to have.

Capt. J.: It was very important to me. If my reputation with the Catholic chaplains was such that they could believe I would act out of this kind of prejudice, then my usefulness in the Chaplain Corps would be minimal. The fact was that by this time many of our priests knew me, had worked with me, and generally speaking did not believe that I would act merely out of prejudice.

Q: Are there any other aspects of your tour of duty there at Parris Island that we should put on tape?

Capt. J.: I don't think so. It was a great tour, a tour I enjoyed tremendously. I enjoyed my general, I enjoyed our chaplains. They were tremendous. And, of course, I enjoyed being again with many old friends, especially among the drill instructors. My door was open and there was rarely a day when a couple or three drill instructors didn't drop in for a cup of coffee and to swap the latest lies, you know!

Q: In October of 1953 you left the recruit depot and reported to director of the Marine Corps educational center at Quantico.

Capt. J.: I reported to the director of the Marine Corps educational center. I was assigned there to produce some resource material for the character education movement, with a special view to seeing whether we could produce something for officer training that could be inserted into the curriculum, let's say, at OTC in Newport or the Marine Corps schools in Quantico.

I ran into a lot of old friends again there, specially General Pollock, who was number two man there, and ended up producing, in effect, a book entitled Ventures in Self-Understanding. The object was to help the young officer have experiences of self-recognition, experiences where he would recognize various facets of himself.

Q: Was this published by the Marine Corps?

Capt. J.: It wasn't published actually. It was reproduced by the Navy. So far as I know, outside of some experimental work that I did myself with the material, it was never put to use, and that may have been a wise decision. I had a lot of fun writing it, learned a lot, and enjoyed in the process relating to numbers of Marines and discussing various aspects of the subject matter with them, and incorporating many of their insights into it. Except from the standpoint of my principles, goals and interest, it was for the Navy not a very productive year.

Q: This was the Marine application of that character education period that the Navy was involved with?

Capt. J.: Yes, the Navy was involved with it. The thought had been that if I produced something that was worth doing in the Marine Corps officer training curriculum, we could then talk with Marine Corps headquarters about using this material in officer training. Once I'd finished writing it I had no further staff responsibilities with regard to what happened in the future, and I don't really know what did happen. I suspect that at some point it fell through the cracks, that whoever was responsible up in the chaplains division looked at it and thought probably it wasn't very promising for its purpose, or there was a failure in staffing with Marine Corps G-3. These are all speculations. I don't really know what happened.

Q: Character education, as such, was still in the hands of the Chaplain Corps, was it?

Capt. J.: Yes. There was a BuPers and later, I think, a SecNav instruction, both of which specificed the responsibilities of command to provide these programs and specified the availability of chaplains to help implement them.

Q: Did this also involve leadership training?

Capt. J.: Strictly speaking, no. Theoretically speaking, no. Practically speaking, sometimes, depending on where you were. Down at Parris Island, for example, we were involved specifically in leadership training with regard to drill instructors. This was regarded as being a rather important aspect, their preparation for their job. In other places, the line itself provided one or another kind of leadership training independently of what we were doing.

Q: Tell me a little more about this educational center at Quantico. What was the scope of its effort?

Capt. J.: I don't know that I can describe to you as of today what happens there. In my time, the educational center had several institutions. It had Marine Corps schools, which covered various kinds of instruction. It had the junior course, the senior course, PLC, platoon leaders' course. Marine Corps schools, in addition to being a great educational center and training school for Marines, is the source for military doctrine. Marine Corps schools was the place of origin for the doctrine of the amphibious assault and of vertical envelopment, where the various developments of the doctrines were tested. It is still the place where the serious strategic thinking of the Marine Corps tends to center.

Q: I would think it would be inherent in the situation, then, that chaplains should be attached there and involved?

Capt. J.: Chaplains are attached but not involved very much at all in the strategic area. In my day they were not much involved with the basic function of the school. I don't know that they could have been. At least I was not attached to function, so to speak, as a chaplain, but to perform other duties.

Q: I suppose if it did develop in that direction and chaplains were attached there effectively that they would put more emphasis on making a Marine Corps chaplaincy, wouldn't they?

Capt. J.: Yes, and, of course, I've told you my feeling about this.

Q: And how Workman felt about it?

Capt. J.: Yes. Workman felt differently than I. I daresay he was right. On active duty I would have enjoyed seeing that development take place and would have opted to be with the Marine Corps, rather than with the Navy, although I loved the Navy, too.

Q: You were there for a little bit less than a year and then you went with ComDesLant?

Capt. J.: Yes.

Q: Was this something you sought or was this something that dropped out of the sky?

Capt. J.: A friend of mine, Bob Coe, now retired, was the detail officer then and he had spent some time in World War II with Marine aviation. He got in touch with me and said:

Glyn Jones #3 - 240

"You haven't got enough Navy duty on your record to give you good chances for promotion, so you ought to go back to the Navy."

I didn't disagree at all. Then the next thing I knew I had a set of orders to ComDesLant, who was then in Newport. He was Admiral Hartman - C. C. Hartman, a tremendous guy.

Q: A very quiet gentleman!

Capt. J.: Very quiet, very precise, very humane, sensitive, strong. I'd never served with destroyers before, so I had a lot to learn and didn't have much time in which to learn it. Neither before, except in BuPers, had I ever served with a large staff. So the whole business of staff skills, staff knowledge was new to me. I had to learn that as well.

We had, to begin with, thirty-five chaplains, most of whom were in destroyer squadrons. A considerable part of the force at all times was deployed to the Med. The chaplain couldn't possibly cover the ships at one time. He would ride a ship for a period of time then move to another ship and ride her for a period of time. The squadron was broken up, one part in Newport, Norfolk, and another part in the Med. That meant he was separated again from his ships. So we decided that we would have to improve and strengthen very greatly our program of lay-led religious services. This we did.

Q: What was its status at that point?

Capt. J.: We had some lay leaders but basically the program was not complete, it was not well organized, and it didn't provide for giving skills to the lay leader. So I prepared an instruction that Admiral Hartman signed designating places in Newport and in Norfolk where every week we held lay-leader schools. The instructions ordered commanding officers to select lay leaders of the Roman Catholic, Protestant, and Jewish faiths, and of other faiths, if this seemed feasible, to be sent for training when ships were in port to these schools and then function on board the ships.

We also established centralized sources of supply, materials, for the use of lay leaders. Most of these materials were provided by the churches. The military ordinariate, the JWB, the Episcopal church, and other denominations provided things like prayer books, for example, and other aids to the work of lay leaders. We even got supplies of canned sermons, which I found to my surprise were much more readily available than I had anticipated, but they served a very useful purpose. We selected among them and found those that had a reasonable degree of quality, reproduced them, and sent them out on schedule to lay leaders.

Q: They also supply confidence, don't they?

Capt. J.: Indeed they do. The lay leaders, curiously enough, always at first were very glad to receive them. But once they started to get into the stance of the work, so to speak, they tended increasingly to want to produce themselves their own things, which was much better.

Q: Naturally. They came from the heart.

Capt. J.: They came from the heart. These young people were often highly motivated. We ended up having to modify the instructions to caution commanding officers in selecting lay leaders against the choice of fanatics. We found that in a few cases this happened and then the prestige of the program immediately plummeted. It became important to say to the Cos that their selections need not necessarily be the best speakers around. They should be men very highly respected on the ship who did it on a voluntary basis, but were designated by the commanding officer. The commanders tended to feel happy about that instruction because they found themselves in the very unhappy position of selecting people in a profession of which they were not experts and tending to select the people most wanting to do it, who were not always the people who could best do it. They trod a line but I think very well.

We were available, of course, as resources to them, and not infrequently it meant the commanding officer would send a man in, or an officer in, to talk with us, and would want us to express our judgment about them. Occasionally, we weeded somebody out that way, more frequently the men they sent in seemed to us to be very good people for the job.

I would say that we averaged training 400 or 500 lay leaders a year.

Q: My, what a considerable number!

Capt. J.: There were reasons. One was that there was always a turnover in destroyers. Another was that lay leaders tended to recruit other lay leaders, so that we ended up requiring that there be three in a ship but sometimes the lay leader would come in and he'd have in two or three other guys saying the CO said it was all right for them to go to school. These were one-day schools. So a ship might have half a dozen lay leaders.

Q: This proliferation put some responsibility on the chaplain, did it not?

Capt. J.: Oh, indeed. These people, of course, reported first to their commanding officer, but their performance had to be satisfactory in the judgment of the squadron chaplain. If it failed to be satisfactory or if the man compromised his moral character, these became grounds immediately for his dismissal from the job. That happened not often, but on occasion it became necessary to discharge a lay leader.

Q: But, on the whole, this system did aid the chaplain to spread his authority and his usefulness around?

Capt. J.: Tremendously. It did a lot of things. It certainly did that. It expanded the sphere of influence of the chaplain, once we got lay leaders into all the ships. They turned to the chaplains for technical and professional guidance. They also tended to help the young chaplains in meeting their ecumenical responsibilities. Almost all of them were strongly inclined to want to meet them but didn't know how. But all at once they had in every ship now a Protestant lay leader, and they had in every ship a Catholic layman who was responsible for counseling the commanding officer and guiding the chaplain with regard to providing Roman Catholic services, for looking for a priest, for setting up the altar when a priest would come and celebrate. This kind of thing.

This, I think, not only expanded in space the influence of the chaplain, I think it tended to expand it in depth, equally important. The lay leaders also were introducers of the chaplain to the rest of the crew. If any question came up regarding the chaplain, one of them could always be found to give an opinion. They would tell the chaplains what was happening in the ships so the chaplains had a sort of, I think legitimate, intelligence organization. They also brought to the chaplains sometimes complaints about which the chaplains could do something. I think it was a tremendously useful ministry.

Once in a while a lay leader would get in over his head. We had to watch this, especially with regard to counseling. We tend to forget that in a ship or in a school a vast amount of counseling takes place by the nature of the case among peers. Most of the counseling that takes place in a ship is from one sailor to another. We had to be sure that a sailor who was given an official designation, as the lay leader, for example, did not by virtue of that fact begin to be seen as a man competent in counseling. In our school one of the things we said to them was "watch out, don't counsel, here are the referral points, however, you may use. If somebody comes up to you with this problem you may refer him to this" - we put all this in writing - "or you may refer him to this one or that one." So that they could actually do something for youngsters, but we tried to keep them from giving too much of their uniformed opinion.

Q: I suppose that required a certain amount of viligance, didn't it?

Capt. J.: It did, but we ended up getting the character of man by and large as a lay leader who was aware of his shortcomings and had sufficient humility to live within his limits. So it was never, I don't believe, a serious problem, but it was a problem from time to time and one of which we had to beware.

Q: What other aspects of this destroyer command come to mind?

Capt. J.: Destroyermen are sui generis. They are the real sailors.

Q: Elaborate on that.

Capt. J.: You don't have to ask them who are the real sailors. They will tell you!

Q: That's pride in their service.

Capt. J.: Oh, it's very good. They're beautiful people. They're small-ship sailors. They're a very different breed of cat from the cruiser sailor and the battleship sailor or the carrier sailor who himself is a different kind of a man. By virtue of the fact that the destroyerman is a small-ship sailor he is almost always a man, enlisted or officer, who has vast amounts of responsibility, who has very important jobs to do, very like our nuke-sub sailors, I would say, in that respect. They know everybody in the crew. Once they've done a tour in destroyers, the tendency is that they don't want to go any place else. They liked destroyer duty.

They also had the feeling at that time that in some sense they were a kind of forgotten man in the Navy. They operated off by themselves a great deal. They didn't have many of the amenities of the big ships. They had to undertake missions that were tremendously demanding. Sometimes they had very little maintenance time when they got into port. So they had somewhat of a put-upon feeling and this fierce pride that I have mentioned.

They welcomed chaplains. This, you know, is a strange turn-around. I can remember not long before my time in destroyers when the hardiest prejudice of destroyer sailors was that it was bad luck to have a clergyman aboard. They believed it as an article of faith.

Q: Its origin?

Capt. J.: I don't know its origin. I have the feeling that its origin may be biblical, but of this I'm not sure. I forget where I was when this happened, but several years before when the first chaplains were put into destroyers it was as an experiment. The bureau was not about to accept this as policy and it was examined very closely with a view to whether the prejudices of destroyermen would permit it.

The first couple or three men had fairly rough times, but they checked the crews to see what their feeling was and the personal feeling toward the chaplain overcame whatever previous superstition they may have had. The reports were favorable, so gradually during Stan Salisbury's time we started to feed chaplains into destroyers. They'd always been in tenders, of course. That was the only chaplain the destroyer sailor up to that point had seen.

When Admiral Burke came he wanted to know about everything and he wanted to know about religion. He called me in and said, "What are your people doing?" which I thought was great, and I told him. He said, "Are you doing the job?", and I said, "No, we aren't, but I think we're doing as well as we can do with what we have. We aren't doing the job that these boys need."

"What do we need?"

I described to him how the chaplains were separated from their charges by the accidents of deployment and so on and I said:

"We need one chaplain to every division of destroyers." He said:

"Prepare a letter to CNO asking for the billets." So I

said: "Are you going to be able to offer any compensatory reductions." You know how that works.

Q: Sure.

Capt. J.: Billets aren't established on a cold dare. There are only a certain number of billets authorized in the Navy every year, never enough to fill all the needs. So commanders asking for new billets have to do two things. They have to justify - you understand this, of course. And the second thing they have to do is, in most cases, to provide a compensatory reduction, that is, they have to surrender a billet somewhere else on the force in order to do this.

Arleigh Burke is just the most honest guy in the world. He said to me:

"What do you think?" I said: "I don't think that you can give up thirty-five billets to get thirty-five chaplains. Or if you could, somebody in CNO would say, look, why were you overstaffed all this time with these thirty-five people that you can now surrender."

He said, "I agree."

So I said: "I think you ought to give up a nominal number of billets and let me write in the letter that it's obvious you can't give them all up or else you would have been keeping thirty-five people who were not justified."

This was the line we took. I think he was willing to give up ten, as I remember, and then in the letter I wrote, in effect, that obviously he couldn't give up thirty-five billets because this would indicate that he had thirty-five bodies he didn't need any more and that was not true.

Nothing happened. Admiral Burke was then selected to be CNO. Admiral Joe Daniel had come in to replace him. Then one day I got a frantic call from the Chaplains' Division. "Admiral Burke has just asked for a copy of the letter he sent from Newport asking for billets for the destroyer divisions and we don't have a copy. Would you send us a copy." He had this young aide who was a commander, now he's a vice admiral, Tom Woschsler, who had always supported us strongly. He was a destroyer skipper before he became CNO's aide, and when he got there he said to Arleigh Burke:

"You know, you want to do something for destroyers and Glyn Jones wrote a letter for you and you signed it asking for those billets. Before we left we hadn't heard anything."

So Arleigh Burke said to him: "Nudge them. Find out what they're going to do about the billets." He did, he nudged them and, of course, once the CNO is expressing interest "what are you going to do" indicates that you'd better say yes, and they looked and saw whose signature was on the letter! So we got the billets for the divisions, a chaplain in each division.

Q: A good way for them to begin a career, too?

Capt. J.: I think it's a great for most of them, certainly. They're thrown on their own, they were responsible to a squadron commander of some seniority, a very senior commander for a captain, who was their own commanding officer. They had to maintain diplomatic relations with eight separate commands and use good judgment in the process. They slipped once in a while but the response I tended to get from the destroyer skippers was one of real enthusiasm.

They dreamed up new ways of transferring chaplains from ship to ship. It used to be the old breeches buoy, remember, then some of the ships got helicopters.

Q: And life became easier!

Capt. J.: Sometimes. One or two crashed! They called it the holy helo! That meant chaplains were a lot more mobile than they had been before. They could go forty miles to a ship to hold services and to visit the ship if they had to.

Q: Where did this assignment take you other than Newport?

Capt. J.: Once every quarter I had to go on an inspection trip. It was not called an inspection because I was not in the line of command, so I couldn't actually inspect and it was called a visit. But, of course, everybody knew that I was going to report what I saw to Arleigh Burke or to Joe Daniel.

Q: So there was spit and polish attached to it?

Capt. J.: To a degree, but destroyer sailors are not very strong on this. The second time around I think people started to see me

Glyn Jones #3 - 251

more in a pastoral role than a reporting role because I think the questions I asked were the questions that they themselves wanted some answers to. How's the chow? We had just started three years before to send people up to the Cornell Hotel School and the days of slab, scoured roast beef topped with red lead were ending. Not all destroyers had good cooks yet, though, and sometimes the chow was awful.

Q: This was a Navy program?

Capt. J.: It was a Navy program for training their cooks. Now I think Navy food even when I retired would compare favorably with any good food anywhere. But this was not true then.

Questions of how about the families, are deployments hurting the families? How about drink? Are you having trouble here, wife-beating and this kind of thing? From time to time there would be things of this sort coming in - officer problems. I'd go around and visit. Sometimes officers felt they could talk to me when they didn't want to talk to someone in the very close comradeship of the wardroom. There was a lot of that.

We had great admirals as well who with the different DesFlots. I'd get down and visit them and they invariably wanted to use me and wanted to care for their men. You may remember Admiral Fahrion -

Q: Spike?

Capt. J.: Yes. Then there was the man who commanded the Greer in

World War II, off Iceland, in the first action against a submarine. He was Admiral Lawrence Frost, a distinguished white-haired man. He was really concerned. He's say, "Where are you going?" And I'd say I was going to do this and this and this, and he's say to me:

"Well, I think I'll go over with you. I should be going over myself. It's about time." So he'd go with me and introduce me to the skipper, if I didn't know him.

Capt. J.: I had a very moving experience. I went to a destroyer, the Robert E. Owen, commanded by Bob English, one of these hell-raisers, full of beans, the kind the crew likes, who kept the men on their toes. I got out there and walked aboard the ship and I was tremendously moved. I had seen this boy killed. Owen was a sargeant in my regiment when we landed on Cape Torokina, in Bougainville. The Japanese had a gun position there with a seventy-five firing right down the slot. They knocked out several of our boats. Owen jumped into the frontal opening of their position, right alongisde the gun, and bayoneted the Japanese who were inside. He came out the back entrance and there he was shot and killed. They named this destroyer after him. I told Bob English this and he took me at once to see the placque commemorating Bob Owens. Then he said, "You've got to do something. You've got to speak to the crew. You've got to tell them about it."

So he mustered all hands, introduced me, and I made my little speech about Bob Owen, my memories of having known him before he was killed, and how he lost his life. Those kids listened as if they were in church, simply a pall of silence during that brief recital.

I don't know where Bob English is now —

Q: That ship meant much more to them after that, didn't it?

Capt. J.: Oh, I think it did. He wrote to me afterward. He was quite a writer. I think he'd written short stories and novels. He wrote to me saying that there'd been a lot of discussion. All at once the ship had come to mean a great deal more and had been personalized. The men for whom many ships are named tend to be forgotten. The men rarely know who they were, but the men knew who this one was.

Q: This took you into the Med, too, did it?

Capt. J.: Yes. I didn't go into the Med the same way. I went down to Norfolk and Charleston and to Gitmo and San Juan when we had exercises down there. I went to the Med largely to correlate activities with the Sixth Fleet. The CinCNavEur chaplain in those days was based in Naples and we were in the business of providing services to the Sixth Fleet, ships, men, everything else. Once they crossed a certain datum line in the South Atlantic, just this side of the Gates of Hercules, they left our operational control and came under the operational control of Com Sixth Fleet, so these chaplains were then no longer my chaplains. But I still had to provide things in getting them ready to go, so I did go over and talk to the man whom eventually I succeeded a couple of removes later who was the Sixth Fleet chaplain.

Q: Did you have any problems in terms of supply for your men?

Capt. J.: No, I don't think so, none that I can remember that were very important. The basic things we had easily. There were other things that we tried to get and were sometimes successful and sometimes not so successful. Things like tape recorders, films, this kind of thing we tried to make available. What we did in Newport and Norfolk was to designate a particular tender as the supply center, to which chaplains would go and draw these items as they needed them and wanted them. So, to a degree, each man decided what he wanted and took out what he needed.

Q: What use would a chaplain make of photographic equipment?

Capt. J.: Tape recorder, you mean?

Q: Or a tape recorder.

Capt. J.: These were used a lot by lay leaders. They used them to provide accompaniment for the singing of hymns, for example.

Q: Oh, I see.

Capt. J.: Sometimes sermons would be taped and they could be used if the lay leaders wanted them. It gave simply another dimension to the work of the lay leaders. But the chaplains themselves also used them.

Films were mainly films produced by the Chaplains' Division in the Bureau of Naval Personnel. They had to do with various moral problems in the Navy. "To Be Held in Honor," for example, was a film about marriage, an awfully good film. There was a film about gambling. John Scarne, the famous card virtuoso, appeared in this film.

One of the interesting sidelights on this is that Eddie Hemphill, a friend of ours, was technical director of it. He had a scene in a compartment where men were being invited to gamble, and the man who was inviting them was a one-hash-mark seaman. Of course, that would speak loud and clear to them, to every sailor.

Under Admiral Burke I learned a very important thing. Make sure that you're right. Or, to put it another way, people may sometimes place more credence in your word than you do yourself. I remember something that worked out well for me that taught me this lesson.

I'd been visiting the hospital in Newport, which is an old building, as you know. I noticed that down in the cellar of the place there were chairs lining both sides of the passageway which were filled with wives - a dismal place, an awful place. I went to see the hospital people and said: "Can't you do better than this? Especially for the wives of seagoing people? It's rough enough having to come here and then to be put up in such a miserable place."

They said, "Gee, chaplain, we would but we just don't have a place." I went back and reported the next day to the flagship. The admiral saw me and said, "Come on in. How are things going?"

"Well," I said, "we're having problems up at the housing park." There was a mobile home project up north in Melville. While I was talking to him about this, I said, "And I wish they could do something in the hospital for a waiting room. A lot of our wives are going there and waiting around in that miserable dungeon."

He said to me, "Get your hat." Just like that. Aye, aye, Sir, I got my hat. He walked me off the ship, we jumped into his car, and we went to the hospital. He walked down this passageway, dimly lighted, and he looked at me and said, "This is a disgrace." He went up to the commander of the hospital who really was shaken out of his boots, you know, when he saw Admiral Burke arrive, and he said:

"I've just been walking down your cellar way and I do not accept this treatment of the wives of my men. You find a proper waiting room and find it immediately." Then he turned on his heel and walked out.

Admiral Burke, you know, was not the kind of person to be that abrupt, but he was angry. He said to me:

"I want you to go there a week from today and come back and report to me."

There was a building just outside one of the lower doors to the hospital that was being used for a greenhouse. Somebody, maybe the commanding officer of the hospital, looked at that place and said, "No longer a greenhouse. Let them make it a waiting room," and they did. It was a lovely well-lighted waiting room. They had some magazines in there and decent chairs. That solved that problem.

But be careful what you say to Arleigh Burke. He may do something!

Interview No. 4 with Chaplain Captain Glyn Jones, U.S. Navy
(Retired)

Place: The U.S. Naval Institute

Date: Wednesday morning, 24 July 1977

Subject: Biography

By: John T. Mason, Jr.

Q: Well, Sir, we begin Chapter 4 today and this also begins your tour of duty with the Armed Forces Staff College in Norfolk. That was in August of 1956. You were there for three years.

Capt. J.: Yes.

Q: Tell me about it. Tell me about it in some detail.

Capt. J.: First, this was the longest tour of duty I ever had in one place. It was also one of the most pleasant, but there's not a great deal to say about it. The college had a fairly large staff and faculty, and a small administrative unit. There were two classes a year, each of five months in length, and 205 students drawn from all of our armed services, from the State Department, the CIA, and some from foreign services, French and British in particular. They were to be indoctrinated in joint staff techniques.

Q: Who was the head of the college at that point?

Capt. J.: The commandant when I arrived was General Schlatter of the Air Force. He'd been a fighter pilot and had commanded the fighters of the Eighth Air Force in Britain. He was a wonderful, free-wheeling individual.

Later on, our own Admiral Wellborn became commandant, so that I served under two magnificent gentlemen.

Q: What did you think of Charlie Wellborn?

Capt. J.: It's very hard to keep out the superlatives. He was a man of great charm, a small person of commanding presence, a first-class mind, and a person of the greatest empathy, and here he is (pointing out a photograph). I have that very picture at home signed by him. I had never served with him before, but, of course, he had been DesLant. When he arrived and found that I had been the DesLant chaplain we had a great deal to talk about.

Throughout, both from General Schlatter and Admiral Wellborn, I received every possible support of my ministry. The ministry itself was conventional. I had Sunday services. I was in charge of the library. I ran an adult class on Sunday mornings, which rapidly grew and became very well-received. I taught Christian theology. I taught another class, a course in Christian ethics at a fairly respectable level. These were very, very bright people, even though they were not schooled in theology.

Q: The men and their wives?

Capt. J.: The men and their wives. The attendance, I guess, would be in the vicinity of seventy or eighty.

Then, in due course, we started a weekly prayer group. This was for the men alone. We gathered once a week at a quarter of seven in the morning in the cafeteria. We had breakfast, a speaker, then devotions and at eight they would go off to their offices. This started in a very modest way as well, but in due course the attendance got to be eighty or ninety, and it taxed the resources of the cafeteria.

Q: What was the nature of the prayer group session?

Capt. J.: First, it started in a rather personal way. It was an intimate thing. But then, as it grew, we expanded the program. Sometimes, the officers and enlisted men provided the program. Some would be prepared to speak and give Christian testimony. Then we would have speakers from the outside. Sometimes the speakers were controversial.

At that time, there was a tremendous controversy about the opening of the schools in Norfolk. They had been closed over the segregation question. I invited Stuart Grizzard, who is now at the National Baptist Church in Washington, to come to speak. He was on his last legs in his own church because he had preached the gospel about race. But he came out and spoke to our people - told them what he had said and what was happening to him, described the reaction of his own people to his ministry. Very soon after that he was thrown out of his church.

We had other people. The mayor of Norfolk was invited down to speak as were other clergymen and chaplains from other places. All in all, it was one of the richest experiences in my time at the Staff College.

Q: Going back to your class on Sunday mornings, what did the people who attended seem to be interested in especially?

Capt. J.: They were interested in several things, if my memory is right. First, a higher percentage of these students than of the service as a whole were committed Christians. Why they should have been I don't know, but they were. Many of them felt a deficiency in their intellectual understanding of the Christian faith. The Christ figure was strong to them. When you came to the creeds, to the history, to an intelligent formulation for the Christian of today, they felt themselves in deep water.

Another concern of theirs was the ethical demand of the Christian faith. Many of them, I think, had learned before they came, but some of them learned perhaps under my preaching, that a great deal of what happens in the life of Christian churches is not wholly biblical. There's a tremendous tendency, as you know, in the church to ignore the prophetic teaching of the Old Testament. This question was especially germane at that time in Norfolk when we were facing this race situation. So they became concerned about Christian ethics.

In addition to this type of ethical concern, they were concerned about such questions as war, peace, marriage. Marital problems, sex, liquor, were practical problems in their lives. They wanted to know if the Christian faith had anything to say about these issues.

I used a sort of middle-of-the-road set of textbooks in ethics - Paul Ramsay from Princeton and Georgia Harkness, people of this sort.

They were interested, too, in the Bible. They knew the Bible was good....

Q: They had a copy at home!

Capt. J.: They had a copy. They believed that it was authoritative, but they didn't really know why. They didn't really know very much about the way in which the Bible was organized, how it came to be historically, or what it had to say. Some central notions in the Bible had eluded them completely.

I found, for example, that the idea of progressive revelation unlocked a tremendous number of doors. All at once it became possible for them to read the fifth chapter of Judges and to understand it in situ, so to speak, and to see how there came to be a difference between that and the sixtieth chapter of Issiah.

Q: So it was revelation and response on their part at that time?

Capt. J.: Indeed, I think so. Once we got involved at these

levels, I typed out manuscripts of everything that I had to say. At the end of every class there was a run on what passed for a xerox machine by people who wanted copies. They would take the whole pile of things and reproduce them and pay five cents, or whatever it was, a page! I've had correspondence from some of them saying they've used this material themselves in teaching.

A good friend of ours is Major General George Pickett, who was a tank commander in Europe under our famous man - what was his name?

Q: Patton?

Capt. J.: Under Patton, George twice received battlefield promotions. He was a rather nominal Episcopalian. He went to church and, you know, he didn't worry too much about many of these things. But then he became a senior officer and he had a number of considerations to keep in mind. He had his children late. He was being promoted rapidly so he had greater responsibility. He came to our church and, in due course, to these classes. These sort of hit him just where he lived. He was one who reproduced my outlines. He was a member of the permanent AFSC staff, so he got the whole shot, so to speak. Later he had the Second Division in Korea. He thought for a while, after retirement, about going into the ministry but decided not to. Nevertheless, he's now active in the church. We correspond regularly, and he's been using these materials in teaching in his own church.

Q: You said that they were interested in knowing more about the demands that the faith made upon individuals. How did they react as you elaborated the form of the demands?

Capt. J.: Here was an ambivalence, I think. This is one man's impression, you understand.

On the one hand, they reacted with great pain to some ethical aspects of the Christian faith. Another dear friend of mine who was a member of the faculty at AFSC came every Sunday to church. One Sunday he listened to a sermon I preached with regard to the school situation in Norfolk, in which I said to my people very simply that the attorney general of the state of Virginia was lying to them, the governor of the state was lying to them, and that there would have to be a resolution of this in terms of the truth. I ended up giving the teaching "neither Greek nor Jew" with an illustration about a black man in Virginia who went alone to the Communion rail. Then a man came alongside him to receive. He was General Lee. Well, my friend Felix listened to the end. Then he got up and stamped out. He said: "I've never heard such a thing in my life."

The next day I saw him and he said:

"I'm never going back to your church," and he told me why. He said, "I'm going to the Catholic church." Well, I said:

"You're jumping from the frying pan into the fire. You aren't going to win anything by that."

So there was that kind of response. The more general response was one of honest and painful wrestling. Some of the things that they found out contradicted many years of conviction on their part. If they took them seriously it would mean real reorientation of their lives. And there's no kidding that this was not entirely pleasant.

On the other hand, there was this feeling of revelation, of things beginning to fall into place, things beginning to make sense. I think that this came to many of them as a sense of relief. They'd been living out something that they hadn't completely understood. Now even the painful understanding brought them a sense of relief and release.

Q: Was this a unique experience for you in the chaplaincy or did you meet this sort of thing elsewhere?

Capt. J.: I had experienced this elsewhere. Every chaplain does. At Parris Island our weekly Bible study was attended by many of the chaplains and many of the officers. The general was especially interested, who was Silverthorne, a practicing Christian, and he felt some shocks from this. His own faith had tended to be sincere and strong but simplistic.

We did the Book of Amos on one occasion there. We spent several weeks on it, and the Book of Amos shook the old man out of his pants.

Q: I would think it might.

Capt. J.: It really did! Yet, I have to say that he believed he was receiving the truth about God's word. His view was that the truth had to be accepted whether it was pleasant or not.

The thing that shook many of them in this area, I think, was the concept that the Christian faith applied to society. They didn't have any trouble in believing, many of them, that the Christian faith taught you shouldn't drink whiskey or shouldn't play cards or dance or shouldn't run off with a choir singer. They tended to believe this kind of thing. But when you ran into the notion that the Christian faith was seriously involved with the concept of justice, justice in society for all men, when they see the Old Testament putting forth a picture of God judging nations, this they found difficult. A tendency especially among service officers is to set the nation at a point where it is really beyond judgment. To find suddenly that it is being judged is a rather painful thing. You know, the academy chapel mystique and this kind of thing.

Q: Which could be right or wrong.

Capt. J.: More sophisticated than that but nevertheless emotionally that's generally where they are. To look at, say, the Book of Amos and then to apply it to our country here and now and suddenly to realize that it's speaking in a contemporary way to us, this is a little bit shocking. It moves you from the picture of "Let us now go to church, and the brigade marching to the chapel on Sunday morning, to the relevance of the Faith to what people do in the office, in the barracks, out on the street.

I didn't hold these classes in every place I went. The two places, it seems to me, where it was most meaningful were Parris Island and the Staff College. I think it was more meaningful in the Staff College to more people because the general level at which one could approach the material was higher. I could make broader assumptions about the intellectual power of these people than I could of the mixed group, say, in Parris Island.

Q: And yet Christianity speaks to all levels?

Capt. J.: Yes, indeed.

Q: So how do you deal with the enlisted man?

Capt. J.: You do the best you can. Don't underrate the enlisted man -

Q: No.

Capt. J.: The thing about the Staff College was not that you had a cross section of officers, you had the very cream, just as you do at the War College.

Q: A selected group, yes. Elite!

Capt. J.: Well, indeed, the elite. I could make some assumptions about them as a group. The same material, it seems to me, could be taught in a somewhat different way to any group of enlisted men or to any other group of officers or dependents or what not.

At the Staff College it seemed possible to teach it at a more demanding level and to get down a little farther into the roots of things than you might otherwise be able to do.

Q: So you say your tour there was just a general run of chaplaincy?

Capt. J.: Yes, nothing unusual about it.

Q: But you found a special opportunity?

Capt. J.: Yes. I don't think I found an opportunity that other chaplains would not have found. I don't know either whether other chaplains before me had not done these things. It's very conceivable that they did. But these were things that brought me particular satisfaction. I think also to some of the people it brought a great deal of new insight about the faith.

Q: Did you have any opportunity within the community outside of the Armed Forces Staff College?

Capt. J.: No, I didn't. Very little there, and the reasons are rather mixed. Once you go on schedule in a school, like the school I'm in now, it's a twenty-four-hour-a-day affair. You can't sign up to do any considerable number of things off-base. This isn't to say that I was working twenty-four hours a day, but I had to be available. I had lots of calls, lots of things to do at night, people would come over and want to talk about something, especially once I had gotten to be known. It was an unusual job, too, in that it took quite a lot of administrative planning, much more than the average single Navy chaplain job does.

Q: You had to...

Capt. J.: We had to rebuild the whole religious program every five months. This meant that I had a Sunday school of about 120 kids. I had to staff that. I had a choir that ranged from twenty to forty. I had to staff that and I had to find choir masters. I had a group of acolytes that ranged from twelve to thirty in number, and I had to recruit them. This meant that I had to plan carefully. I had to get my publicity out to the new students before they arrived and outline to them what I needed. I had to ask for volunteers.

I was visited last week by Colonel Paul Becker, USMC (retired), who is now the comptroller for the University of Delaware. Paul and Claire stayed with us overnight, and, in passing, he said that he remembered getting a package from the Staff College telling all about the community. He and Claire looked to see if there was anything from the chapel and, sure enough, there was my little packet and announcement of the things I needed, choir singers, a new choir director. Well, he'd been the choir director wherever he'd been. So he said to Claire:

"Give the chaplain a buzz and see if he's got a choir director."

She did and I didn't. Paul had the job. And the same with

Aileen Hoffman. You know Carl Hoffman, he's a Marine general now?

Q: Yes.

Capt. J.: Carl is a great trumpet player and so we had a lot in common because I used to be one. They got the little packet and Carl -

Q: It was like a welcome wagon!

Capt. J.: It was, indeed. Carl saw that I needed singers and he could sing, and Aileen was a conservatory-trained choral conductor. They arrived and they gave me a buzz and I was in business for that class.

During the six classes that I was there I never failed to get either a semi-professional or a professional choir director.

Q: Isn't that interesting!

Capt. J.: There were so many. These were people who had a high quotient of service motivation, of wanting to give. I think this was another factor in their being selected to attend the college. I never had any trouble in getting not only enough Sunday school teachers but teachers, generally speaking, far superior to the run-of-the-line you find in a church. Simply tremendous people. And the acolytes were falling all over each other.

I had an early eight o'clock Communion. Then I had a later morning worship service which generally was in the free church Protestant form. I used acolytes at both the services. They waited in line, hoping that somebody would break a leg so that they could have the job!

Q: That was in the day before they had girl acolytes?

Capt. J.: Yes, it was indeed. We had, as you've remembered, I'm sure, the experience a couple of times of having an acolyte in the chancel - it was a small chapel, always crowded -

Q: And they passed out?

Capt. J.: Yes. They'd look at the cross and the candles would flicker and, in due course, they'd pass out!

The tone of this in terms of the experience of all Navy chaplains, I think would be very conventional. It would not really be deserving of much comment.

Q: And yet you are a very innovative type of person, so what were some of the things you did that were innovative, that were out of the ordinary run?

Capt. J.: I really don't think I did very much that was innovative. I did things that were apparent to do, that I think most Navy chaplains would do. I had one interesting experience that probably doesn't belong here.

We had a softball league. The staff were ten years older than all other teams - couldn't run, couldn't throw, couldn't hit - and they were regularly at the bottom of the league. One day I got a call to come up to headquarters. There was a conference of all colonels and captains about what was to be done about the softball team. This was very serious. These people didn't like being liked. The end conclusion was that we had to have a single philosophy of softball, we had to have a single manager and that I was going to be the manager!

Q: Not because you were chaplain?

Capt. J.: No, no, it had nothing to do with that. There had to be one boss, and it was I. I decided that. Our philosophy would be not to throw anything hard to these people. We were going to throw them slow junk. It was not going to be for strikes. We'd throw them high and slow inside or slow and low outside, and let them hit. We used the fast-ball only as a change up.

Well, you know, it was amazing. The young enlisted team, they teed off on this slow junk. They were driving them a mile foul. If they ever hit them fair they were up and high and out. We won the league. We lost a game or two. We never scored much ourselves, we were winning 4 to 3 or something like that. These people were frustrated by being able to hit the ball and not having much to show for it.

This sort of helped my prestige a little bit!

Q: Yes! How did Wellborn fit into this picture of worship?

Capt. J.: In terms of?

Q: In terms of worship. Did he participate?

Capt. J.: No, he did not. This is not to say that he didn't some place else. This I don't know. I know that he and Schlatter alike simply gave me every support that I could ask for. There was nothing that I couldn't have if I said I needed it.

The administrative command was commanded by a Navy captain. He was a Navy administrative guy, Frank Acker. He was there for a couple of years with me and was a simply outstanding commanding officer. He talked to me every week. We didn't have many enlisted men, but he wanted to know what I was doing with them, he wanted to know how the housekeeping of the school affected the morale of the students. Living conditions were bad. We had these old, old buildings.

Q: It's different now.

Capt. J.: Oh, yes, it's an entirely different thing now.

We had six apartments in each building. The buildings were identical in their structure and in their planning, and this led to some embarrassment sometimes. The first week I was there I went to pay respects to Admiral Briggs, who was the Navy assistant commandant. The Admiral invited us to stay for dinner, but we had children at home, we had to go, so he said:

"Well, you'd better take off your shoes," the water was running so hard, "roll up your pants, and I'll give you a raincoat."

So I got into this rig and drove home, walked up to our apartment, opened the door, and found we were in a strange place. There were strange people there. Out came this man whom

I recognized as a senior Air Force colonel on the staff. Here he saw me, shoeless in Gaza, so to speak, and wearing two stars on my raincoat, and he did a triple take. I'm sure he was wondering what kind of a chaplain they had!

Frank Acker was most responsive to the needs of the students and could always be approached. He was not a hard driver on the people who worked for him but had very high expectations, and this, of course, permeated the entire little command. I thought made it really one of the most effective administrative commands I think I've ever seen.

Frank retired and went to be assistant to the president of Brown University for a number of years. Then, I think, when he got sixty-five or whatever, he retired.

Q: We've come to the end of that very happy period at the Armed Forces Staff College in 1959 when you received an assignment overseas. How did this come about?

Capt. J.: Very routine assignment. I received orders to the staff of the commander in chief, U.S. Naval Forces, Europe, to be assigned with the naval administrative command in Naples, Italy. I was to be a pastor in Naples and also the staff chaplain for CinCUSNAVEUR in London.

Q: This was simply a staff force?

Capt. J.: Yes.

Q: That means you were the senior person on the staff in Italy?

Capt. J.: Yes. I was also the senior chaplain in the European area.

Q: Your rank at that point was what?

Capt. J.: I had just made captain.

I had a little chapel in Naples, which was a very interesting situation again. Once a quarter I had to go to London to report to the admiral. I had responsibility for the Sixth Fleet, and so I called regularly, visited the ships, both at sea and when they came in, and went on inspection tours with CinCUSNAVEUR staff. If they went to Asmara, say, I'd have to fly there or tie up with them somewhere, go to Istanbul to visit Karamursel, and I'd have to tie up with them.

Some years before we had a billet in London, a chaplain on the staff of the commander in chief, and for reasons I don't now recall - maybe I never knew - that billet was deleted.

Q: To make way for a line officer?

Capt. J.: Perhaps. In any case, the chaplain at Naples was given additional duty to the CinCUSNAVEUR staff.

After I'd been in Naples for three months, I made my first visit to London and went in to see the admiral, who was H. Paige Smith, a great man. He had been a former Chief of Naval Personnel. He wanted to know how I was getting along. I said to him, in effect:

"Admiral, if you were getting as poor performance from other parts of your staff as you're getting from me, you'd never stand for it."

Well, he was a little surprised and said:

"What do you mean?"

I said:

"Your chaplains and the ministry to the fleet are being neglected in a shameful way because you don't have a chaplain here."

Q: In London?

Capt. J.: In London. I said: "There's no way in which during a brief quarterly visit I can do the coordination with your staff that I need to do. There's no way in which I can relate to the Army and the Air Force commands on the continent as I should. There's no way I can take care of the Sixth Fleet."

"Well," he said, "what do you recommend?"

I said: "I recommend that you establish a billet for a staff chaplain here in London."

"That," he said, "is very hard to do. The staff is hard up for people."

I said: I understand, Sir, but I'm the only one of my kind." In other words, if you don't have a bird like me, then you're minus him completely.

Then he questioned me about whether I thought the Chief of

Chaplains would give them a billet from contingent unallocated, that didn't require the C-in-C to surrender a billet I said I didn't think so. I pointed out in addition that the Chief of Chaplains was not too happy about the billet having been deleted before and didn't feel the burden of proof was on him. I left with him a paper in which I'd written all of this.

In due course I got a dispatch from London asking me to prepare correspondence to CNO and to the chief of Naval Personnel asking for the establishment of a permanent billet in London.

Q: Smith saw the merits of this then?

Capt. J.: He did, he agreed, and he gave up a number.

Q: He did give up a number?

Capt. J.: Yes, he did give up a number. I wrote in that paragraph saying that compensatory reduction will take place in such and such, and I left that blank for them to fill in and they did. He signed it. It went in. About six months later we got a dispatch establishing a billet in London and ordering me to it. This I hadn't contemplated. I was a brand-new, makee learn captain, I was very happy in my billet in Naples. We had a very interesting experience there in terms of the establishment of the development of a congregation there and I was enjoying this a great deal. We had just gotten settled and lived in a building on the very high skyline of Posillipo called Palazzo Rosso,

Red House. We were on the eighth floor. From the front of our balcony we could see Capri. There was the whole bay and Vesuvio! Now I had put my foot in it and we had to move!

I relieved a tremendous guy in Naples by the name of Vaughan Lyons. He had relieved another great chaplain by the name of Eddie Hemphill.

Q: I've heard about him.

Capt. J.: Well, he's a great guy. Eddie had his congregation in a theater, the Arco Belano Theater, in Naples. In due course, though, he felt he had to have a church, so he made an arrangement for the use of the Anglican church there in Via Aquia. He rented it and moved his congregation there. It was a very curious arrangement. He wasn't allowed to use the church for celebrating the Communion, he couldn't use the altar. In due course, though, Vaughan came. He thought the church was way off the beaten course of things, the congregation was very small. He decided to move from the church to the cafeteria of the Forrest Sherman School.

Q: What was the Forrest Sherman School?

Capt. J.: It was the American service high school in Naples. The week before I reported he did just that. At the first service I attended, the attendance was tripled from what it had been in the church because this was in the center of the American population.

So, when I took over, the attendance continued to rise because people could finally get to church without any great difficulty until the cafeteria was completely filled.

Again, I started an adult class. We hadn't had any structure to the congregation, so I did what we had done at the Staff College. I organized a chapel council made up of eight or nine people.

Q: A vestry sort of thing?

Capt. J.: A vestry, precisely. We called it the chapel council. They would meet monthly and advise me, and would give directions about the utilization of the money and make recommendations about programs. These people in the Staff College were mixed, most of them were staff and faculty officers and two or three enlisted men, chiefs, perhaps, you know. But here almost all of them were senior officers of the several services who were either up at NSA or down at the NATO command.

Q: CinCSouth?

Capt. J.: CinCSouth. Cat Brown was there at that time, and he was very nice and very helpful to me.

So I was having a ball with these people. I had a great choir. We had four professionals, one to man each part, so to speak, and then a large number of volunteers, and a lot of them sang very well. And we had regular visitors from the ships as they came in who would come to church up there. It was really a going organization and we were having a lot of fun when we had to go to London. So, in due course, I was relieved.

As a quondam professional musician I had one moving experience. Our organist, Genarro D'Onofrio, was an Italian state treasure. He couldn't leave the country without permission and was paid about $4,000 a year simply for being alive. One Sunday after church, while I was removing my vestments, there came to me some glorious lorelei on the violin and organ. I hastened to the music and was soon introduced by Maestro D'Onofrio to the violinist, Aldo Ferrarese, concertmaster of the Scarlatti Orchestra in Naples and a virtuoso specializing in Paganini who had appeared with most of the world's great orchestras. D'Onofrio, who knew I was a hack fiddler, announced that fact to Ferrarese. The latter immediately insisted that I had to play on his instrument - which had been Paganini's own. No ancient Hebrew approached the Ark with greater trepidation, but at last, and with the greatest delight, I surrendered to his urging and Naples was regaled with my rendition of Bach's air for the G string.

Q: Would you focus on that congregation that you built up there or that was built up at Forrest Sherman? What were their particular interests in worshiping there?

Capt. J.: It was a different congregation from the Staff College. We had a lot of enlisted men in that congregation, many of them senior enlisted men, first class and chiefs. We had a lot of officers. We ran a Sunday school and this in itself attracted people. In the adult class, one had to make haste rather more slowly. I think they were just as interested in pretty much the same kind of questions. One dimension, I think, that was different or additional to the interests of the Staff College people was that these people were abroad. They were away from home and were very aware of this. There was a two-fold thing of new experiences and what, in Welsh, we call "hiraeth," homesickness, longing. Worry about what would a couple of years in Italy do to kids. All of this kind of thing was a dimension that we didn't have to think about at the Staff College.

I had a lot of counseling to do.

Q: You always had had!

Capt. J.: The growth in the congregation there had little to do with me. It had to do, I think almost entirely, with the relocation of the services to a place where the people could reach them. Once that happened, the people sort of came out of the woodwork.

Q: And also that factor that you mentioned, the homesickness, they were drawn?

Capt. J.: This was true about the community as a whole in other ways, too. The communities tended to be very close. Some people went into the Italian community, but, as with many Americans, most people did not. They tended to be an enclave.

Q: It was because of an alien culture, was it not?

Capt. J.: It was. It wasn't, I didn't think, that different from our own. There were many symbols there with which we were familiar. Of course, it was a Roman Catholic country but we got along very well with Roman Catholics. We had no problems. In my own case, I worked with Father Farelli, who was the priest who took care of the scugnizzi. The scugnizzi are the boys and girls of Naples who have no parents and who live nobody knows how, really, in the city, by stealing, begging, and so on.

Q: Sleeping in the doorways!

Capt. J.: Sleeping in the doorways. Some of them would be taken up by Fagin-type characters and would beg for them. There was one case I remember of a young boy, ten or eleven years old, who had a broken hip that hadn't been set. He was begging. An American officer saw him and took him to our people and asked whether something couldn't be done about this. Our people said, on the side, sure. They broke his hip and reset it and the boy disappeared.

Several months later this officer and I were walking down the street and here was the boy sitting in the same place and his hip was rebroken again. This kind of thing. You know, you wouldn't believe it, but this took place.

Q: It was to his advantage to - ?

Capt. J.: Well, he was captured again by one of these Fagins -

maybe the same one - and he gave what he made to her or to him. Father Barelli took over some of the old bombed-out places in Naples and put these kids in there, gave them a place to sleep, had soup for them, and required that before they could sleep or eat, they had to bring in an empty bottle. And so he started a huge trade in bottles, which brought him enough money to support them. During the time I was there, he had between 500 and 600 boys. No one was forced to remain there, but they came and they stayed and he influenced them and saved them, I'm sure, from many difficulties.

The curious thing was that the cardinal wouldn't support him. He didn't punish him in any way, but he just wouldn't support him.

There was a Protestant orphanage down south of Naples that was run by Italian Methodists, which we also supported. To that orphanage Navy men from the ships go down to work as they come into port. I went down and paid my respects to the cardinal, who was a very nice old person. He couldn't speak English, but my Catholic buddy spoke a bastard kind of Italian and so he introduced me.

Later, I told my friend I didn't see that there was around the bishop the normal organization that you find in an American diocese. Didn't see Catholic Charities.

"Oh," he said, "we don't have Catholic Charities."

"What happened?"

Well, what happened was that Castoldi, that was the cardinal's name, spent every morning dispensing alms personally. That was his understanding and the church's understanding -

Q: That was charity. Therefore, his failure to support the -

Capt. J.: That's right. Father Barelli was outside the system, you know.

That was a very fascinating learning experience for me in that I did have these relations, with the orphanages in particular. There was a Catholic orphanage called Casa Mia. The Protestant orphanage was called Casa Materna. I don't know that Father Barelli's orphanage had any name. He was a charming man. If ever I saw a committed person, a person totally Christ-like in his life, it was Father Barelli.

Q: You found in your efforts with these orphanages that the American service men were willing to participate in things like that?

Capt. J.: This has always been so. If the American people only knew one-tenth of what our soldiers and sailors and Marines do in this respect, they would be amazed. From our own command, which did not have a large enlisted contingent, we used to have enlisted men go down every week to do all kinds of things. An electrician would go down to fix wires, you know, and everything else. They'd be building, adding on to the buildings. Cooks would go down and help supervise and improve the kitchen. Things that you couldn't even imagine these guys would go down and do. And, of course, they had the reward of having the kids come out to them.

You'd go down there and you might see a sailor sitting there and in his lap would be a little boy or a little girl, and this to them was the real reward. They did the same thing for Father Barelli and for Casa Mia. Not only our kids did it, but sailors would come over from the ships. The ships knew about these places. Some ships would take collections before they came into port and would come and make offerings, give gifts. That still takes place.

Q: Is this out of character when they're in the States?

Capt. J.: No. They do the same thing in the States. You have a different situation in the States. Two-thirds of the crew, when it leaves the ship, goes home, lots of married people. While they're on the beach they are in a much more characteristically civilian than military posture. But when they go ashore in foreign ports they're literally going ashore. They see people more needy even than people they knew here, and they're simply moved to do something about it.

The chaplains help, but I don't think that the chaplains are the ones who necessarily structure these things. Somebody goes out to see Casa Materna, goes back to his ship, and says:

"Say, I just saw something out there you ought to see."
Then they go to the chaplain and say:

"Chaplain, can't we do something?"

Q: You're saying that this is inherent in the nature of the

American?

Capt. J.: I think so. What I'm saying is, I think, somewhat more specific. It may be inherent in American nature, but I'm convinced that it's inherent in the nature of the American serviceman. Somewhere, from some source he is motivated to want to help the needy and the unfortunate.

Q: How do you differentiate between the civilian and the serviceman?

Capt. J.: I don't know that I can. I feel that I'm not able to speak with much authority about the civilian, you know, as I feel I may about the serviceman. You look at the United Fund and that kind of thing and it's very obvious that there's a great deal of this in our population at large. But I've seen it, I think, more dramatically with the Marines and with our sailors.

Q: What sort of impact does this have on the foreign country?

Capt. J.: On the country, I don't think very much.

Q: On the people?

Capt. J.: On some of the people - how to say this? There's a sense in which Casa Materna and Casa Mia are isolated from the mainstream of Neapolitan life, so when a sailor goes there there isn't anyone very much to see what he's doing. The people of Naples, by and large, I don't think are aware of this kind of thing. And it's not done for public relations on the part of our people.

Q: I would hope not!

Capt. J.: Oh, it isn't. You may see something about it in the ship's paper, appealing for people to go to Casa Materna on Saturdays at twelve, but beyond this you won't find it. So I would doubt that it has much influence at all on the populations at large.

Q: Tell me about your relationship with the Sixth Fleet, and how you supervised this task?

Capt. J.: George Anderson commanded the Sixth Fleet during part of this time. He had a fleet chaplain and my function was go to inspect, but more importantly it was to pay a pastoral visit to the admiral and his chaplain to find out what I could do to help. If I had proposals for things that I felt the chaplain should do, I'd clear them with the admiral and his staff - and there were things that I felt should be done - and I would prepare two, three, or four instructions. One I remember on pornography in the ships' stores.

The chaplain in London had brought to me half a dozen books that were on sale - unbelievable. I'm a pretty strong First Ammendment guy, you know, but this was impossible. So I went down to this guy and said: "How come you're selling this stuff?"

He said: "Well, the supply people in the States order it.

We don't buy things by title. We just get a huge order and it's included in the order."

So I prepared an instruction for Admiral Smith to sign and I wrote to Washington and I sent these things, as a matter of fact, to the Chief of Chaplains and said:

"I think you ought to talk to somebody over there, but we're sending out this instruction."

Then I would go down to Admiral Anderson and his chaplain and say:

"Do you have any objection to this? Do you concur in this being done," and he, of course, concurred.

Then I had instructions about instructing lay leaders, setting up schools to instruct lay leaders, which I had done before in Norfolk -

Q: And up in Newport?

Capt. J.: Up in Newport and Norfolk, instructing people who were giving character education presentations, and before that kind of instruction was considered cleared I would take it down to Admiral Anderson. Sometimes he could have modifications to suggest and sometimes he didn't.

My main involvement was pastoral, and I was interested in what happened on the beach, what was the VD rate, how were the families getting along, all of that kind of thing. But it had to be a pastoral concern that didn't wander into the jurisdiction of Sixth Fleet.

Q: This is a very fine line, isn't it?

Capt. J.: It is, indeed.

Q: You might say something about that whole area. I mean the pastoral concern of the chaplain, how can this be supervised by a line officer who may not know too much about that whole area?

Capt. J.: Of course, they had their chaplains and they also had chaplains on the beach at Nice, so that I had a professional structure through which I could work.

The essential distinction, I think, is this. The command has the power to inspect. I did go on inspection trips with our own staff, of course - but this comes badly from the clergy, from a chaplain. The power of the chaplain in these circumstances is moral, and not authoritarian in the sense of coming down the chain of command. He does have behind him the full power of command authority and people know it. But I think that he must be very sensitive to the things that need to be done, but he must approach them not in the sense of saying this is what the admiral wants, my admiral wants, but in the sense I've been around the Sixth Fleet and I've observed these things and I've talked to your chaplain about them, and we agree that some stresses are needed here and here and here. He would listen and he'd be glad. But these were in the form of suggestions and not in the form of inspection reports. When I went on inspection with the staff I had a report to fill out and I was doing a very different kind of activity.

I don't know if that distinction means much.

Q: It does. I would think that it would be very frustrating, however, to make these suggestions and they have no greater power than that?

Capt. J.: No, I didn't feel frustrated at all. I didn't feel frustrated even though sometimes not all of them were accepted. This was my pastoral experience in other parts of the work of the church.

If I felt something was radically wrong, and this has happened, it happened more in DesLant than it did with the Sixth Fleet, I would go to the commodore and say:

"I think this is wrong and I think it must be changed," and if the commodore gave me a bad time, then I would say, as I had to on several occasions:

"I will put this in writing and I will send it to the admiral via you, then you can make your case with the admiral." And most times he would back down and say, "Wait a minute, let's be reasonable," and most of the time they were reasonable.

Q: You talked about the employment of lay leaders in the Sixth Fleet -

Capt. J.: Yes. They were doing what we'd been doing for a number of years. The problem, because of the turnover of personnel, was to replace those people and to keep available a backlog of capable people. Once we got the backlog, the lay leaders tended to schedule themselves in sequence so the same person didn't do it every Sunday, or they tended to do things together sometimes, three or four of them, which was a better thing than having the same person do it every Sunday.

Q: Yes, and, after all, they were lay volunteers.

Capt. J.: Oh, they were volunteers. They couldn't be assigned to us without their consent.

Q: One of the points made by Admiral Smith in a memo of his was that the chaplain will inform the commands about the spiritual needs of units without chaplains?

Capt. J.: Yes. This was an instruction I had written and that the admiral signed. This placed the chaplain in the position of making sure that local commands let their chaplains get off the ship. For example, here you have a cruiser that might be escorted, say, by three destroyers, none of which carry chaplains. Well, it was the obligation under this instruction of the cruiser chaplain to alert his captain to the fact that he had obligations to these ships. It was the captain's responsibility to see that. The religious needs of the destroyers were met.

This kind of instruction was always well received. If destroyers weren't cared for it was never, to my knowledge, a voluntary not caring. It was simply an oversight, it got lost in the wash kind of thing. But once the chaplain knew that he had the obligation to tell his skipper that the skipper was responsible for these destroyers, the skippers complied. They arranged helo hops and everything else to get the chaplains over.

Q: Another point was to exert every effort to secure a ministry for personnel of other faiths?

Capt. J.: Yes.

Q: Was this a real problem?

Capt. J.: No. This was only putting into writing the old Navy tradition, if you have a cruiser with a Protestant chaplain he must make every effort that he can make to make sure the Catholic and Jewish and other personnel, when it's possible, receive their ministry. There was a time, long back, when Navy chaplains were not zealous in this, put it that way. They would do what was required, but since before my time the Navy chaplain has taken this as a very serious responsibility long before the churches got into this understanding - a very serious responsibility to see that personnel not of his faith were cared for as often and as well as my people. So it became routine.

When I was in Naples, for example, we'd get dispatches from ships saying they were arriving and were in need of a Protestant chaplain and a Catholic chaplain. We had three chaplains there and one or more of us would be involved every Sunday going down to the port to hold services in those ships. Then occasionally we'd be visited in our chapel by chaplains from the ships and they'd bring some of their men.

Q: While you were in Italy, stationed in Italy, there were some interesting things that occurred?

Capt. J.: Yes. Some of them I wasn't involved in. There was an earthquake in North Africa that took place while I was in Morocco on an inspection visit with ComFairMed, but there wasn't anything I could do about it. I went to the admiral and volunteered to go down and help if I could and he said if he thought there was anything I could do he'd call on me but they couldn't see anything, and he was quite right.

Q: The fleet did do something about it, though?

Capt. J.: Oh, indeed. They flew in personnel, doctors especially. There weren't any Christians down there. There were Moslems involved. We had some aircraft problems. We had an old R-4D that was the staff aircraft for ComFairMed. She was taking a basketball team to a tournament when the gyrocompass went off. They went fifty miles off course. They were flying in cloud and all at once, they saw before them mountains there was no way to avoid. This lieutenant, a mustang, a great pilot by the name of Jenson, took over the controls. He mushed that aircraft in, turned her nose up so that he hit right on the bottom of the aircraft and just kept going right on up the mountain.

Q: So he could land on the mountain!

Capt. J.: He did, with wheels up, you know, and ended up on the edge of a cliff. Nobody was seriously hurt. One of the people aboard was a clerk from my office and he lost all the fillings from his teeth. Then they were rescued in a day by a Spanish shepherd who got up there.

We lost power in an aircraft ourselves at Rota one day. We were taking off for Naples and getting power on, and somebody reversed the power sources and when we got up we'd lost compass and radio and everything. We had again an old mustang pilot. We were about 9,000 feet in cloud and we veered into the shore, got in and found the beach. Then he flew by line of sight, visual, you know, back to Rota. He was curving around mountains and all the rest because he had to keep visual. Then he had to buzz the tower to get their attention because he had no radio, and we got in with no problem at all. But there were an awful lot of people who were very angry.

Q: I suppose so. Did we have a chaplain at Rota?

Capt. J.: We had two chaplains at Rota.

Q: Does this constitute a different kind of service?

Capt. J.: No. The chaplains at Rota had two basic responsibilities. First, there's the air station, of course. Also, we had our new tender there and they had to see that she and the nuke subs were cared for.

I remember going to Rota and the Catholic chaplain, Frank Adams, saying to me:

"You ought to visit the Protestant church in Sevilla." So I said fine, and he took me in there, showed me the church. No outside sign was allowed. Then he said:

"The minister runs the Humbert and Williams bodega, where sherry originated. Let's go see him."

We went to see him. He was a charming man. He ran the sherry bodega and told me about what it meant to minister to Protestants in Spain at that time. He found the national government was hard on them but local people, Catholic people, tended to protect them so far as they could. He had a congregation of about 200. He was accompanied everywhere he went in the bodega by a very evil-looking man whose name was Ferguson. I don't know, he may have been off-scouring of Wellington's armies.

When the time came for us to leave, the minister said to me:

"I want to show you something." He showed me the books of the bodega - 1793, raided by pirates, everything gone, and they restarted in 1793. Then he said: "I want to give you something," and he brought out a velvet box and in it was a 1793 bottle of brandy. Can you imagine that? Used in the making of a sherry.

You run into a a lot of interesting things of that sort, but every sailor does.

Q: Was there any relationship with the Luisitania Church in Spain?

Capt. J.: No, not that I know of. Between this congregation?

Q: Yes.

Capt. J.: No, not that I know of. So far as I could ascertain, it was an independent congregation. I had to do with the other people in Italy, the Waldensians, 100,000 of them up in the northern mountains. They're very highly respected. They're almost together in one community. The head of the church had an office in Rome. Shortly after my arrival I went up to pay my respects to him. He came down to speak to my church and to my adult class, a highly cultivated, well educated, theologically sophisticated person. When I left Italy, he heard about it and wrote me a beautiful letter. He also sent me a Bible which he transcribed in his own hand, asking blessings upon my preaching of the gospel, which I still have.

Q: Going back to Rota, I was curious to know whether there was a new angle to the ministry to submariners, now that they serve in Polaris submarines and are at sea so very long?

Capt. J.: There are a couple of chaplains who can give you authoritative pictures of this. One is Neil Stevenson. If I'm not mistaken, he is now in the office of the Chief of Chaplains. I knew him when I was assigned in Washington and he was on the staff of SubLant down in Charleston. He was, I guess, absent from the staff but he was down in Charleston working with nuke subs, trying to work up programs for the use of these people who were long times at sea, to find special means of caring for their families. They had to make adjustments for this service. But I myself had no experience at all beyond relating casually at Rota to the submariners.

Q: Did you have any contact with Malta when you were there?

Capt. J.: No, I had none at all. I had a lot of contact with Sicily. We had a command down there at Sigonella, a naval air station. I went down and visited it regularly, and when their new chapel was built, I was invited to come down and preach the dedication sermon. But Malta I had no relations with.

I got around to Morocco, Asmara, Istanbul, Athens -

Q: Did you get to Wheelus base?

Capt. J.: I didn't.

Q: It was still in use, though?

Capt. J.: It was still in use, but I didn't get there. Then up into Germany, Bremerhaven. I'd go regularly to the two commands in Europe, once I was in London.

Q: And you went to London in 1960?

Capt. J.: In 1960. I reported to the staff and had a great time with that staff. They were beautiful people, and, of course, Admiral Smith. His No. 2 man was Reynolds Hogle - Admiral Reynolds Hogle, a big, bluff, direct sailorman, and very, very sharp. I enjoyed both of them.

Q: How did you go about your duties as force chaplain when you came up there?

Capt. J.: For one thing, once the new billet was established, the admiral wanted the title to be changed, and so he had it registered as fleet chaplain, so that there were three fleet chaplains.

Q: Atlantic, Pacific, and —

Capt. J.: And NavEur. His reasoning was that the largest operational fleet that we had on this side of the world was the Sixth Fleet, so I had a large obligation to ships at sea and should have the title "fleet chaplain."

I had an operational responsibility and the fleet chaplain, Atlantic, had both an operational and an administrative responsibility, so that ships coming to Sixth Fleet crossing an op line outside, say the Canaries or wherever, then came under our command. At that point my personal responsibilities began.

LantFleet did a great deal with training and other things of that sort. We were a fleet in being that was operational. Of course, Second Fleet was the source fleet from which we got our ships. For that reason, Admiral Smith said he wanted the surgeon to be known as the fleet surgeon, and the chaplain as the fleet chaplain, and we were.

Q: What about that flow back and forth from Second Fleet to Sixth Fleet? I mean the six months' service or whatever it was?

Capt. J.: Yes.

Q: What about that in terms of your command?

Capt. J.: So far as I know, it worked very well. I coordinated my work with the Lant Fleet chaplain. If we had needs, and we did have needs, I would communicate them to him. For example, a very minor thing, I concluded after visiting Sixth Fleet that people were always running out of equipment, losing it or whatever, and then having to wait long periods of time for it to arrive from Lant Fleet. So I communicated with the Lant Fleet chaplain, who was a wonderful man by the name of Merle Young, and asked him if he would concur in the concept of establishing a permanent chaplain supply source in two places, aboard one of the tankers, perhaps, and in Naples, so that we could promptly replace any items the chaplain needed. He concurred wholeheartedly and we made the arrangement. Admiral Monroe at that time was commodore of ServForce, Sixth Fleet, which is where we put the supply dump. He concurred wholeheartedly and so we had a better supply situation.

That kind of thing called for coordination between us but it was never any problem.

Q: Roughly, how many chaplains did you have under your command?

Capt. J.: Well, I didn't have them, of course, under my command. They were my professional responsibility, but they were under individual commands. Counting chaplains - I'm not exact in this, this is an estimate - counting chaplains ashore - and the number at sea fluctuated, I would say that it was in the vicinity of twenty.

Q: Also, what about the responsibilities on the continent of Europe, in Germany - ?

Capt. J.: Yes, we had one chaplain in Bremerhaven, we had one in Nice, and I had to be responsible for them. We had also a housekeeping chaplain with the administrative command in London who was the local pastor. In London I had no pastoral responsibilities at all. I simply went to church like everybody else.

Q: You were getting too high up in the chain of command to have pastoral responsibilities!

Capt. J.: Well, it was the first time - no that isn't true, I didn't either in DesLant. I was really so tied up in DesLant it would have been impossible, and most of the time in London I was, too. I felt a real sense of deprivation both times, not having pastoral responsibility.

Frank Garrett, who later became Chief of Chaplains, was the chaplain in London and did a fine job.

It was a good year. I enjoyed it. But then I got sick and had to be sent home.

Q: Where were you living in London?

Capt. J.: We lived in a little village in Surrey, 25 miles south of London, called Claygate. We were involved in a number of ways in the life of the village. I got to know the local Anglican priest very well. He was a very innovative man and that year, for the first time, was having an every-member canvass. The town was by the ears. It had never been heard of before.

Q: An established church!

Capt. J.: Yes, indeed. Well, it was the established church, but this was a Christian church and it was led by a Christian man. He had the educational task of training and teaching his people about stewardship and he didn't duck it. He was such a strong and loving person that the people took it. It shook them.

What he did was call six of his men in and he said:

"I've got something I want us to pray about." They said okay, and so they all knelt down and he prayed that these people would learn the meaning of Christian stewardship. Then they sat and talked about it, and they said: "We have responsibilities as laymen."

Each went out and gathered together six people from the parish and prayed about it and talked about it and, in due course, they covered the whole parish. Then they had a parish meeting and talked about it. The people had been flipping a little bit, but one thing that helped was that it came from themselves, you know. They decided to do it and so it was done for the first time while I was there.

Our next-door neighbor was Bill McKay, who was one of the first six, and when he found out I was a minister, he'd come over and we'd talk about the every-member canvass. He knew that it was commonly done in the States but it was the first time for them.

They went out, as many of our churchmen do, two by two and visited every house in the parish. They'd been told in advance, so they were there, and the thing was an overwhelming success. It worked like a charm.

Q: Has it taken over elsewhere, do you know, in England?

Capt. J.: I don't know. I wasn't there long enough to see very much farther than that. I would hope that it did.

Q: Your residence in that village, was that your own choice?

Capt. J.: Yes. We could have lived anywhere within reach that we wanted. Ruth looked around for several weeks until we found a place owned by a British Army officer, and rented it. We had a great time.

Q: What about the burden of traveling? I mean such a large area to be cognizant of.

Capt. J.: Oh, you mean traveling around the continent and Africa?

Q: Yes.

Capt. J.: I did quite a lot. There were always limits because of budget, but the admiral was very generous. If I said I had to go some place it was done. The man who had the money was what we called in the Marine Corps G-1, the administrative officer, Captain Dick Mugg. He always provided it. Sometimes it cost him a sum we couldn't apply for. Up on a visit to London when I was living in Naples, I started on the way home and our aircraft conked out in Paris. This was a Navy aircraft. It was Saturday and I had to be in Naples Sunday to preach and to hold services. So I had to take Air France to Rome, then train from Rome to Naples. I arrived about six in the morning, so I got there in time for service. That kind of thing couldn't be anticipated.

I didn't find the traveling difficult as long as I was convinced it had to be done.

Q: What sort of relationship did you have with Washington, the Chief of Chaplains, when you were in that command? I mean how close were you?

Capt. J.: So far as I know, I had a good relationship.

Q: I mean in terms of his knowledge of what you were doing?

Capt. J.: The chief's?

Q: Yes.

Capt. J.: First, I reported regularly to him. Then I made sure that any official acts of mine were sent to him in terms of copies. When I issued instructions, for example, to CinCUSNavEur and Sixth Fleet with Admiral Smith's signature, I'd send the instructions over to the Chief of Chaplains so that he would know what was happening.

Then a very curious thing happens in the way of correspondence. Some of it is very good but some is very bad. Chaplains, outside of the law, communicate unofficially with the Chief of Chaplains in the form of personal letters. This, now has some degree of sanction, so that I guess the naval authorities feel that chaplains have to have some means of communication. I suggested long since that this type of correspondence be legitimized, that it be called, for example, professional official letters, technically official, or something of this sort. It might be in informal form, but then it would be legal. There's always the possibility of a chaplain unwisely writing things in these letters that would be deleterious, damaging to other chaplains, damaging to some commands - sending official information unofficially and illegally. I felt there should be control by designating a new form of correspondence.

Q: How did that grow up? Simply because the Chaplains Corps was small in peacetime?

Capt. J.: Yes, I think it did, and because they were scattered. When I entered the Navy there were, I think, only 92 chaplains. They were all over the world. Very rarely did you see two in one place. I think they did it at first as much as a means of fellowship as for communicating information. The Chief of Chaplains had to know in some way but they didn't want to usurp, as they saw it, channels of official communication for much of the information that they sent. And so they set up unofficial means.

Q: Has it been legitimatized?

Capt. J.: Not to my knowledge, and I think that's a mistake. I think it's very much in the interests of Navy commands to have a type of technical correspondence among the chaplains, between the Chief and his chaplains.

Q: Professional to a professional.

Capt. J.: Indeed. I myself would see no difficulty in having it legitimatized. I think people would look at it closely and might have corrections and ideas that I don't have, haven't reached, but I think it could be legitamized. Then, the writer of the letter could really be held responsible for what he had written. Files could be seen by interested people who might have a legitimate interest in them.

Q: I suppose it fluctuates, does it, with the personality of the Chief of Chaplains?

Capt. J.: No, I don't think so. I don't think it does. I think there's a tendency on the part of many chaplains, especially junior chaplains, not to write very much, and even a fear of writing. Then, there's a tendency of other chaplains, and I'm one of these, I imagine, when something seems hot to me to write to the Chief and say, hey, I think we ought to do this or we ought to do that. This has generally been well received, not always agreed with, but the chief was glad to have the views of his personnel.

Q: Do you know if there's any parallel, say, in the Medical Corps?

Capt. J.: I think that there is one essential difference that at some point we're going to have to look at anyway, I think, between the Medical Corps and the Chaplain Corps. That is that the Medical Corps exercises technical control of its professional area. The Chaplain Corps does not. There can be intra-bureau correspondence between the Medical Corps Headquarters, Bureau, and doctors in the field. This is a technical and legitimate type of correspondence.

In the case of the chaplains, of course, the Chief of Naval Personnel is the Chief of Chaplains in the Navy. The Chief of the Chaplains himself is a minor functionary in the personnel administration structure of the Navy. This sounds like pretty strong language, but it's the case. The Chief of Chaplains has no technical control over his professional area per se. He makes suggestions to the Chief of Naval Personnel and performs certain ceremonial functions, but the decisions are made by the Chief of Naval Personnel.

My desire to have this changed was one among several reasons why I asked the Chief to be released from the bureau in 1951.

Q: Yes, I remember when you did that.

Capt. J.: The Chief then was not inclined to want to change it.

Q: Did he see the validity of it as an argument, as a position?

Capt. J.: I don't think he felt any resentment, to put it that way, at me for holding these views. His answer to me, however, was that the Chief of Naval Personnel does very well by us. That didn't answer my question. I don't like to be in a position where my technical and professional fate is in the hands and in the control of people who don't know my profession.

Q: And who assume in a sense a lady bountiful attitude toward you?

Capt. J.: Their attitude is great. I have no personal complaint against them. The fact is that the Chief of Naval Personnel doesn't know my business and he shouldn't be running it.

Furthermore, it's demeaning to the Chief of Chaplains. He's in an organization of personnel administration which is a smaller category than is the ministry of religions. He's equated with officers clubs and promotion, recruitment, and so on, which have no bearing at all on the ministry of religion.

Very slowly there have developed sentiments in favor of doing what I believe should be done, namely, assigning the Chief of Chaplains, at the EXOS level, to the office of the Secretary, just as the Judge Advocate General is assigned. The Judge Advocate General has technical control of his own professional domain, and the Chief of Chaplains should, too. Even the Chief of Information operates under the Secretary.

Chiefs have attempted to do little things about it. George Rosso, an excellent Chief of Chaplains, got an agreement from the Chief of Naval Personnel that he could communicate directly with the Secretary of the Navy on matters of religious interest. A lot of people have forgotten that until a few years before George Rosso every chaplain in the Navy could do that. Every chaplain was required to write an official report of his activities to the Secretary of the Navy. But here the Chief himself was getting back a little bit of what every chaplain had a few years before.

Q: What is the difference between taking it to the Secretary of the Navy rather than the Chief of Naval Personnel? I mean they're both non-professionals in terms of the clergy?

Capt. J.: Yes. This is a very important question, and it has to do with the ambiguity of the chaplaincy itself. Chaplains in the field necessarily have to be under military command. Nobody questions that. I've been under it all my life, almost. The question is where should the ministry of religion in the Navy be organizationally placed.

The Secretary of the Navy is no more professionally qualified than the Chief of Naval Personnel, but he is the dominant civilian authority. I believe strongly that the chaplaincy should be placed under civilian authority in the structure of the Navy, and the civilian authority by law is dominant in this country.

Q: Yes.

Capt. J.: This is not to say I don't like the Chiefs of Naval Personnel. They're great men. But by the nature of the case, they behave as any people would behave in their structures. They behave to keep their own power, to maintain their own area of control. So they have fought consistently against any attempt, and no really serious ones have been made, to give autonomy to the Chaplain Corps under the Secretary. To give us, in other words, the same thing that JAG has.

When I came to the bureau in 1961 or '62 - 1962, I guess it was, I suggested to our then Chief that we write an official report, an annual report, from the Chief of Chaplains to the Secretary of the Navy, not via BuPers, as had been gained by George Rosso. Remember that, until five years before, every chaplain had submitted an annual report to the Secretary.

I helped prepare the report, we sent the report to the Secretary of the Navy, and what do you imagine happened?

Q: He sent it back or sent it to BuPers?

Capt. J.: No, he accepted it, but he sent a copy to BuPers, which was perfectly all right.

Q: And you had not done that?

Capt. J.: No, we had intentionally not done this, to make sure that we had a direct connection with the Secretary. Immediately there came down to our office a brief note from the Chief of Naval Personnel ordering us never to do this again. This, of course, was a direct breach of the promise to Chaplain Rosso.

Q: And his reason?

Capt. J.: He gave no reason. He didn't have to.

Two years later, I had written to Frank Garrett - this was after my retirement - saying I hoped he would do something about this, because it seemed to me that the integrity of the ministry of religion was involved, leaving all personalities aside. He talked to the Chief of Naval Personnel about it. The new CNP said, in effect, "I don't see why that can't be done." Arrangements were made, and Frank wrote me that CNO and the Secretary had agreed to place our office at the EXOS level, the Secretary's level, where we'd be running our own show.

I waited and didn't hear anything about it. Then I found out what had finally been done. Frank wrote me: it's been decided as a solution to this difficulty, to get away from many difficulties that would evolve if he went to the Secretary, that he would report not only to the Chief of Naval Personnel, but also to the assistant CNO for personnel. He, as you know, also happens to be the Chief of Naval Personnel.

This was touted as a great victory, a great step forward in liberating the Chaplain Corps. It was, of course, only one more defeat in the attempt to reach the power for doing our job in the Navy. This would have been the view, I believe, of Saint Reinhold Niebuhr!

Q: The Secretary was not - ?

Capt. J.: No, no, we never got into him.

Q: What is your prognosis of this situation?

Capt. J.: It's hard to say. If the churches really knew where we were fixed and about the inhibitions on the ministry that stem from it, they would immediately move. However, for a number of reasons, they don't move. One is that they don't know. The second is that many of the chaplaincy representatives are former chaplains who like the status quo in the services. Thirdly, the churches put these chaplaincy committee chairmen in the background. They're not a very large concern to the churches. The only church that I know that gives serious importance to it is the Roman Catholic church with the Military Ordinariate. The Catholic Church at this point, I think, has not moved because most of the priests who have come to high position in the armed forces, in the Chaplain Corps, tend to be very conservative in pre-Vatican II tones. John O'Connor is a gifted inter-regnum and his innovations are unique in my time, but the power situation is essentially unchanged.

Q: What about the Episcopal Church with a bishop for the armed forces?

Capt. J.: I met one bishop, Bishop Lewis, whom I found impressive. The best man, I think, the Episcopalians ever had was Bob Plumb, I felt, was very knowledgeable -

Q: He's a friend of mine.

Capt. J.: All right, then you know Bob Plumb. He was very knowledgeable. He knew where all the bodies were buried. He was a real diplomat, a first-class man, but at the time he ran things, he had to have the cooperation of other churches, especially in the General Commission on Chaplains, and most of the other churches weren't interested at all.

I think there's another side. The Chaplain Corps is now really training its chaplains. We're getting commander chaplains and captain chaplains for the first time who are really trained for their work and who have sensitivity to problems of this sort that, generally speaking, the chaplains of my day did not have. It may be that from this new bunch of trained chaplains who've been trained in the last five or six years there will come a movement in this direction.

Q: What is the advantage to be derived by BuPers in keeping the setup as it is?

Capt. J.: No advantage. The disadvantages to our Corps are legion. First, the present arrangement represents a low and Erastian doctrine of the ministry. Chaplains are defined as mere agents of the state with no autonomy in spiritual matters. A second serious consequence is in budget. Our Corps does not have, nor does it defend before Congress our own budget. We only participate at a low level in a Bureau budget for personnel administration. Local decisions about budget are not made by chaplains but by line officers of the Bureau. When across the board cuts are made we can make reclama only to the Bureau. Thirdly, there is spiritual leadership in the Chaplain Corps even if the Chief of Naval Personnel cannot provide it and the Chief of Chaplains is refused the wherewithal to give it. Throughout my time in the Navy there were unofficial "Chiefs" outside Washington to whom the Corps turned for guidance. Will Thomas probably exercised more spiritual authority from Annapolis than he ever did as Chief Roland Faulk had the same power as "West Coast Chief of Chaplains" at San Diego and chairman of the Chaplain Research Board in Washington. When there is a vacuum, power will move to him who uses it.

The most important disadvantage to our Corps is that any local chaplain who understands the dynamics of power can easily and readily effectuate his objectives even if they are contrary to the policies of the Chief of Chaplains. I have myself done this, always regretting that there was not a central agency to promulgate policy which had its own integrity. Indeed, one of the few comforts remaining to a Navy chaplain in this Erastian situation is that the Chief of Chaplains cannot prevent his ministry if he knows his business. Yet, this is not effective administration but anarchy, yet it is to this we are condemned until our dignity is respected and restored.

Q: The Chief of Chaplains does not have anything to do with congressional committees?

Capt. J.: No, unless he happens to be called for some reason. But he doesn't routinely go up and defend his own budget. I think that is all radically wrong and has got to be changed.

Q: You said that one important element in this whole struggle is that the churches should be cognizant of the situation. Why aren't they cognizant? Is it because they're not that concerned?

Capt. J.: Churches are run by human beings. They love power as all other human beings love power, and in the dynamics of power churches differ very little from General Motors.

When the man who runs, let us say, the section on the ministry in one of the churches begins to look at his area of concern, he may have 2,500 churches under him for whom he must provide direction and who answer to him or to someone else within his system. Outside of this domain, which he controls, he has other clergy who belong to the flock but don't belong to him. They may be in VA hospitals, they may be in the armed forces, or they may be in the missions and answer to the guy at the next desk.

With the churches out of sight is generally out of mind. This is not to damn them too much. There is a formal kind of concern on the part of the churches. They do visit their chaplains. They send representatives out from denominational headquarters to call, but there's no serious understanding of the dynamics of power within the military structure. And, as long as the churches don't remain interested, I don't think anything much will be done. One hopes that the newly trained chaplains will understand that they need not only divine but also human power -- which is also God's --

to fulfill their ministry. Only when they communicate the need for such power to their churches will there be a change. That power means being placed in a structure where they can get a high signature on what needs to be done, based on a structure where they can justify their own budget and get the money they need on their own merits. All that kind of thing is needed to support the ministry in the Navy, and that's what we don't have now.

Q: You said earlier that the churches tend to have as their representatives former chaplains -

Capt. J.: They do, for the most part.

Q: - and former chaplains have no real concern. Why don't they have the same feeling that you have, having been through the mill?

Capt. J.: I imagine there are many reasons. These are all good men to begin with. The man in my own church, as a matter of fact, is one of the very, very best, who is very realistic about these things and really knows where the bodies are buried. Many of the others do not. The bishop of Military Ordinariate is a retired Navy chaplain, for example, as the previous one had been a former Army Chief of Chaplains.

I imagine there are many reasons why they aren't concerned, the chief of which, I think, is that they don't understand the dynamics of power. Many of them, I think, are pietists. They don't want to believe that the church uses power and that there are struggles for power within the church, and all of the rest.

Q: It seems to me at the moment that's the weakest link, isn't it?

Capt. J.: I think so.

Q: And through education you hope to rectify that situation?

Capt. J.: In the church, you mean?

Q: Yes.

Capt. J.: It doesn't look very good to me at the moment. Many of these people who hold the chaplaincy positions in the church are retired service people; they are people not inclined to get involved in daily slugging for power within ecclesiastical circles. They're put off to one side within the ecclesiastical organization. They are big fish in small ponds to their chaplains and they're rather content with this.

Most churches do have a representative for chaplains but he has a very low priority in their scheme of things. Until he represents a serious priority, I don't think anything is going to be done by the churches. The sad thing is that we have - I can't tell you how many now, but I would guess in the vicinity of 3,000 clergymen in the armed forces. That's a larger number of clergy than we have doing an awful lot of things.

Q: Yes, indeed.

Capt. J.: You would think that the church would say, hey, wait a minute, we have got a tremendous investment here of manpower and we want to know what it's doing. Is it preaching the gospel and ministering to people or is it running the Navy Relief Society?

Q: Your comments on this subject throw a new and interesting light on your address to the graduating class in Newport on the subject of power.

Capt. J.: Yes. I was trying to say something like this to them. The thing that is disturbing to me is not that our corps always wins in the struggle for power. It is that we should consider it legitimate to struggle for power, because we need human as well as divine power to get done what we have to. The civilian community is a different milieu and a different sort of situation entirely. We're talking about a tightly, hierarchically organized structure in which things get done by assignments of power, assignments of authority and responsibility, precision in the sense of holding people to their responsibilities. In this context our Corps is drifting off in the realm of personnel administration and being effectively ignored and bypassed. And it means to me a lack of serious understanding of our calling in the service, a sadly inadequate doctrine of the ministry.

Q: When you were in London, you became interested in the subject of fitness reports for chaplains. Do you want to talk about that? You made some recommendations to the Chief of Chaplains, I believe.

Capt. J.: I did. I recommended, after a considerable amount of groundwork, that a technical professional fitness report, in addition to the present one, be submitted on chaplains by their technical supervisors, namely, by senior chaplains.

Q: In addition to the line officers' reports?

Capt. J.: In addition to the line officers' estimates. My thinking, very simply, was that the present fitness report is submitted by officers of very good will and high integrity who lack professional competence to hold an opinion in the area of the chaplain's performance. As a consequence, we find them variously addressing aspects of the chaplain's work which they consider important but which may have nothing to do with his ministry - his doing well as a tour officer, that kind of thing, in additional duties. And, of course, chaplains, being human, tend then to put their attention on this type of work which brings promotion and good comments from their seniors. This leaves chaplain selection boards, then, with reports that are one-sided, unprofessional, incomplete, and inadequate for making selections.

What is needed in addition to the present report is a report from someone of experience who is competent to judge the professional performance of a chaplain. This report, I believe, should be made by the senior chaplain nearest or in the organization of the chaplain being reported on. It should be set up in such a way as to ask questions precisely about professional performance and to seek answers that will help a selection board particularly to understand more about the functions of the man as a minister or a priest or rabbi. It should be sent through channels.

Q: The commanding officer who makes out the other fitness report would see this?

Capt. J.: He should see it, and this for a number of purposes. One is that he deserves to know the professional evaluation of a professional on his chaplain. Furthermore, this would be a highly useful educational device. It would tend to teach commanders over a period of time what it is that the chaplain is supposed to do and to begin to help them develop judgments on his performance in these fields.

Of course, it would be very useful administratively in other ways than selection. The Chief of Chaplains would have a tool that would tell him about the professional strengths and weaknesses of chaplains, helping him to assign them where they can correct situations, where their strengths can be used. This would give new focus and power to the total ministry of the Chaplain Corps.

Q: What about the situation where there's a divergence? A man has been awfully good in areas where his line officer superior approves, and yet he's awfully poor in the pastoral sense which his professional superior disapproves of?

Capt. J.: This is precisely the kind of thing that this proposed report would seek to uncover. If we find that a man is doing very useful work indeed in areas that are tangential or irrelevant to the ministry, but neglecting his ministry and his own professional growth, we want to know about it so that we can call him in and say, "Look what's happening to you. Let's get back to the ministry."

Q: In light of what you have been saying about the situation with the Chief of Chaplains under BuPers, would it not be something of an opening wedge in getting a change there?

Capt. J.: I don't think so. I don't think that it would seriously involve the power structure in such a way as to persuade them that the Chief of Chaplains should be professionally cognizant over his own people.

Q: Don't you think the educational process in time would do that?

Capt. J.: Well, in a sort of archeological way! It might wear them down, but...

Q: This is eons in time!

Capt. J.: It might take eons of time but I don't see it really seriously affecting that issue. I see it as having merit in its own right. I see it as having merit especially - of course, for the Chaplains Division and also for commanders.

As I mentioned in this letter, when I discussed this matter with our staff in London -

Q: This is the letter you wrote to the Chief of Chaplains?

Capt. J.: Yes. The C-inC's staff immediately seized on it. All of the staff heads came and talked to me about it. They were concerned about matters that hadn't occurred to me particularly. Their first and chief question was: had they been fair to their chaplains. They admitted immediately that they weren't professionally competent to judge the chaplains' performance.

Q: A mea culpa attitude?

Capt. J.: They were beginning to get it. Up to this point they hadn't had it because they had done the best they could. The Navy had taught them they were competent to judge everybody. You know, the nearest thing to God in this world is the captain of a ship, and all at once the question had been raised - they weren't competent to pass judgment. They're professionals, and once they saw the dimensions of this case they immediately admitted they weren't.

Q: What then?

Capt. J.: The first thing was to look back and think, gee, I've written reports on a lot of chaplains. Have I been really fair to them, did I really understand what was happening?

This, to me, speaks volumes about the integrity of the reporting seniors in the Navy, the vast bulk of whom are line officers. The average line officer takes a tremendously serious view about his responsibilities in reporting. This is important because I wouldn't want this proposal to be considered as an attack upon the past integrity or lack of integrity of line officers. This had nothing to do with that. The integrity is there, it's always been there, but the professional competence to pass judgment has not.

Q: What was the reaction in Washington to your suggestion?

Capt. J.: It was as if it had fallen into a deep well and finally you could hear a little thing at the bottom saying, "It has arrived!" Merely an acknowledgment.

Q: Why do you think there was no enthusiasm for it?

Capt. J.: That I don't know. I do know that before this time I and other chaplains in the Marine Corps had routinely prepared fitness reports on chaplains and had sent them via the command to the Chief of Naval Personnel.

Q: Yes, you did that with General Silverthorne.

Capt. J.: I did it with General Silverthorne.

At this time in the office of the Chief that practice was disapproved. It was not liked. But, of course, that was worlds apart from this proposal. Not at all the same thing. Maybe they confused the two, I don't know.

One of the big problems we have with things of this sort, with new ideas, is that during most of my time in the service, because of its lack of power to do what needed to be done, the Chaplains Division basically saw its job as being the administration of the status quo. What changed anything very much was not welcome.

Q: They didn't want to open a can of worms by attempting it?

Capt. J.: And they didn't want to attempt doing what they felt was futile. I had the distinct feeling, over many years, that this was the basic orientation of the Chief's office. I think there have been some very useful changes recently in that direction, in that regard.

Q: Has this subject come up since you raised it in 1960-61?

Capt. J.: Not that I know of.

Q: Inasmuch as you've talked about fitness reports and your proposal for reform in the area, I thought you might like to say something about the specific reasons why this came as an issue at that point, when you were with CinCNavEur?

Capt. J.: There were a couple of instances in which chaplains under my jurisdiction received reports made in all good will and honesty which failed to recognize their abilities or to reflect what they had done in the squadron. As I looked at this, I observed in each instance that the problem at hand was the lack of competence on the part of the reporting senior in understanding what a chaplain was supposed to do. There was no means from my position to rectify this injustice. It seemed to me that there was value in the reports that had been submitted, but they were incomplete, and that the way to complete them was to get a professional evaluation from one competent in the ministry upon the work of these men which would give us a total picture.

The sad thing in these instances is that I think in at least one case the mediocre report resulted in the man not being promoted, when, if he had been properly understood in the beginning, he might well have had a very promising career in the Navy.

Q: How did Admiral Smith view this proposal of yours?

Capt. J.: I never talked directly with Admiral Smith about this proposal. I know that Admiral Hogle, the deputy to Admiral Smith, felt it was a very thoughtful one.

Q: Yes.

Capt. J.: It seems to me that at the time I sent the letter, Admiral Smith was away on some kind of business. The letter, as you see, was written informally and was not sent through channels. Here again is the issue of technical-professional chains of correspondence. Yet, I don't think that that might have made very much difference in the outcome.

Q: The letter is, indeed, an example of what you were talking about previously in correspondence with the Chief of Chaplains. We'll leave London. You were there, unfortunately, for only one year. You left in September of 1961.

Capt. J.: Yes. I had for some months not been feeling well and began to run a regular temperature. I finally had to be hospitalized and was sent to Weisbaden, first, and then to San Diego Naval Hospital, where finally it was necessary to do exploratory surgery. The doctors found that I had two abcesses on one of my lungs which had broken and inflamed the lung with pneumonitis germs. So they cut two-thirds of my right lung away, and my health immediately returned.

Q: Was this a situation that had been developing over a period?

Capt. J.: In my last year in college I weighed about 180 pounds, and then during the summer I got sick, lost 50 pounds, and I never regained it until after this operation, when my weight once more went back up to normal weight for a man of my size. It was because I had pneumonia at that time and these abcesses had formed.

Q: And you were carrying that situation all those years?

Capt. J.: All those years, yes.

Q: Without ever having it erupt?

Capt. J.: Without having it erupt. The precipitating factor in London was that I had a pneumonia and it was during that these abcesses finally broke.

So for a matter of, I'd say three or four months, in London I tried to do my work while not being well at all and running a temperature every day, the doctors not being able to pin it down to anything. And they weren't able to, indeed, in San Diego, where they thought it might be coccidis-mycosis, thought it might be cancer or TB. Nothing worked out and, finally, the surgeon, Jack Fleischaker, an old shipmate of mine in the First Marines, came in and said that they'd like to do exploratory surgery and find out, and they did. That's what they discovered.

Q: How distressing. It was certainly a hiatus in a very active career. How did you feel about your career at that point?

Capt. J.: Oh, I felt my career had ended. I couldn't see, before the operation, any opening and my doctors didn't see one to a return to good health. But, of course, after the operation, once the doctors found out what the problem was, then the solution was very clear and I quickly returned to good health and have remained in good condition ever since.

Q: What did that do to you as a person at that time, suddenly to be confronted with the end of a career, the end of active service? How did you react to that?

Capt. J.: I think with considerable misgiving. Up to that point I had been thinking only in terms of remaining in the Navy. I love the Navy. Of course, during that period before the operation, there came all kinds of possibilities, being medically retired and other possibilities. It was not a very pleasant period.

But I had some very interesting experiences in the hospital.

One had to do with my concern about how the hospital was run. My doctor said to me that I was to sleep through every morning until I woke up, but there came every morning at 4:30 a corpsman who drew my blood. After several days of this, I decided to find out who had written the order that required that my blood be taken at 4:30 when my doctor said I should sleep until I woke. I chased it down and I finally found the answer in the blood lab. The order was signed by a third class corpsman.

So I wrote a letter to the admiral, who was a real great guy. I forget his name. I told him this and I said, "It seems to me that in terms of priorities the importance of people in this hospital runs something like this: charwomen, ward laborers, corpsmen, nurses, doctors, patients. When the patient eats and when he sleeps depends on when the charwomen are supposed to report. When his blood gets drawn depends on what some third class corpsman writes down in the blood lab."

Well, the old man came down to see me! He was great. He wanted to know who I was, and he said:

"You sounded pretty mad!" And I said:

"No, I'm not mad, but I think I'm trying to reflect to you not the table of organization of the hospital, but what is actually important in this hospital. And the most important thing in this hospital, by which everything else is determined, is the time the charwomen report to work."

"Well," he said, "that would mean...."

He double-checked and, sure enough, the third class corpsman had written this requirement and, of course, the admiral found out why! Because the third class wanted all the blood there at eight o'clock, when he reported! It's all very simple.

Q: What else? You said there were several other things that were interesting that happened in the hospital.

Capt. J.: Let me see. I don't know that I can think of much more beyond the fact that a chaplain, like a doctor, never goes off duty. Once I was established in my room and it became known I was a chaplain, in due course, there started a little dribble of people coming in and sharing their problems, until it became more than a dribble. I started to get an actual clientele, almost.

Q: Sapping your energy!

Capt. J.: It was, and so I finally called the senior chaplain of the hospital and said:

"You know, I'm getting too much work here. How about your guys checking up a little more often, on this deck, anyway, to see if they can steer some of it away."

They were very good. I think probably what they did was to go round and tell the patients that I was sick, too, and that if they needed help they would be glad to come up, because it ended in due course.

Q: I wonder if you had another experience, if you learned in reverse, so to speak, from a pastoral point of view, that you were in the hospital, you were on your back, and you were receiving ministration from others, if this wasn't a very revealing thing to you in terms of your own ministry?

Capt. J.: Oh, I think it was indeed. Revealing, first, about myself. I think maybe the character of sin in some of us is that we assume the mantle of infallibility, invincibility, the general presumption that, while others are frail and weak, we, after all, are strong. I'll tell you what I learned in the hospital about myself. It was that I was awfully weak. And that was a very discouraging discovery. I was physically weak and I was by no means as strong spiritually as I might have been. I'll tell you what came to my rescue.

A beautiful old passage that you know very well from the New Testament - "When I am weak, then I am strong. My power is made perfect in weakness." God's only chance with most of us comes when we have been driven to our knees. All at once I had to reverse some courses and decide where the strength lay and where the weakness lay, so to speak.

Of course, that had an effect on my ministry, as any suffering does. I hope the effect was to make me more understanding and compassionate. Before some things in life, nobody's strong, we're all weak. If we offer our weakness to God, there's the possibilities that in us His power may be made perfect.

Q: I found a very difficult lesson to accept, from my point of view, was that I had to in very good grace accept the ministrations of others, when I had felt that I was the minister. There's an ego involved in this sort of thing, and it was a valuable lesson to me.

Capt. J.: I don't think I had much difficulty at that point, because I think in some ways I had long been used to accepting the ministrations of others. Not at that depth, by any means. Yet there were so many ways in which chaplains and laymen and officers had ministered to me on the ordinary occasions of life that I think, on the question of being willing to accept, I was basically there. My problem was that I didn't have to accept in extremis before this, if you follow me.

Q: Yes, I do.

Capt. J.: I was accepting as one who was pretty strong accepting from others who were pretty strong. Now the character of the ballgame had changed and I had to accept a dimension to my life that had hitherto been immune to complete weakness.

Q: My lesson came when I was in seminary, so I was just on the threshold of the ministry!

Capt. J.: Oh, my heavens!

Q: Well, fortunately, you came out of it very well indeed.

Capt. J.: Fortunately.

Q: Did you have an opportunity to maintain much contact with the outside world, with the chaplaincy outside of the hospital, or were you too ill to bother about that?

Capt. J.: One of the beautiful things about the Chaplain Corps is its pulling together in times of crisis, in times of crisis for the country and in times of crisis for an individual. I was overwhelmed by the concern of the chaplains.

Q: A fraternity?

Capt. J.: Yes, indeed, a fraternity.

Q: Well, your recovery was a positive thing and so you had to look forward to a resumption of your career?

Capt. J.: Yes.

Q: Were there any obstacles to that?

Capt. J.: No. The doctors felt that it was only a matter of time before I'd be ready to go on active duty again, and they reported this to the bureau. They asked my preference. I had no great preference.

Roland Faulk was in the district.

Q: He was the senior?

Capt. J.: He was the district chaplain. John Shilling, the chaplain at the Naval Training Center, was due soon to go. He was one of the really great people of our corps. Roland asked for me to replace him. So in due course I was ordered, first, to the district, where I spent three weeks or a month convalescing and helping Roland run the office, and then I moved over to NTC to be the senior chaplain.

Q: What were your relations with Roland prior to that time?

Capt. J.: We'd been old and good friends. Of course, while I was at the Staff College and in London, he'd been on the West Coast, so we hadn't seen each other for two or three years, but our relationships had always been close and intimate.

Q: Tell me about this new job. It began in March of 1962.

Capt. J.: It was a great job. At that time we had a high recruit load. We had twenty-one chaplains and also twenty-one enlisted men in the department. We had three commands to care for, the administrative command, the recruit training command, and the schools command, and these chaplains were assigned to the various commands. We had a big schedule of divine services and we had a heavy counseling load. The chaplains were very busy giving required presentations in character education at all levels. So we had a very busy operation. Wonderful commanding officers in all of these commands. Captain D. I. Thomas was the Center commander, and no one could work for a greater man.

I think the chaplains were much appreciated. Everybody there felt the chaplains were an essential part of bringing the young man through boot training or through school training.

Q: There was such a rapid turnover, wasn't there, of personnel?

Capt. J.: You mean of personnel on the base?

Q: Yes.

Capt. J.: Well, of course, in recruit training there's a tremendously rapid turnover. The schools command was somewhat less. The schools ranged in length, I think, from about eight weeks to forty-four weeks, so that you'd have some people who were there a long time. The people in the administrative command were there for normal tours of shore duty, so you had the normal rotation of people.

The more senior chaplains, lieutenant commander and above, were there for permanent tours of duty, but the more junior chaplains were sent to us for six months of quasi indoctrination, so to speak, and experience before being sent to sea. They'd come from the chaplains' school, four or five at a time. We would have four or five detached and sent to destroyers or the mine force or other places. Each group would be with us for six months.

I thought it was a good idea. It gave them a practical grounding under supervision of beginning to live with naval officers and sailors, and some feel for the routines of Navy life, which don't after all differ very much from ground command and life at sea. By the time they left us, I think they were pretty well oriented, not greatly experienced but at least they knew what to look for. They knew the difference between six bells and the mail buoy!

Q: You speak about counseling as being a heavy part of the duty of the chaplains.

Capt. J.: Yes.

Q: What nature did it take? What direction did it take, largely?

Capt. J.: It depended on where one was. In recruit training, for example, a great deal of the counseling had to do with the adjustment of the recruit, homesickness, for example, very little in the way of family counseling, except if there was trouble between his father and his mother. But when you came to schools command, you began to run into very typical Navy family problems, individual problems of drinking, trouble between husband and wife, the effects of separation, occasionally unfaithfulness, all this kind of thing. And, of course, the man who, one way or another, was wrecking his own career. In permanent personnel, administrative command, you found very much the same kind of thing. These were more stable for the moment, however, and you had more leverage to pull to try to do something.

Q: Did San Diego itself have some influence on the recruits? I'm mindful of the fact that my eyes were opened walking along some of those main streets in San Diego.

Capt. J.: Our recruits didn't see much of the main streets. They didn't get out very much. I don't know that it had a great effect on them. I think it tended, at that time and somewhat before to influence other sailors who went out on the town. Recruits had to be back in early, but other sailors could go out. Of course, there were lots of things to do there, many of which could get a guy into trouble. And the average sailor, as you know, is rather inclined sometimes to try things out. So we would have problems.

San Diego itself, however, about the time we were there or a little before had really cleaned up the town a great deal and it had become something other than a sailors' liberty town. The city was doing more and offering more. There were interesting places for the sailors to go besides that garish strip down by the waterfront, and I think it became a much more interesting liberty town than it had been before.

Q: Has it maintained that higher level since?

Capt. J.: That I can't say.

Q: It was during this time that you began to work and think with Roland about the problem of compulsory attendance at chapel, wasn't it?

Capt. J.: It was. I had been concerned about it for a long time with the moral issues, the wrongness of coercing conscience, of the psychological damage that was done to men, and with the constitutional issues that were involved. My more active involvement at NTC came about in a rather interesting way.

We had only one chapel there. We held thirty-five services a Sunday, and they were held in all kinds of places. We had three services a Sunday, for example, in the boxing ring. So I surveyed the situation, got Roland's advice, and my chaplains looked it over, and we felt that we needed two chapels in addition to the one we had. A huge chapel at the Recruit Training Center, a chapel holding, perhaps, 2,000 people, and then a smaller chapel at the Schools Command.

So I prepared the paperwork to ask that planning for these chapels be begun and that they be built. I went in and checked the command's priority list for construction, and chapels were way, way down at the bottom, the last thing. They weren't going to construct anything. But I still put in my paperwork, and Captain Thomas called me in and said:

"Glyn, there's no realistic chance." I replied: "How about changing your priorities? I've seen the list and chapels are at the bottom and I don't think they ought to be at the bottom. What's the use of having 21,000 men and not having the churches to take care of them?"

"Well," he said, "you know, up there they take a very dim view of this."

Q: He meant in Washington?

Capt. J.: In Washington, yes.

"They don't at all," I said, "they require these people to go to church. This is a very important thing."

Well, he hemmed and hawed a little bit, and that's as far as we got.

So I prepared an official letter to the Chief of Naval Personnel requesting that a huge circus tent be sent to me. I drew a plan and said I was going to ask the command for permission to put the circus tent right here next to the road with a sign on it "Navy Chapel." That didn't go over very well. But I said again to Captain Thomas:

"Now, wait a minute. You know, you guys are riding two sides of this thing. If it's important enough to coerce our men to attend church it ought to be important enough to give us a chapel."

"Well," he said, "you don't understand." I said: "I understand very well. I'm the guy who has to try to minister and I understand what it means."

So I went to Roland. Roland had been thinking about this. The way in which compulsion was structured was very simple. Religion was defined as training. God was defined as a training agent. The worship requirement was placed on the training syllabus, where it said on Thursday at four o'clock they will go up on the grinder and march for one hour, Sunday at nine o'clock all recruits to church. Just like that.

So I prepared a letter to Captain Thomas - and he was getting a little gunshy by this time - in which I proposed the following revision to the recruit training program:

"Delete item 28 (c) on page 305." He looked at it, and there it was. Nowhere else in writing in the whole blame Navy was there a requirement, except in the curriculum required by the Training Division of BuPers.

Q: Didn't they have something at Bainbridge also?

Capt. J.: Bainbridge also had it. I think they did it the same way we did. BuPers was the one that put it in the training manual.

Well, Captain Thomas said: "Okay, I tell you what I'll do. I'll write a letter to the Chief of Naval Personnel. I'll say that unless he objects I'll delete this provision of the syllabus."

This thing hit Washington. It was rather esoteric. It didn't say anything about church attendance. It just mentioned the Training Division syllabus. They read it and they really blew up. They called D. I. Thomas on the phone and said, "Don't you touch this thing." Then they wrote a letter giving some pious thoughts about why required church attendance ought to be retained, but adding in the letter that compulsory chapel was being restored to Bainbridge, where on local initiative it had been cut out. Of course, it also said in the letter:

"You understand that if you were to do this at San Diego it would have the most serious repercussions on affairs at the Naval Academy."

This, of course, was a sad mistake on their part. There was no way by which in official correspondence Roland and I could have raised the issue at the Naval Academy to the Chief of Naval Personnel. But now that he himself had raised it, we were able completely to exploit it. You're quite familiar, I think, from that point on with the correspondence that evolved, and of course the crux of the thing came to be the academy.

I have a friend who was in JAG at that time and the question came up: can these people write about the Naval Academy because they have no responsibilities there. And JAG's answer was, well, it's in the context of the discussion and so they can. This man also reported to me that the then JAG said that compulsory chapel attendance, regardless of the law, was going to continue while he was JAG. And that was the attitude of high command at that point on the whole issue.

We then wrote other letters. We wrote to SecDef, got a flip reply from Kennedy's young friend, Paul Fay, who was then assistant up there. Nobody took it seriously. The philosophy was, let him bounce against the bulkhead.

An additional problem was that the midshipmen couldn't get into court because of the doctrine "de minimis non curat lex," (the law will not deal with trifles). To get standing in the court, the midshipman had to have a significant part of his taxes affected. He paid, of course, only one half of one mil, if anything, in taxes to support religion in the Navy. But that was changed by a court decision which said the classes affected by any given exploitation were entitled to bring the matter to court.

Q: This then became class action business, didn't it?

Capt. J.: Yes, indeed.

Q: Which is now a fairly common thing.

Capt. J.: A very common thing. Very soon several midshipmen and one cadet instituted a suit. The ACLU gave them legal assistance. In due course - I don't know where they heard it but they heard from some place that I had had dealings within the service on this question - they called me. I sent them a copy of my letter to SecDef. Then they asked me to come down and testify in federal court. I did. Bob Drinan, the representative from Massachusetts, testified, Earl Grill, chaplain at American University, and I forget who else, but several people. We were before Judge Corcoran and he ruled against us. The ACLU appealed and at the appellate level, we won. The character of the decisions was such that the government took one look at them and decided to accept the appellate court's decision, which did away with it.

Q: As I understand it, the first efforts were within the chain of command, but then they got outside of the chain of command and into the courts and through the Civil Liberties -

Capt. J.: Yes. That became possible only when this principle De Minimis non curat lex was done away with with regard to compulsory government religion. Class action suits could be submitted then.

It was very interesting that, while this case was being tried - while it was being prepared even, all these men were discriminated against within the academies by being given extra punishments and were deprived of privileges. It was necessary for the court to issue a restraining order preventing the academies from treating these young men that way.

Q: Were these young men sincere in bringing up the issue?

Capt. J.: This is a hard question to answer because it goes to motive. I don't know that all of them were. I'm quite convinced several of them were, so that for purposes of the court case there was enough genuine concern and sense of outrage at being exploited to justify it being heard.

I think some of them joined in to get on the band wagon or as a prank and that kind of thing, but I don't know how many.

In talking with other midshipmen, however, I found that the vast majority of midshipmen wanted the practice ended. A lot of them said if it were ended they would for the most part go to church, though they might not go every Sunday.

Q: I don't think the evidence bears that out.

Capt. J.: No, I don't think it does.

Q: I think it's very pathetic, at least the times I've been there.

What about the Navy's point of view that it was a part of their training, an essential part of their training, to understand?

Capt. J.: By this time, I'd been in the Navy twenty years and I had been in the bureaucracy quite a bit. I understood that not everything the Navy says represents the deep inner concern that should be involved. In other words, the Navy sometimes says things in a self-serving way. As a Christian I was outraged, for example, at any attempt by anybody to define religion as training. The Christian faith is not training to accomplish human ends and for anyone to use it so, in my book, is to commit sacrilege. It is to take a divine end and use it for human purposes. This is demonic. I didn't put this in my letter, but this is the way I felt. I felt that the use of God for human ends was just the reverse of the meaning of the Christian faith. I myself couldn't understand for that reason how any chaplain could accept assignment to the Naval Academy. Some of our very best chaplains refused, absolutely refused to go there.

This is why the chaplaincy of the Naval Academy became a touchstone, among others, for the selection of Chiefs of Chaplains. A chaplain who could accept this position in good conscience was "SAFG." He would settle for an Erastian definition of the priesthood or ministry. That's a very cruel thing to say, but I'm convinced it's true.

Q: Well, of course, under other circumstances, I suppose a man who serves at the Naval Academy as a chaplain has a chance to establish contact with all sorts of people in high command and elsewhere, so he does have a favored spot.

Capt. J.: Yes, he does, even if all things were kosher. But all things were not kosher. The Chiefs of Naval Personnel certainly knew this and they were going to be very sure that the men that they got were safe. And they were. They got safe men. These people were all good people. It may sound as though I'm saying that the Chiefs of Naval Personnel or the Chiefs of Chaplains were a bunch of crooks. They weren't. They were very fine ministers and good people, but they were insensitive to the moral realities that are involved in today's world, or else they could never have worked, under those circumstances, at the Naval Academy.

Q: As one reflects on the rule as it existed before the court's decision, it seems, on the surface at least, somewhat compatible with the custom as it had evolved over the centuries of -

Capt. J.: No question. Completely consistent with custom. We took our custom from the Royal Navy. Of course, in Britain there's never been any kind of a constitutional provision forbidding compulsion in religion. Generally speaking, they have not practiced that, but they did in the Royal Navy and we took our practice from them. One of the reasons for gathering the crew on Sundays was to read the Rules of War on one Sunday and another Sunday every month to read the code of the ship, the rules that applied within the ship. And then on another Sunday they'd have divine service and we were following -

Q: Read the Ten Commandments on that Sunday!

Capt. J.: Read the Ten Commandments in a sense, yes. We followed that tradition. How we got to it is completely understandable and we can be sympathetic about it. However, it's very interesting to see how all the tradition is of compulsion. There were complaints from Navy chaplains, among others, but nobody listened. They didn't have to listen.

Q: As you were carrying on your correspondence with Washington, what was the position of Captain Thomas? Did he remain there?

Capt. J.: Oh, yes. Captain Thomas got very interested and probably had no strong feelings. Once he saw what was happening - he had his orders from the bureau and he executed them - I think he began to feel sympathy for us. On the basic issue I don't think, perhaps he changed a great deal. He was a great man.

Q: That was a major issue you got involved in out there. Were there others when you were at the training center? There was the issue of the chaplaincy in naval hospitals, was there not?

Capt. J.: No, I don't recall anything else.

Glyn Jones #5 - 345

Interview No. 5 with Chaplain Glyn Jones, CHC, U.S. Navy
(Retired)

Place: His residence in Mt. Hermon School, Massachusetts

Date: Thursday afternoon, 27 October 1977

Subject: Biography

By: John T. Mason, Jr.

Q: This is a delightful day to come and visit you, Glyn!

Capt. J.: A great day to have you, Jack.

Q: And to hear some more of your very interesting story. Last time, we broke off as you were winding up your tour of duty in San Diego. Having been ill and having recovered successfully, you were now contemplating a move to the office of the Chief of Chaplains in Washington. Would you tell me something about the background to this? Off tape, I believe, you told me that you had thought you would retire but you were persuaded to continue. You then said that before being ordered to the Chief's office you wanted a discussion with him of these twenty-five points of interest to you and of general interest to the Chaplains Corps. I want to know about them and the background of your going to Washington and deciding to continue in the service.

Capt. J.: I was planning to retire in San Diego. One day

I got a phone call from the Chief of Chaplains and the deputy was also on the line. Both of these men were very old and dear friends of mine.

Q: They had word that you were planning to retire?

Capt. J.: I had informally talked with them about it but I hadn't yet reached a stable decision. They asked me to come to Washington for duty. They felt I was seriously needed there. I did not want to go and told them this. They asked me to think about it and write them a letter about how I felt. So I did. The letter contained these twenty-some matters that I felt should be prosecuted by the office of the chief of chaplains, objectives that we should seek.

Q: What did they think your main contribution would be in Washington at this time?

Capt. J.: They didn't say. I said, and they knew this, that I didn't want to come to Washington unless we had an activist posture, unless we were going, as an office, to move in these directions. I sent the letter to Washington and it was circulated in the office of the chief, where it caused understandable anger in some quarters. You don't in the Navy write a letter setting forth the conditions under which you will accept a set of orders. It was a strictly personal letter to old friends, of course, but was still susceptible of that interpretation.

Q: This was the reaction of some of the men?

Capt. J.: Yes, it was.

Q: Did they take it as an implied criticism?

Capt. J.: Yes. I think they felt that I was infradig in writing such a letter and that I was not properly respectful of the chief. If I'd had any other kind of relationship with the chief than the long friendship we'd enjoyed, they might well have been right.

Q: The chief at that time was?

Capt. J.: Floyd Dreith. Jim Kelly was the deputy.
My hope was that the arrival of the letter in Washington would persuade the chief that I was not the man he wanted. Though we were dear friends, we differed very fundamentally in our temperaments and our philosophies. Floyd is a man with outstandingly high intelligence. He is a Missouri Synod Lutheran and he tends to be a supporter of the status quo. He was not a shaker and a mover, and, of course, I was proposing specifically that we shake and move.

Q: And Jim Kelly wasn't particularly a shaker and a mover?

Capt. J.: In some ways, perhaps. I would say that Jim and Floyd had more in common philosophically than I had with either of them. So my hope and expectation was that they would look at the letter and say:

"Here's old Jones again, raising hell. We don't need this up here, we've got enough trouble."

But about a week later, to my shock, I learned from Roland Faulk at Com II that my relief had been ordered. Then I got another phone call from both of them saying that they had read the letter, that they agreed that they would move on these things and that they wanted me to come.

So I had locked myself in a box.

Q: Had you anticipated this box?

Capt. J.: No, I had not. The first time they called me, I said to them that one of the reasons I didn't want to come was that I wanted to retain their friendship. I could foresee that if I went to Washington we would soon be embroiled in a series of encounters over these issues. I was bound to lose. Furthermore, I was bound to lose not only the issues but very possibly their friendship, and this I didn't want to do.

In any case, they said come, and I went.

Q: They wanted to be moved then, did they, in these directions?

Capt. J.: No, not really. They had another problem that would have prevented them from moving even if they wanted to. It was this other matter which especially moved Jim Kelly to want my help.

Q: So you had locked yourself in a box and you had to come?

Capt. J.: I did have to go.

Q: And this was in January of 1964, was it?

Capt. J.: I think I reported in February of '63. I may not be exact here.

Q: I think the date is 1964?

Capt. J.: Yes, you're right.

Q: What kind of title did they give you?

Capt. J.: They invented a prestigious title. I became the assistant for administration. Supposedly, I was to conduct the administration of the office while the two admirals were set free for larger matters, recognizing Red China and so on.

There was not much of a job to this because the desks pretty much ran themselves. It's a small office and doesn't represent a large administrative challenge at all. In effect,

I did nothing serious or meaningful during my year and a half there, except to try as I could to help the deputy and to help the chief.

Q: Ruthie moved back with you?

Capt. J.: Ruthie moved back. We left two of our children in school in San Diego until June, then they joined us.

Q: You came with some hope that you might accomplish something?

Capt. J.: No, I didn't believe that anything could be achieved. I didn't think realistically that the things I wanted done would be accomplished. I did come with the hope that I would be helpful in ways that Floyd or Jim would like to have me helpful. I'm not at all sure that I was. It was a rather undramatic and unutilitarian conclusion to my career.

Q: You certainly did accomplish something during that period in Washington. You didn't sit at your desk without doing something, so tell me what you did.

Capt. J.: I tried to move on some of the things that I wanted done. I persuaded the chief, for example, to send an annual report to the secretary in accordance with CNP's concession to Chaplain Rosso. We sent one and, as you remember, we were promptly ordered by the Chief of Naval Personnel not to do it again.

Q: Were you able to do anything in the area of personal communications with the chief, the interchange of letters that you spoke about last time?

Capt. J.: No, I was not able to do anything on that. I attempted to. Unfortunately, by the time I had done the work on some of these things, the office for other reasons had become almost chaotic. Communication between the members of the office had broken down. There were personal tensions that had come into existence, some of which I've no doubt I caused. I hadn't wanted to be the cause, but my arrival had become the cause.

In due course, the chief retired under pressure from CNP. The office was in such a shambles that the Chief of Naval Personnel ordered in a senior chaplain against the wishes of Jim Kelly, who had not yet been named the chief. This man functioned in the central personnel administration of the office, namely, writing orders. This chaplain was brought in so he could personally report to the Chief of Naval Personnel everything that happened in the office.

Q: Who was he?

Capt. J.: His name name is Slattery.

Q: He was there on a temporary basis?

Capt. J.: No, he was permanently assigned. It's my understanding that the Chief of Naval Personnel later independently ordered him detached from the office for some alleged cause.

Q: Who was the chief of naval personnel?

Capt. J.: Semmes.

Q: And this new man had authority over Kelly?

Capt. J.: Oh, yes, indeed. He was formally placed under Kelly but he was reporting directly to the Chief of Naval Personnel, around Kelly, so to speak. Jim was in an untenable situation. Here was the consequence of the low doctrine of the ministry and the Erastianism imposed on the Chaplain Corps by the Navy with the consent of the churches. It was the ultimate debasement, the farthest Babylonian captivity of our Corps. From this humiliation you can understand my insistence that the Navy chaplaincy must be organizationally placed under the civilian authority, the Secretary, rather than under line officers.

In January it was decided that Chaplain Dreith would retire but he did not do so until June. During those six months Jim Kelly had no assurance that he would be named chief. Then, of course, there came the necessity for a selection board to name a new admiral, and it happened that my name was among those to be considered.

Under these circumstances I had no desire to be an admiral

in the chaplain corps, or to live the life that a chaplain admiral lives. I felt that what a chaplain admiral did was ceremonial and not substantive. Furthermore, I was distressed by the events that had been taking place in the life of the office and did not conceive that my participating in the selection process would be of any great benefit to the Navy either. So I wrote a letter to the board asking not to be considered.

Q: Isn't that unique?

Capt. J.: I don't know if it's unique. It's the only one I know about. I don't know whether there have been other officers who have written to the boards asking not to be considered.

The board met and selected a former Naval Academy chaplain to be the second admiral.

Q: Who was that?

Capt. J.: That was Cy Rotrige. He served for a time in Washington and then as Fleet Chaplain, Pacific.

In the meantime I remained in the office, put in my papers to be retired on the 1st of November. When September came I was pondering some job offers. I had a very interesting one with my denomination at their headquarters, directing a project called Metropolitan Associates. This outfit infiltrated

Christian witness into the structures of the city, into the industries, into the politics.

The other offer was to come here to this school. I had other opportunities that were not nearly as attractive as these. And so I decided to take this job.

In September I used my terminal leave to come here. Then I went down to Washington on 1 November to be retired.

Q: Had Kelly been selected at that time?

Capt. J.: Kelly had been selected to be the chief, I believe in June. The second admiral had been named at the same time and took over in June.

Q: That was then a short period in Washington and you didn't really succeed in accomplishing very much because of the circumstances?

Capt. J.: That's right. The sad thing was that I was torn. I wanted to do what my friends wanted me to do, if they wanted me there. I liked and respected them both. On the other hand, I knew perfectly well that there was a fundamental contradiction in philosophy here that temperamentally I would not be able simply to sit there and not attempt anything.

As it turned out, the situation was worse for a number of reasons that I had expected. I don't feel I was useful.

Q: Was there any discussion at any time of any of the points that you had raised in your communication?

Capt. J.: Only with Jim Kelly. There was no discussion with Chaplain Dreith, except for the matter of the report to the secretary. Jim was so beleaguered by the whole sequence of events that he simply did not have it in him, at that moment, to take any action.

Q: Nor the authority, I suppose?

Capt. J.: Nor the authority, indeed.

Q: But you could have sowed some seeds at that point that materialized later when he became chief?

Capt. J.: Not to my knowledge. Again, Jim and I remain very close friends. He would be the first to admit, however, that we have not always seen eye to eye, nor have we necessarily felt it was important that we should. But when we came together to an office of this sort, with the contradiction in philosphies, then something was bound to give. What had to give, of course, was I. There's no way a subordinate can force his chief to do what he doesn't want to do. Nor would I want to force it, for that matter.

Q: That was in a sense very frustrating.

Capt. J.: It was, indeed. The one good thing about it was that I didn't feel on balance that my career had been useless. I don't know that it was such a great one, either, but I felt I had been used for some good purposes. I felt great satisfaction in my friendships and in whatever services I'd been able to perform. So, although my career ended with this frustration it didn't end with a bang but it didn't end with a whimper, either.

Q: I recall reading one of your articles that appeared in a magazine called "The Link" in January 1957 and dealt with the nature of the church. In that article you advocated to your readers that, whatever the job, look upon that job as a calling. Then you went on to say that every job a man does or is assigned is a part of his worship of God. So I expect that, in reflecting on your own career -

Capt. J.: Yes, I feel this very much. I feel even the calling to Washington, which I didn't want and which I thought was unprofitable in the terms on which I wanted the job done, was nevertheless in its own way a valuable illustration of the same thing.

There's no reason in God's kingdom why the call should always be something that you desire.

Q: Or a success?

Capt. J.: Or a success, in certain mechanically worldly terms. It's still a call, so you have to go. You do what you can.

Q: As you reflect on your career in the chaplain corps, what are the high points in your worship of God?

Capt. J.: There are so many that it's impossible to enumerate them. And some of these things, I think, are not necessarily pleasant to think about.

The other day, for whatever reason, Ruthie and I were talking about an old and dear friend of ours, the late Frank Sullivan, who had been my Catholic colleague in my first regiment, the 3rd Marines. I remembered his fondness for a young lieutenant named John O'Neil, who had been with him at Boston College. Suddenly it occurred to me that John O'Neil has been dead for thirty-four years. He was only twenty-two when he was killed on Bougainville. It's almost impossible for me to think of John O'Neil as having been dead for thirty-four years. And many others. Norman Wait, a boy from Brookline, and many, many other boys who were killed back then. To me they're eternally youthful. There's no way I can imagine what they might have been today, twenty-two plus thirty-four, you can add it - a mature man having succeeded or failed in one or another important thing in their lives. They never had the chance.

Q: You know that title of a book <u>Time Must have a Stop</u>, and I suppose it stops in one's memory when a man dies.

Capt. J.: Yes. Once we embarked on this conversation, I thought of other men who'd been dear to me and who were killed. John Hancocks, for instance, a lieutenant in the 1st Marines in Korea. Don France, an altar boy and acolyte in Christ Church Cathedral in Atlanta, an Episcopal church - a beautiful boy, a captain in the Marine Corps. He used to visit our home in Camp Lejeune. He was getting ready to marry. Then suddenly orders twenty-four hours to embark for duty beyond the seas. He never married. He was killed on the retreat from the Chosen Reservoir. Well, he's been dead now for twenty-six years, so he would have been about fifty-two or fifty-three had he lived.

Those are very low points in my memories, but in other ways maybe eminences in my career. Experiences with people long gone, which were great experiences and which I shall never forget. Slug Marvin, Hector DeZayas, Gunny Greer . . . Dulce et decorum est . . .

Q: And experiences, I would dare to suggest, in terms of accomplishments that you thought were right?

Capt. J.: Yes, to some extent, I think so. My relationship with Don France was broad Christian brotherhood. We lived together with John the Baptist Craven, whom I've mentioned, sharing all the Christian assumptions. Little John Hancocks was not a Christian. He was a very good man. His life was the Marine Corps. I had come to understand and appreciate him, too. He gave many things to me. He and his kind in the Marine Corps.

Then other experiences. I don't know if I've mentioned this in our conversations. I was in a battalion in Korea that was surrounded by an entire enemy division at a place called Kojo. We were finally moved to a hill by the seashore. One of our companies was deployed 400 yards ahead of us. They were badly hit, at night. We couldn't get to them and they had to break out and try to get to us. They couldn't do it until the morning. Then they came in, carrying their dead and their wounded. Their captain was Wesley Noren, another great Marine, a wonderful, gentle person.

I went to the lines and outside the lines to meet them along with a couple of other people, the doctor and the battalion commander. A Marine came running over to me and said:

"You're responsible for my salvation." I couldn't understand what he was talking about. He said: "When we were under attack, I was sure I wasn't going to make it and then I remembered that you were here. The last time I was in this kind of trouble, you were there, too."

It turned out he was a Marine gunnery sergeant by the name of Salisbury who'd been in my regiment in World War II. Then we had a patrol that ran into a bad time. I heard about it and went up to the lines to try to find where they were coming in. I went out with another patrol to meet them as they brought in their dead. One of the men coming in was PFC Salisbury. This was in 1943, and all those years he remembered that I had met him. Then that night he recalled I was here again and somehow he had a vision that my presence represented his hope.

Q: These recollections of your ministry as a chaplain are pastoral.

Capt. J.: Yes.

Q: Pastoral relationships with individual people.

Capt. J.: Yes.

Q: There were other things in terms of the chaplain corps itself and its function that you accomplished during the course of your career. Some of those events must be high points, too, must give a sense of satisfaction to you?

Capt. J.: So far as the chaplain corps is concerned, I don't know really of anything in particular that I accomplished.

Q: At the training school?

Capt. J.: Yes. I conducted training sessions for my chaplains in San Diego. I had these young chaplains for a six-month tour before they went to sea, tried to give them the basic administrative skills so that they would be able to function aboard ship, or maybe on a PhibRon staff, or wherever they were sent. I had done the same thing, I think, in other places in DesLant, but these are things that other chaplains did, too.

Q: But this was done on your own initiative. I mean, there was no -

Capt. J.: There was no formal training program, as such, established, say, by the Bureau. Now there is, and this has been a tremendous step forward. Many other important developments have taken place under the leadership of John O'Connor.

Q: Is it done along these same lines?

Capt. J.: No, I think it's a much better and much more sophisticated thing than I ever attempted.

Q: But under the circumstances in which you functioned then, it didn't necessarily have to be sophisticated?

Capt. J.: No. Sophistication wouldn't have helped in San Diego.

Q: Just tell me, in brief, what you did, what you taught them in that six months.

Capt. J.: I taught them how to write an official letter, how to staff a proposal so that all the people who had an interest in it could add their chop to it in presenting the matter to the commander whose signature was needed, how to obtain supplies, how to arrange for the services of other chaplains when they were needed, how to get transportation when you wanted it, how to prepare a budget - all simple things.

Q: Basic tools.

Capt. J.: Basic tools for the ministry, yes, exactly.

Q: And in a situation like that, a sophisticated approach, it seems to me, would have been useless.

Capt. J.: That's right. The grand strategy, you know, of war would have meant nothing to these young people, but this kind of nuts and bolts thing was, I think, very useful to them and enabled them to function when they went out.

Q: But you say currently there is a more sophisticated program?

Capt. J.: Yes, indeed. Navy chaplains now have a school at

Newport in two echelons, the primary one being for new chaplains. The most important one is the second echelon for commander chaplains. This really prepares these men to function in the Navy with as much expertise as any line officer or any supply officer, where, before, this kind of thing was lacking. Chaplains didn't have it. So I think we may expect the quality of performance by chaplains in administrative billets and in the office of the chief radically to improve, because at last they have the skills with which to get the job done.

Q: I see.

Well, upon retirement you did accept this appointment at Mt. Hermon School and have continued there until the present time?

Capt. J.: Yes.

Q: Perhaps at this point it would be very fruitful if you would become somewhat philosophical and talk about some of the issues that mean something to you, some of the things you've worked on in retirement. I know one in particular. You sat on a special committee to formulate ideas on the draft.

Capt. J.: Yes, that is true.

Q: And some of your philosophy, I think, is apparent in the report that was issued by this committee. Would you tell me about that?

Capt. J.: Yes. This was a committee formed by President Johnson to advise him on what to do about the draft. My memory is that it met sometime in 1967, but I'm not exactly sure, while the Vietnam conflict was on. It had 100 members, many of whom were prestigious - Senator Kennedy, for example, Margaret Mead, Milton Friedman, the Chicago economist, people of that quality. The head of Selective Service, General Hershey, attended the meeting.

On the last day of the meeting a motion was placed before the committee recommending that the draft be abolished, and that we move on to voluntary armed services. This was my position and I supported this motion. But Hershey rose and said it was his understanding that the committee was not to make any recommendations. That, of course, would have meant complete futility. There was no point in our meeting if we were not to make a recommendation.

Q: Just study the question and do nothing about it.

Capt. J.: And say nothing, that's right.

In any case, when the meeting broke up there was a bit of confusion. Before it broke up the question was put, and out of 100 members almost 90 voted in favor of abolishing the draft. People as disparate in their economic philosophies, for example, as Milton Friedman and Senator Kennedy, both agreed on that. Some professional military men also argued in favor of abolishing the draft, even though the official Army position at that time was that they couldn't continue functioning without the draft.

I was always glad to have had a vote in that and to have used what little influence I have in opposing the draft.

I think it's important you should know why I opposed it.

Q: Yes, I hoped you would talk about that.

Capt. J.: For a number of reasons. One is that it doesn't work. It produces ineffective soldiers for too short a period of time. They never become professionals. The second is that it's unconstitutional. Our constitution says that no American citizen may be held in involuntary servitude without having been convicted of a crime. This, of course, is what we were doing through conscription. We were defining it, this honorable service, as involuntary servitude. I found this unbearable. I've known too many honorable men over twenty-four years who took this profession seriously, who voluntarily sacrificed themselves and their time for the sake of their country, to accept such a definition of military service.

Q: Where does the defense of the country enter into the

picture?

Capt. J.: I felt the country was better defended by volunteers. It always has been. Hershey and others at that time said that the draft was the historic method by which the country was defended. That was never true. We went to the draft in 1863 for a year and a half. We went to the draft in 1917 for a year and a half. We went to the draft in 1940-41 for five years. For the first time in our history, in 1946 or '47, whatever it was, we entered into a permanent peacetime draft. This was completely contrary to the traditions of the country, as I understood them, and was a very bad precedent.

Another reason why I opposed the draft was this. The draftee was paid so little, paid considerably below the minimum wage, that the difference between his pay and the minimum wage was an unwilling contribution on his part to his own enslavement and a terrible inequity.

So, for these reasons, I opposed the draft and I continue to oppose it. My feeling is, I think, that if, when the country is in trouble, we cannot rally enough Americans voluntarily to defend it, there are a few ways of doing it otherwise.

Q: Then we fall and deserve to fall?

Capt. J.: I'm afraid we would, you know. We must have enough civic virtue so we will defend our country and try to keep the peace, and we can't make up for it by forcing people. Napoleon tried it and he was a better general than most we've had, and he failed.

Q: Another interest of yours that has been manifested from time to time, especially in retirement, is civil liberties and the constitutional rights of man.

Capt. J.: Yes. I'm very interested in this matter for a number of reasons, and my interest was expressed in the Navy to an extent over the question of compulsory chapel. But the matter is broader than this, and my interest, I think, springs first from my convictions as a Christian and from my belief as to what a man is, from the nature of his dignity, the God-given character of his rights. So we're not merely talking civil liberties in the sense of freedoms that are awarded by a state or enshrined in a written constitution. We're talking about natural rights, and we find this in almost every Christian tradition. The Thomists were very clear on it, you remember. The Protestant theologians, in their turn, all understood that man is a child of God and has certain divine freedoms that he didn't invent and that are bestowed upon him. As a consequence, I believe that anything that interferes with these is morally wrong.

Of course, that conviction is reinforced by the bill of rights and our own constitution. All at once, these divine rights have become political rights guaranteed by the constitution within this particular national state. Again and again they say how man's natural rights may function and may be assured in this particular political context. As a consequence, I belong to the American Civil Liberties Union. I'm very sensitive to the continuing attacks upon the bill of rights and attacks upon people in an attempt to take away their rights.

One of the terrible things about Watergate was not that we were dealing with bad men. The constitution assumes that politicians cannot be trusted out of sight, and, as a consequence, has set up a system of checks and balances. The thing that was so terrible about Watergate was that these men were subversives. They were destroying the basic fabric that holds our political society together, taking away the rights of people and seeking to take away still more rights, arrogating to themselves powers and authorities without limitation, which no one under our government rightly possesses.

Q: Do you envision any limitation on the natural rights of man in our modern world, when we think of the potential enemies of our country and of any democratic country, monolithic states without any belief in the natural rights of man? Do you envision any limitation upon our own, those we enjoy in this country?

Capt. J.: From time to time, temporarily, for overriding reasons, the security of the state. That question has been muddled again by Watergate, when national security was made the reason for all kinds of criminal behavior. It must never be so. Yet there are times, I believe, when to defend our freedoms we must give up for the time being the right to say everything we know in public. For example, the right to tell everybody where the ships are going, that kind of thing.

Q: How is this to be determined?

Capt. J.: I think it has to be determined politically. By politically I mean I think it has to be determined by people whom the people vote into office, by officials who are responsible to the people. Sometimes it has to be determined juridically. I know and you know cases where this has been done. Sometimes the determinations are disastrous. For example, I shall never forget the national panic when a Japanese sub threw a couple of 3-inch shells into Long Beach, California, and we imprisoned a whole NISEI population. Something short of that, you see, can be defended. That cannot be defended, not in any civilized state.

The problem that we confront, of course, is that to the extent that we compromise our own principles, to that extent our enemies are winning. They don't merely win on battlefields. They win when they impose their principles on us. While we sometimes have to compromise them for our own reasons, we must be careful never to do so to such a degree as to represent a victory for the totalitarian.

You were raising the question about the contradition

in democracy.

Q: Yes.

Capt. J.: One, I believe, is the action of a Congress that's not responsible, or not responsive, to the whole people. Members of Congress are responsible to small segments who have special interests.

Q: Not looking at the real merits of an issue and backing it and putting it into effect?

Capt. J.: Yes, indeed. Winston Churchill said that he was in favor of democracy because it was the least evil form of government. No political scientist, to my knowledge, has ever held democracy to be an effective or an efficient form of government. It is merely the form that allows the people to have a government the quality of which they deserve. They choose it for themselves and it's as bad or as good as they are, as wise or as unwise.

So I don't believe we must expect of democracy many things that Mussolini did very easily. We like to have trains run on time and if we shoot engineers the way he did we can make sure of this. But we don't want that kind of solution. So we must live with contradictions, ambiguities, uncertainties. We are looking at Congress and saying, "Imagine what Congress could do if it were made up of really competent men of integrity." Well, it isn't. There are some good men there and there are some men not so good. They're about what we deserve, and they do about what I think a realist expects them to do.

Is it cynical of me to say, or realistic as I think it is, that we shouldn't be surprised that Congress behaves this way? On balance, I don't think they're as bad as they could be, even though they're not as good as they should be.

Q: What about the rule of law, the role of the code of laws in our land, as they come in conflict with the rights of the individual man?

Capt. J.: That is a very complex question to which I have few answers. Allow me to suggest one or two things.

Q: Yes, do.

Capt. J.: Law has as its purpose the administration of justice. One of the ends of justice is to ensure men their rights. In its actual administration in any country, including ours, law almost always becomes the possession of a special class of people, it begins to take on the characteristics of that particular class and to defend their interests. A man can steal a million dollars on paper on Wall Street and get thirty days. He can even lie to a Senate committee, as our attorney general did, and get off with probation. Let a black man steal two loaves of bread and he'll be locked up. The law is unfair.

I would like it if the law were more fair, if it did dispense equal justice, if the eyes were closed, and the scales were balanced. It isn't the case, and it isn't the case in the whole spectrum. The legislature of Massachusetts is probably the most corrupt political body in the country. The courts of New York - you've been reading the stories in The Times recently, what's been happening with the jurists there. We end up with corrupt policemen, two policemen in Northampton caught commiting armed robbery, one having taken $35,000 from a store, and now the chief has resigned and the whole force is under investigation. Who's to watch the watchers?

So the picture of law being the stern impartial arbiter in our society simply has never been the case. Vide the corruption of the FBI. The law belongs to him who has the power.

Q: What about the law in terms of providing an ordered society in which we can all function with safety?

Capt. J.: The law seeks to do that. For lots of reasons, I think it fails. Some of the reasons you can see when you contrast us with Great Britain. We're a vast, sprawling society with all kinds of cultural, moral, religious backgrounds. England is smaller, more nearly a homogeneous country. In our society, the police are armed to the teeth and fail to catch more than one in ten offenders, and we don't have the space to incarcerate even them. Many of them are actually put out in the street, many of them fail to be convicted.

I can remember my father telling a story to the contrary. He went back home to Britain, sailed on one of the Cunarders. The day he sailed a man was murdered in London. Dad stayed twenty-one days in Wales and sailed back. The day he arrived in New York the London murderer was hanged. Now, there's a real deterrent, not in the hanging but in the quickness of the response. I don't think anybody's ever proved that capital punishment deters, but what does is the sure knowledge that you're likely to get caught and, if you do get caught, that you're swiftly going to be tried and sentenced. That, of course, we don't have in this country.

Q: Well, and in part do we not have it because Civil Liberties will enter into a picture and insist upon various aspects of a man's civil rights being honored and this prolongs the whole process and takes it from one court to another? How does that jibe with the total picture?

Capt. J.: There is truth to this. Some procedures are delayed because, say, the ACLU or some other people object to the unconstitutional tactics of police or prosecutors or even judges. These things they do on behalf of the civil rights of plaintiffs. Quite as often, however, you find this procedure of delay being used intentionally by lawyers as a means of putting off the evil day and perhaps, in the end, staving it off finally, getting away with it. You find this not only in terms having to do with civil rights, but you find it in white-collar crimes. It was a great day in the morning that the Watergate defendants were tried and convicted and jailed. Two of them waited for their appeals to go through. These went through promptly because they happened to be the defendants. If it had been someone else, those appeals might have taken two or three years, and they would have been delayed.

Q: And also it raises the side issue or question of the expense of a prolonged attempt to inflict justice.

Capt. J.: Yes, indeed.

Q: It becomes almost unbearable upon the man accused.

Capt. J.: It does, indeed.

Q: And upon the state and the taxpayer.

Capt. J.: Absolutely. And, once he's convicted, look at the expense. I read somewhere a few days ago that it costs about $10,000 a year to incarcerate one criminal. There is the amazing cost of the problem of sorting out who should be incarcerated and who should not. The prisons are universities of crime. The indeterminate sentence deprives the prisoner of any motivation for getting out because he doesn't know how long he must stay behind bars. He has to prove himself rehabilitated, and how can he do that when he's in prison? All of this kind of thing has entered in.

Q: What about the role of the media in this whole picture?

Capt. J.: There's a profound dilemma with regard to the media, and it arises again and again. The first amendment assures the freedom of the press, but the press is not free merely to the guy who owns one, as one wit said. The press is free for us. It is we who need the free press because it is we who are informed by the press.

On the other hand, there's the Sixth Amendment that ensures a man a fair trial. We find these two amendments in conflict again and again. Judges seek to put gag rules on reporters. Obviously the way to ensure a fair trial is to allow for a change of venue, but judges are reluctant to do that and you don't find it very often.

We had a murder in Greenfield last year. The murderer finally got a change of venue to Worcester and was tried. I imagine he got a fair trial. But here is the kind of dilemma that exists in free society. Again I think that what we have to do is not to reduce human freedom, but by political measures try to reconcile these contradictions, recognizing that we've got to have both of them, the freedom of the press and the right to a fair trial.

Q: But isn't there such a thing as unlicenced freedom of the press, a lack of accountability on the part of the press very often in reporting things?

Capt. J.: Yes, I think so.

Q: Widespread coverage and not necessarily true.

Capt. J.: I think there is sometimes. The thing that bothers me about that is the inability of people in many cities to get an opposing view, when you find all the papers in the city owned by one man. And especially when you find that the local radio station and the TV station are owned by the newspaper.

In San Diego, for example, there is an absolutely miserable rag called the San Diego Union. I feel that it's completely irresponsible in its treatments of news and in other things. Why? Because it has no competition. In Manchester, New Hampshire, we have the same situation with the Union Leader. In other cities I think we have responsible newspapers - the Atlanta Constitution, the Cleveland Plain Dealer, The Times - but where you run into one-newspaper cities I think then you run into a temptation to go to extremes.

Q: On the other hand, such a small percentage, we're told, of modern-day people read newspapers for their news. They derive it from television and radiocasts.

Capt. J.: Yes.

Q: In that case, you have immense networks, terribly powerful networks, blanketing the country with one point of view. Isn't this comparable?

Capt. J.: I think it is, and I think it's very dangerous. What to do about it? You know we have a mythology in this country that seems almost impermeable, which, it seems to me, applies in this situation. We talk in favor of free enterprise, competition, the law of the market, supply and demand determining the price. You will hear big oil and steel and automobile companies talking this language. But these are all people who determine administered prices. They're not subject to the free market in the slightest. They do everything in their power to destroy private enterprise. They build huge conglomerates. You find now that an oil company may also be in half a dozen other enterprises, all tied together. They reduce competition. And increasingly we run in the top echelons of our economy into huge, monolithic organizations, which are not responsive to economic laws, they're not responsive to law itself.

J.P. Stevens in South Carolina, for example, since 1935 has successfully broken the law with regard to the Wagner Labor act. No one has prosecuted that company. We find the same kind of thing in many instances.

Now, to come back to your illustration. It's happened in news, with regard to television. Two or three very large outfits, all news in the country sent out through six or eight people in New York. I think it's a very dangerous situation.

Q: I can see the possibility of it not being so terribly dangerous if there is this sense of accountability on the part of the newscaster or the man who manipulates the news or whatever; if he is trying to be strictly honest and unbiased. But is that always the case, and how do you achieve that sense of accountability?

Capt. J.: I'm afraid you've set an impossible question. I'm sure that men like Walter Kronkite and Eric Severeid have high professional standards as they write the news and give it out. I'm not saying that they don't. Nevertheless, as a Christian, I understand the recalcitrance and self-interest of men and, in spite of their professional standards, I don't think they can be trusted.

Q: You mean the fallen state of man?

Capt. J.: The fallen state of man. I think our constitution proceeds from the assumption that man can't be trusted out of sight. It also proceeds on the other, grander assumption that only man is fit to govern himself. It weds these two irreconcilables through a written constitution that puts checks and balances on governmental actions. Because he can't be trusted no one can do anything that isn't checked by somebody else.

This is the problem that comes to me as I think of the media, especially of the media with no check on them. Who's to check the AP or Walter Kronkite? Unless you have some option, and you don't have an option. And that's why I feel it is dangerous.

Q: It does raise this question in my mind. At least in this time a man through his own inventiveness and his cleverness and his magnificence has developed systems that almost take the place of God in a sense in our lives.

Capt. J.: Yes, indeed. They overwhelm Him. Supposedly they're His creatures but they become his gods. Increasingly, He finds Himself their creature. You mentioned the news media, but you can look at the computer or you can look at the satellites or any number of systems that we have created. The systems that we have created to serve us increasingly become incapable and incompetent. The Post Office, for example. The railroads, a prime example of government welfare to large industry. The government gave them all the land and the tracks and everything else, then they were looted by their managers. Finally, when they were totally destroyed, they were turned over to the government to be run.

Q: In this picture in our modern lives, where are the natural rights of man in the order of things? Man has taken his natural rights and has developed the system that challenges God. Where are his basic rights in this picture, in the order of precedence?

Capt. J.: One reason I belong to the ACLU is because I feel somebody should be speaking out for the rights. I don't always agree with the ACLU, but somebody, I think, should be speaking up. I think that a large number of man's natural rights have simply been submerged by our culture. Let me give you an illustration from the media.

A few weeks ago, several churches objected to the screening of a play intended for television, a soap opera, because it was excessively brutal and pornographic. The media barons immediately started to cry out "censorship." I looked at this with some interest and asked myself the question, "Why don't they cry out 'censorship' when they forbid me on commercial television or radio from hearing the Boston Symphony? When they cram the cultural ethos of Nashville, Tennessee down my throat? When they give me no option but the literature of the Hollywood script writer?" Who's censoring whom?

Everything that's dear to me in verse or drama or music is forbidden on radio and television, unless I turn to their public forums where I may listen to and see excellence in the arts.

Q: Public television, yes.

Capt. J.: Or I may like to get some jazz or I may hear some verse read well.

Q: If you happen to be fortunate enough to live in a place where there's an outlet.

Capt. J.: If you're that fortunate. If you're not, then you are censored from any decency or excellence in communications. That, to me, is a problem having to do with man's natural rights. It strikes you in many ways.

I was talking to a friend of mine who lives in Georgia - did live in Georgia - about a place where we might retire. He said:

"Georgia's a great place, a beautiful place, housing is cheap, and you'd like it. You'd like the people." I said I was sure I would but said:

"Let me ask you a couple of things. How about public libraries?"

"Oh," he said, "in that part of the state, no."

And I said: "How about public television, good music stations?"

"Oh, my heavens, no."

All right, I can't go to Georgia. I've been censored out of Georgia, not through any choice of mine. This is where, it seems to me, our rights again and again are violated. I'm not saying either, you understand, that everybody should have my tastes. I'm willing to allow Nashville, Tennessee, to debaunch a certain number of people part of the time.

My complaint is that I don't want them to do it all the time to the exclusion of civilized entertainment.

Q: You want them to be exposed to something else occasionally!

Capt. J.: Yes, to something else. Exactly.

Q: I can see this whole issue growing into an international one in terms of cultural things, in terms of the natural rights of man as we know them as Christians and as we know them in a democracy, and the interrelationship of nations today, the differences in national economies and levels. There's a conflict here developing. We see it now, I believe, in the steel industry, U.S. Steel announcing that they had a tremendous loss in this quarter, an unheard loss. And why is this developing? Because of imports of steel from countries where the standard of living is not the same as ours.

Capt. J.: Especially from Japan.

Q: Isn't this going to be a real conflict in the natural rights of man, as we know them here and as they are known elsewhere, unless they get involved with economies?

Capt. J.: Yes, indeed. This is a very complex question. We used to think that it could be solved simply by either of two extremes. One extreme had protective tariffs. The other extreme had free trade. We know very well from the thirties that protective tariffs don't protect anybody. They ruin us all. The ideal is to have trade as free as one may have it, but there has to be, it seems to me, degrees of accommodation here.

Q: Subsidies, you mean?

Capt. J.: Sometimes, perhaps, not always. But sometimes restraints. Sometimes the Japanese saying, "No, we agree not to occupy more than this percentage of your market." They have the same problem with TV sets, for example, and their TV sets are better than ours. This is the thing that's so very disturbing. What's happened to our quality?

Another dimension of this, though, that distresses me even more is the multinational corporation. Here, for example, are the Texas oil people who are succeeding in getting pretty much what they want from Congress. They are giving us this free enterprise talk. But what do we see in Texas oil? We see three or four multinational corporations who execute the wills of foreign governments, who translate into our economy the prices set by foreign governments, who themselves have tremendous tax breaks on the money that they make abroad, who are not subject, in the end, in most ways to U.S. laws. What are we seeing?

What we are seeing is the transfer of sovereignty, in my view, from political entities to economic entities, which increasingly are functioning today as separate states. States not under the control of any political sovereignty.

I may be mistaken. I think people should be going up and down the halls of Congress saying "Who is under the law here? Who is bound to obey the law?" And no one much seems to be getting very excited about it. John Galbraith does. William Buckley calls him out of his mind. Milton Friedman out in Chicago isn't disturbed because he's well paid for his economic advice to the Chilean junta. He says it can all be handled if we simply know how to run the money supply. I think that this is insane, to end up with such a conclusion.

Again, you have tremendously competent men structuring these corporations, getting into economic alliances with foreign powers. Do you know that a U.S. Navy ship was not able to buy Mobil oil in Manila during the oil embargo? A U.S. Navy ship was not able to buy its fuel from an American company!

I think we ought to be a lot less concerned about the Panama Canal as a strategic problem and a lot more concerned when that can happen.

Q: Can I introduce another aspect of this whole worldwide economic picture, I suppose, the report, was it the Saudi Arabian foreign minister who said that if there is another conflict in the Middle East they will use oil, they will use everything, in an effort to enforce their will. This is international blackmail, isn't it?

Capt. J.: Absolutely, nothing but. You recall that during the first of the wars Nasser locked up the Suez Canal.

Q: This also is a part of this complex picture.

Capt. J.: Absolutely.

Q: So we get back to the role of God in the world.

Capt. J.: Yes. He has watched, if Toynbee is correct, twenty-one empires regard themselves with pleasure and satisfaction, twenty-one empires enjoying the goodness of their own works and the prowess of their might, and now they're all gone. It doesn't seem today that Houston, Texas, can be assailed. It seems that Dallas will remain forever. But the mills of the gods are slow and they grind exceeding small.

Q: It's like going back to the one God and His will in this world of ours. How do you envision that being effective?

Capt. J.: We assume sometimes that we are different from the people Amos addressed. Certainly we dress differently and our desserts are richer and we can go from here to there much faster.

Q: And we're much more sophisticated.

Capt. J.: In many ways. But we're not essentially any different. God's got the same problems with us He had with them. We may expect the same consequences if we don't align ourselves with His will. This is why I'm disturbed when President Carter tells us how good the American people are, and that they deserve a government good enough for them. Well, as I said before, I think they're getting the government they deserve and I think they always will. The law, in some ways, is self-executing.

We speak about the wrath of God. We're not speaking about Him reaching down and tapping a cigarette-smoker and saying "I'll give you cancer." He's merely saying that you may receive in this life what you ask for, and if you ask for cigarettes you may receive cigarettes and more. That's a simple principle. I don't think you'd find it understood in many board rooms or in many union offices or in many universities. When you can put a man on the moon, you know, you're entitled to have some respect for what you've done. One mustn't be surprised on the other hand, if you really begin to think that you are the final part of the equation, the ultimate part.

Q: Now we come back full cycle to the Navy chaplain and his role in trying to right some of the errors in our world today. What can a chaplain do in all humility?

Capt. J.: I tried to say some few things to the young chaplains in the graduating class about that.

Q: A couple of years ago?

Capt. J.: This was last year - no, it was in March of this year. Ross Trower invited me out to speak to the class.

One has to begin, you know, with the fact that there is no way one can be God's man without planting himself in an ambiguous situation. It doesn't matter where you are. You can be in a parish, you can be a minister in a prison, you can be Dr. Sweitzer in Africa, or you can be a Navy chaplain, and you're caught up in all the ambivalences and anomalies of the human condition. It would be idle to pretend that there's any locus in the world of which that is not true. So, it's true in the Navy. The chaplain is a man of peace in an agency of war. He represents the one true God to an organization that frequently makes the nation its god. He ministers to men of war who desire peace as ardently as he does. They're caught in the contradiction, too.

I think all he can do is to minister with a clear eye open to the ambivalences of his ministry, not expecting from men more than their humanity can give, open always to his own fallibility, realizing that his needs are as great as theirs.

I think he must be the same man outside that he is inside and that this is the best sermon he will ever preach. He hopes that men will see in him qualities a man can and should have while he recognizes his own imperfections.

I'm not a great disciple of Bonhoeffer's in some ways, but

he has one phrase that I think every Navy chaplain ought to embody so far as he can. That is he must be a man for others. He's not his own man. He's God's man, but he's not God's man merely to be God's man. He's God's man for others. That's his purpose.

Q: Selfless?

Capt. J.: No, that is his self, to be for others. I think he is mistaken if he takes the position that no one else is the ministry in this place. The ministry, if I understand it, is the service of the whole community in healing and making whole itself. That ministry is done in various places by pfcs, and doctors and generals and cooks and truck drivers, and the chaplain is the prototype of that ministry.

Q: But it is a priesthood of all believers?

Capt. J.: It is a priesthood of all believers and I'm convinced also of nonbelievers. Maybe they have their own strange and eccentric priesthood but I have seen too many nonbelievers suffering and doing for others to feel that somehow God isn't using them, too. They may not admit it but from my standpoint they're part of the holy priesthood. Indeed, sometimes, you know, I wish that some believers would exercise their priesthood as well as I have seen it done by some nonbelievers.

Q: Is this not a very difficult point to impart to young clergy who are embarking on a career as chaplains, the fact that they are the prototype for the community but the community is also -

Capt. J.: Its own ministry.

Q: Yes. Is that a difficult concept to accept?

Capt. J.: First I must say that I don't know that I have ever tried to teach it to young chaplains. In the second place, as I look back upon my own youth in the ministry, I think I should have found it difficult to accept. In those days when I was fresh out of seminary the difference between the sheep and the goats seemed quite specific, you know.

Q: One isn't always aware of the power of his own ego, either?

Capt. J.: No, of course. And automatically if you have the doctrine of election you know who's elected first! Of course! I suppose as I've grown older it is to take much more seriously the sophistication of the doctrine of sin while finding much more hopeful the possibilities, it seems to me, that God has built in the human mind.

There are possibilities in every situation beyond our vision, if we can find them and cooperate with them, and that is the grace of God.

What was it old Dickens wrote? The best of times and the worst of times. Someone else wrote that it was the particular virtue of this man that he did the best of things in the worst of times. That, it seems to me, it always the possibility of a Navy chaplain.

Q: I want to think you very much for this very enlightening series. Sometimes you said they were sea stories, but I think you have here far more than a collection of sea stories.

Capt. J.: I hope so. It's been a lot of fun to talk with you about these things. My chief hope is that this can be useful in some way to the Chaplain Corps of the Navy. If it is I'll be very happy.

Q: Thank you. I'm sure that's the case.

Appendix

to

Series of Interviews

with

Captain Glyn Jones, CHC, USN (Ret.)

APPENDIX

Papers that pertain to the U. S. Marine Corps:

1. The Moral Basis of Leadership - speech of Jones at the Marine Corps Recruit Depot, Parris Island - Nov. 24, 1952

2. The Chaplain in Combat - a paper of Capt. Jones (date not determined.)

3. Paper on Military Character Guidance Program - Marine Version - 1949.

4. Memorandum to Gen. Pollack, USMC-Nov.2, 1953 - Character Guidance Program.

5. Letter of Chief of Chaplains - to MGEN Silverthorn, USMC, Parris Island, S.C., Feb. 11, 1952.

Papers that pertain to the Navy in particular:

6. Letter to the Boston GLOBE - Jan. 31, 1972 - subject of Compulsory Chapel Attandance at service academies.

7. Letter from Jones to Chief of Chaplains - Sept. 6, 1961 - on Fitness Reports.

8. Letter from Jones to Executive Direction, General Commission on Chaplains - subject - Status of the Navy Chaplain Corps, May 22, 1962

9. Address of Capt. Jones (March 4, 1977) at the Chaplains School, Newport, Rhode Island

10. Letter from Jones to Chief of Chaplains (Nov. 26, 1962) - subject: A new Chapel for the Naval Training Center, San Diego.

11. Letter from Jones to Chief of Chaplains (Dec. 20, 1962) - subject: Assignment of Chaplains, Naval Training Center, San Diego.

12. CincU SNavEur - Instruction pertaining to Navy Chaplains, Nov. 16, 1960.

13. Memo of Capt. Jones (Nov. 27, 1951) subject: Rank Structure and Assignments in the Chaplains Corps.

14. Memor - Capt. Jones - subject: Navy Relief, Oct. 16, 1951

15. Request for Re-assignment, Sept. 4, 1951

16. Request for Non-Selection - May 24, 1965

17. Two Citations.

HEADQUARTERS
MARINE CORPS RECRUIT DEPOT
PARRIS ISLAND, SOUTH CAROLINA

OFFICERS INFORMATION AND EDUCATION PROGRAM
Class No. 2   24 November 1952

Speaker: CDR G. Jones, USN - Post Chaplain

Subject: THE MORAL BASIS OF LEADERSHIP

Many of you may remember Ernie Pyle's famous description of the death of Captain Wasko on the Italian front. It was dusk when a caravan of mules came down from the hills with the bodies of the men killed that day. The bodies were unloaded along a road, and as the last one was being placed on the ground the mule-driver told the bystanders that one of the bodies was that of Captain Wasko. One by one the bystanders went over to view the body.

The men Captain Wasko had led were still in the line up in the mountains. There who came to see his body were strangers. Yet, as Ernie Pyle describes their grief and their incoherent expressions of affection and respect for Wasko, it is clear that the influence and authority of this young officer had spilled over the bounds of his company. His leadership extended wherever his reputation was known. Ernie Pyle's portrait of the grief of his mourners raises a natural question: What did this man have that made men want to follow him?

The military services are spending a lot of money to find the answer to that question. For the past two years Ohio State University has conducted research to discover what makes a leader. Up to this point they have come up with only one finding. After two years they have reached a definition of leadership-- but they aren't sure it's the right one.

As we think of Captain Wasko, we would like to isolate his leadership qualities so we may teach them to others. But it isn't that easy. In 1949 the Second Marine Division set up an NCO Leaders' Training School. Out of a curriculum of 129 hours, 125 hours were allotted to review in professional skills, two hours were assigned to the study of formal guard mount, and only two hours to the study of leadership. The theory was that much leadership training would take place in the 125 hours allotted to professional skills. That of course, was based on the assumption that teachers were good leaders and that leadership can be taught. The school did an excellent job in teaching and reviewing professional skills. Many of the students believed, however, that it was a case of the blind leading the blind so far as leadership training was concerned.

Now it is easy to criticize. It is better for us to recognize, and applaud, the efforts being made in these directions. We are dealing here with a matter about which we know very little. It is clear to all of us that, to cope with the realities of today's world, we must learn a great deal more about leadership. Obviously you and I cannot in thirty minutes contribute a great deal to the solution of this problem. It is possible, however, that we can analyze the problem and find some general principles which will help us to understand it.

To begin with, it may be instructive to remember some estimates which have been made of our military leadership. Some of you in this room can remember examining Japanese documents which were extremely critical of American leadership, especially on the platoon and company levels. A German writer, General Freytag-Loringhoven, made an interesting appraisal of American military leadership in World War I. He stated that the American was an outstanding warrior "who succeeded in spite of the inefficiency and ultra-conversatism of his junior officers."

During the Civil War, a period when both sides prolifically produced excellent leadership, General Lee, President Lincoln, and General Jackson rated the performance of the soldier in the ranks as being vastly superior to that of his officers. General Jackson said of his men, "My men can do anything." He was not so confident of the ability of his troop leaders. There was rarely a time when Jackson did not have some of his officers in "hack". General A.P. Hill, one of his division commanders who became a distinguished soldier, was constantly in trouble with General Jackson, and was not only placed under arrest but received charges and specifications for a general court martial. General Jackson said of another fine officer, General Richard Garnett, "A good brigade placed under his command will soon become a poor one." A year and a half before that war ended, General Lee informed President Davis that casualties were bankrupting the Army of leadership at all levels.

Older Marines seem agreed upon the fact that leadership poses a greater problem now than it ever has in the history of the Marine Corps. The small size of the Corps prior to World War II and the rigid process of selection did much to assure a high level of leadership performance. The critical years since 1939 have seen problems arise which the Marine Corps today is seriously trying to overcome.

Two weeks ago General Silverthorn discussed two important elements, the material and the intellectual, in the current planning of the Marine Corps. Today I would like to have you consider with me another important component of victory -- the moral fibre of the military organization, especially as it relates to leadership. You and your predecessors have long understood this component much better than most military people. You know from experience that it is the intangibles which cause men to fight well when their equipment is obsolete, their information inadequate, their command mediocre. The larger part of good leadership is the creation and the inspired employment of the moral component in warfare. In Biblical words, it is "to keep the spirit strong when the flesh is weak", and even when the flesh, too, is strong.

The moral foundation of the successful leader cannot be understood by a superficial examination. There is a school of thought which lays great stress upon the qualities of leadership but ignores their roots. The author of a current book on leadership says, for example, "That these qualities exist is enough for our purpose; from whence they sprang and why they exist is relatively immaterial. They will be studied from the viewpoint of their results rather than of their origins, lest their analysis become obscured or entirely hidden in theoretical abstractions." This writer assumes that you can understand a tree by knowing its leaves and ignoring the roots. It is my thesis that we cannot understand these qualities, to say nothing of teaching them, unless we know where they come from.

This writer stresses the qualities of leadership, yet he ends up dealing with theoretical abstractions. He points out that leaders possess loyalty, tact, courage, initiative, and decisiveness. That is true. Yet loyalty is an abstraction. There is no such thing as loyalty. There is only a person who is loyal, and you cannot discuss the "why" and the "how" of this person's loyalty until you get to the roots of his life. We can analyze the qualities of successful leadership. We cannot place those qualities in other people by merely telling them to assume them. It does no more good to tell a man "Be decisive!" than it does to tell a five foot man to be seven feet tall.

All of us want to be courageous, decisive, and considerate. Whether we do, in fact, have these qualities doesn't depend on our recognition of them as good. In fact it depends on our total personality. When we get away from abstractions, that is from considering qualities like loyalty, tact, and courage, we discover that leadership is a function of personality, Leadership is not a composite of several good qualities. It follows from a kind of life.

Many people think that military life develops the qualities of leadership. It would seem to me hard to prove. It is certainly true, however, the military life gives opportunities for the development of leadership. These opportunities are exploited by those whose personalities have the raw material of leadership. In general, we don't create leaders in the Marine Corps so much as we select for positions of responsibility those people who turn out to be leaders. If we are right, then, in saying that leadership is a function of personality, it is important for us to discover what kind of personality produces the kind of leadership we need.

There are many descriptions of the leadership personality. Here is one by Robert Sherrod. He is writing about a young Marine officer by the name of Bill Jones. "Jones's officers and men respected him though he is far from being a martinet. He had a sense of humor which appealed to them all. He could josh with his men without breeding any of the familiarity which lowers the bars of discipline. One day a grizzled sergeant, Dean Squires, of Oklahoma, came in to make a report. Jones looked up and said, "Talk about old men; there's Squires; I've been trying to get rid of him ever since we were in Iceland together, but he won't go away." Jones believed in his non-commissioned officers with a faith they reciprocated. He told me: "I've got gunnery sergeants who have been in 19 or 20 years. They are the men who make the Marine Corps. Those old men take pride in making an officer. One of them said when I was a second lieutenant, "I'll make an officer out of him if it kills me." Jones added, "It almost did."

"Bill Jones had the touch of leadership which is not given to many men. Because of this his colonel and his general relied heavily on him. But the men who knew him best, his orderly, his headquarters company first sergeant, and his battalion sergeant major would have gone through hell for him."

During the First World War, an English soldier by the name of Donald Jankins, wrote an essay about his company commander entitled "The Beloved Captain". There again you have a picture of a man who is a great leader. His leadership does not consist of his mastery of a half dozen abstract qualities. On the contrary, he is a leader because he is a loyal, courageous, considerate, and decisive person. Before the Battle of Waterloo, commend of the allied troops was given to General Blucher. The British troops wanted Wellington placed in command. "Just give us that long-nosed s.o.b. and we'll fix the French", writes a British private by the name of Wheeler. It had taken generations to breed the man who gave the British soldiers that kind of leadership. So, too, with Nelson, who insisted on treating his captains according to the principles he had learned from his clergyman-father. He called them a "band of brothers" and their relation was so close that they fought one of history's great sea battles without a specific prearranged tactical plan. Nelson's operations order consisted of nine words: "The order of sailing is the order of battle."

Now it is possible to teach a man to be a leader if he already possesses the personal raw material of leadership. But that raw material is a lifetime in the making. It is unrealistic to suppose that we can take a 22-year-old man who has been brought up to be a selfish person and can teach him within a matter of months to overcome his selfishness. The fact is that nothing less than a conversion experience can enable such a person to graft into his life the qualities of leadership.

What I am saying, of course, is that leadership training must in general consist of improving qualities which are already present in a person. Here in a recruit training depot we are properly concerned with the teaching of skills. We recognize, however, that the Marine Corps has no monopoly on skill. The difference between the Marine and the soldier and sailor is not in skill --- it is in the slant of his personality. The main purpose of the recruit depot is to give the recruit the character of a marine, to start the process by which the native qualities of the recruit are expanded and transformed into the personality of a Marine. In a profound sense, then, if you, as Marine officers, are not in my business, you aren't really in your own business.

We have said that many men do have within themselves the raw material from which leaders can be made. Where did they obtain that raw material? Some of it of course, they inherited: their size, their general physical bearing, and their native intelligence. The most crucial and decisive elements of this raw material, however, they have learned. They have been brought up in families which taught them habits of thought, feeling and conduct, so that over the course of their formative years they grew up to be loyal, dependable personalities.

It is certainly true that habits learned in the service can reinforce the personality for coping with the specific problems of service life. When General McAuliffe said "Nuts" to the Germans at Bestogne, he was expressing an attitude deeply entrenched in his life since childhood, which was reinforced and strengthened by his emotional and intellectual experiences in the service.

One would like to think that the leadership personality is found only in good men. It is an embarrassing fact, however, that the genius for leadership is not confined to the Nelsons, the Wellingtons, and the Lees. OUr century has produced such remarkable leaders as Hitler, Mussolini, Lenin, Mao Tse Tung, Frank Costello and Al Capone. These men are authentic leaders. They were, and are, persons driven by powerful motivating forces. The leadership personality is apparently like the rain, available to the just and the unjust alike.

Why is this so? I suspect it is because the personal characteristics which make for leadership are neither good nor bad in themselves. Their moral value is determined by their use. Ordinarily, for example, we consider loyalty to be a virtue. Actually, whether loyalty is or is not a virtue depends upon a number of criteria, the most important of which is the object of loyalty. Being loyal has sometimes led people into slavery. You have seen people whose loyalty to a person, a party, or an idea, has led them into stupidity and evil. The followers of Hitler are a case in point.

If these things are true, then we reach a point where we must consider moral values when we estimate leadership and when we try to teach officers and men to be good leaders. The fact is that you and I judge our leaders in moral terms in any case. No man in this room, for example, will accept the leadership of Premier Stalin. Stalin can show all the loyalty, tact, courage, decisiveness and consideration he wants, and we will not follow him. We refuse to follow him because he affronts our moral judgment. On the other hand, though General Shepherd and President-elect Eisenhower may conceivably lack some of Stalin's leadership capacity, we will follow them in preference to him.

The capable leader must be intensely aware of the loyalties, beliefs and prejudices. Undoubtedly this has explained the unparalleled effectiveness of British leadership in their colonial system. It is interesting to remember that a bloody insurrection in India took place when British leaders failed to take into account the natives' religious prejudice against pork.

Experience seems to show, too, that the leader must exercise his authority in ways which his followers regard as morally right or he will lose his hold over them. Because many Confederate soldiers believed that invading the North was morally wrong, straggling greatly increased in the Army of Northern Virginia as soon as it crossed the border into Maryland. The leader must have personal integrity in terms of the moral standards of his followers, or they will desert him. The Confederate troops serving under General Van Dorn tended to have low morale and to straggle and desert because, although he was otherwise a very gifted officer, he was known by his men to be a notorious roue. In contrast, the puritanical General Jackson won the unwavering loyalty and respect of his troops, who came to admire his stern, unbending adherence to a harsh religious belief.

In some senses, Hitler, Capone and Mussolini met these moral requirements, at least for a time. Even thieves have honor of a kind, and the stool-pigeon is the most maligned sinner of the underworld. In due course, however, these men lost the authority of leadership, in some cases because they did not observe the moral code of their followers and in other cases because they ignored the moral sensibilities of humanity at large.

Up to this point we have merely been saying that the leader must take into account the moral convictions of his followers. We have pointed out that a leader of aborigines, no matter how civilized he may be himself, must not offend against the morals of his aboriginal followers. If this is true then one assumes that his personal morality can be tailored to meet the prejudices of his followers.

In a day when the "Brooklyn" mentality of cynicism is common and when personal moral standards are low, that does not seem to pose a particular challenge to the leader.

In reality, we find that the leader must do more than reflect the moral prejudices of his followers. The fact is that followers want their leaders to be better men than they are themselves. Furthermore, they do not want leaders who reflect the moral climate of the times as a matter of expediency. Men sense nothing more quickly than hypocrisy. The leader's moral code, therefore, must be his own and he must live up to it, for you can't "kid the troops". Furthermore, his men expect him to live up to it with more severity than they are likely to show themselves. Marines who were shacked up with native women in the South Pacific during the early years of World War II were resentful and contemptuous of a Marine officer who had a native mistress and occasionally flew her about in an airplane.

There seems to be a sense, then, in which the leader must develop a moral life independently of his followers. I suspect that that is true not because he is a leader but because it is an obligation common to all human beings. All of us have reasons why some things are eternally right and others eternally wrong. It is that obligation common to humanity which the leader must meet in a superlative degree.

This demand takes several forms. No man is a complete human being, for example, who has not come to terms with the universe. No man fully achieves human dignity without facing, and finding some answer to, the basic questions: "How did it come about?", "Why am I here?", "What is the good and what is evil?", "Why do men suffer?" Of course I would like you to find and to accept my answers to those questions. The important thing, however, is that your personality is undeveloped if you have not oriented yourself to the universe. You ignore these questions at the peril of being less than a human being. Let us admit that man can probably lead a squad for some time without finding satisfactory answers to these questions. It seems to me, however, that his leadership must eventually falter if he lacks this kind of orientation.

Furthermore, every leader must, at one time or another, make decisions about his methods and his objectives. Some of these decisions are moral; that is, the leader asks himself which methods and objectives are right and which are wrong. The pressure for a moral decision is not so great at the lower levels of leadership. That it exists even there, however, can be seen by the drill instructors' problem of maltreatment. As the leader grows in power and authority, the question of right and wrong methods and objectives becomes more urgent. He must answer it. Then he is faced with the problem: according to what standard or criterion is this decision right or wrong? We see the matter most clearly, perhaps, in regard to political leadership. Most of us are resentful at the casual morality of politics and we get angry when a politician sidetracks the question.

By the same token, military men must frequently face it. Colonel-General Beck resigned as Chief of Staff of the Wehrmacht rather than degrade his position and his honor as a German officer by serving under Hitler. Many other German officers served Hitler with reservations. Some of them waited the opportunity to remove him from power. There is a profound sense in which the military leader, above all, must be an honorable man according to the canons of an objective moral code.

The chief moral problem of the leader arises, however, out of his dealings with people. The good leader should have a precise, definite code for dealing with his followers. That code arises in the first place from his basic moral beliefs, just as these spring eventually from his orientation to the universe at large. This problem arises at every stage of the leader's transactions with people. It is not enough to attempt its solution by accepting merely the custom of the time.

For example, physical maltreatment has been a commonplace in German armies for the last century and a half. Even in the Second World War non-commissioned officers frequently beat their men in order to gain greater efficiency. Obviously, this custom is rooted in the world outlook and in the moral code of the German people, who are accustomed to authoritarianism in their daily life and do not have a high regard for the dignity of the person. I mention the Germans in this respect because they seem to be at a halfway house between our beliefs and those of the Orient.

Marine officers, on the other hand, do not eat in the field until they know that their men are cared for. We place a high value on human life. We generally believe that our followers must be treated justly. According to what standard do we accept these beliefs and why do we carry them out so generally?

If we feed our men first without regard to a specific standard, then we are sentimentalists. It makes no sense to feed the men first unless we do it according to some code of ethics.

The standard in this case is clear: the Marine officer must be unselfish, he must take meticulous care of his military resources, he must live according to a definite rule which governs relations between officers and men. That standard was best expressed by General Lejeune in Marine Corps Manual, paragraph 4008. It is no accident, in my opinion, that General Lejeune's recommendation is clearly in accord with the ethical standards of the Jewish and Christian religions.

There is one more point at which the leader must make a moral commitment of one kind or another. This is a century which has seen the rise of at least three great nationalistic religions, in Japan, in Germany, and in Russia. These religions are organically like every religion; they have sacred scriptures, saviours, a body of the faithful which is like a church, a code of ethics and sacramental life. They appeal strongly to the mystical element in the lives of their people. They have filled for their followers a vacuum which must exist in every human life devoid of religious expression.

Now we are convinced that these religions are false. We look down at Nazi biology and Communist botany. We abhorr their perversion of moral standards, with its terrible consequence. But, for better or for worse, we have to live with the fact that these religions provide their adherents with terrific motivation. All of you will remember the Japanese infantry who would not surrender. You will remember, too, that many Germans surrendered when the force of military necessity came into play. The S. S. troops, however, frequently fought on like the Japanese because they were essentially religious fanatics.

If the issue reaches that point, what kind of motivating power can our leaders provide to offset that of our enemies? Esprit de Corps will certainly be of great help. In the last analysis, TIME magazine, to the contrary notwithstanding, not even the Marine Corps can be a religion, and nothing less than religious commitment can cope with the fanatic zeal of our enemies. This is what you would expect a Chaplain to say. In spite of that fact, it may be an important question for each one of you to consider.

The critical decisions of our time may take place on the field of battle. In that case, our leadership must rely on skills and on the material compellent, but not only on them. The critical decisions of our time seem increasingly to be made in the area of the intangibles --- in terms of loyalty, fear, discouragement, suspicion, persistence, resolution. The crisis of our age seems to take place in an area which can be affected by leadership. Our country is founded on the belief that we can endure such a crisis if our leadership is realistically founded on the eternal verities.

THE CHAPLAIN IN COMBAT

The first consideration in ministering under combat conditions is preparation. This will involve many factors. The chaplain must know his place in the organization and his battle station. He will be prudent to follow strictly regulations about uniform, since most of them stem from the desire and need to limit casualties. In some circumstances (e.g., the sickbay of a ship) those needing his ministry will be brought to the chaplain. Under other conditions the chaplain's ministry will not be offered unless he is able to take it to the point of need. The professional chaplain will therefore learn skills and practice procedures enabling him to go where he is needed: reading maps and compasses, daily checking with intelligence and operations staff officers, use of cover and concealment for moving from place to place, informing the commander or executive officer as to his planned movements and his estimated location at specified times and coordinating his activities with those of other chaplains under the direction of his supervisory chaplain. It goes without saying, moreover that the chaplain's usefulness depends upon his acquaintance with and his ability to use various available communications systems, especially when serving with Marines.

Equally important to the effectiveness of the chaplain is his attitude and approach to the specialized requirements of the combat situation. The true professional will take risks only when he has no other choice. He looks with contempt upon glory-hunters and amateurs who move haphazardly to the point of action without regard to their own posts of duty. Abandonment of an assigned duty, momentarily quiet, in favor of a supposed need where the firing seems heavier is frequently desertion of the people who may soon need the chaplain's services. The professional chaplain recognizes that maximum coverage of all troops is best governed by his supervisory chaplain, that the need for his services at some other point than his assigned post will be communicated to him and that individual decision on this question can lead only to chaos and the deprival of service to the troops. The seasoned chaplain exercises an economy of movement which consults first the needs of the wounded, next the needs of troops in the line and always the good of the greatest number. He will not hesitate to accept danger when that is necessary to the effectiveness of his ministry. On the other hand he knows that the service of the chaplain is not accomplished by heedless unplanned movement and that frequently the greatest moral courage consists less in seeking the fire-fight than in ministering quietly where one's lines are cast. Over the long haul the average chaplain in combat finds enough action without having to seek it.

Human need is a constant with which the experienced clergyman is familiar, but certain expressions of it in the combat situation are worthy of examination. The world of the man in battle is almost always constricted. It opens up during movement between engagements, but otherwise a man is limited to a small space. Here one easily falls prey to "tunnel vision". Training and discipline mitigate this hazard to fighting effectiveness, but they do not prevent the slow erosion of the man's judgment, wherein he reads immense significance into casual phrases in his wife's letters and gradually whittling of his value system which eventually elevates a hot shave above most earthly treasures and regards death as an incident of professional interest.

Every sane man knows fear. Many combat veterans will remember men who apparently knew no fear, who seemingly gloried and found fulfillment in the uninhibited release of battle. These are the exception, however, and are finally considered by other men, brave above their own fear, to be abnormal. The priorities of fear, if the words and actions of men may be trusted, do not begin with death. Most men first are afraid of emasculation. Some of them would rather die than encounter this fate. In a unit with high morale men are next most fearful of "letting their buddies down". This is frequently highest in the combat hierarchy of value: meeting your obligation to friends and comrades. Then comes death, in her immemorial role, though long exposure to battle may bring a fatalism exorcising this dread. Finally, there is fear of betrayal, not by comrades, but by the "home front": by wife, or profiteer, or shoddy workman.

The feeling of guilt is omnipresent among combat men. Very many of them have resolved the supposed contradiction between their religion and war, but not without experienceing a residue of guilt. Some men must come to terms with the moral lapses of the last fling ashore before battle. One of the most common phenomena of battle is the feeling of guilt experienced by men over the deaths of their buddies. From the depths of grief they cry:" He would still be here if I'd done my job". For the most part this is unrelated to the actual manner in which the casualty occurred. Rarely is the death of a man caused by the precise misfeasance of another individual. The feeling of guilt, despite its delusive character, is nevertheless very real to the survivor. Its strength, where the feeling occurs, is illustrated by the tenacity with which men cling to it and their rejection of any suggestion that it is delusory.

Battle builds a communion as deep and lasting as that of any religion. From intense need men are driven to know each other in depth, to love each other, to depend ultimately upon each other. This deep interpenetration of selves is not merely the bunching of a herd against danger. It is rather the response of men to the personal isolation and loneliness of combat. This partakes of many elements. Some of it may be seen in the agonizing separation of the man from all that he loves - home and the rest. It comes through in the self-inflicted exile of the men who finally reject all they love - who write home, for example, asking their wives to divorce them - so that they may be no longer exposed to the pain and deprivation of being apart. Loneliness is no respecter of rank or persons. The regimental commander and the platoon leader must decide - along - to send some men to their deaths. Amidst all comradeship every man, at the last, personally confronts within himself the specter of his own weakness and frailty before the terror which menaces not only his existence but also his humanity itself.

It is in communion that men seek liberation from loneliness. The strength and beauty of this communion is an anomaly in the strife of men against men, a visible and notable contradiction to the process in which they are engaged. One is not surprised that a man occasionally loses the last vestige of inhibition in the task of killing. No man is ready to experience the surpassing gentleness of men in battle toward each other, the deep compassion they feel and express toward their wounded, their authentic grief and pathetic remembrances over the dead and, once the passion of combat has been spent, their unbelievable generosity and kindness to prisoners and refugees. This flowering of personhood in a least likely circumstance comes to the unprepared observer with the force of revelation.

Finally units are relieved from the line, even removed from the combat area. The human needs of the combat situation ostensibly disappear and on the surface men seem much as they were before. Yet appearances are deceiving. Grief returns in long nights of silence. Feelings of guilt continue their corrosive work, occasionally exacerbated by excesses directed toward escape.

Apprehensions of the next operation are now only too solidly rooted in experience. The man in need is now a combat veteran and his human necessities are grounded in that fact.

This is not an exhaustive catalogue of phenomena observable in combat, nor are these experiences universal among participants in battle. For every one of them there can be cited an opposite: the psychopath who truly feels no guilt, the loner who rejects comradeship, the rigid personality whose value system remains intact to the point of a daily bath and a neatly trimmed mustache. Here, too, are needs, however isolated and individual. It is to men passing through experiences similar to these, however, and through other experiences too subtle or rare to enumerate, that the chaplain ministers in battle.

There is no stock procedure which a chaplain may learn in order to minister effectively under combat conditions. A few general statements may suggest useful approaches to this ministry. The mere presence of the chaplain, more than anything he says, is itself a ministry to men under these tensions. The chaplain is that charismatic person representing what will remain real after the guns are still. He should therefore visit his men as often as possible. It is his professional obligation, of course, to be with the wounded, but this role has another and profound meaning to his men. In the aid station the chaplain exercises not only his own priesthood but vicariously that of countless other men who would comfort their comrades if they could. There he represents not only the healing power of God but also the human love forged in the communion of battle among this wounded man and his comrades. This he will learn from conversations during every visit to the line.

The wise chaplain will not attempt to communicate within value structures which men, for whatever reason, have discarded in battle. Without forsaking or compromising his own values he will speak and commune with men where they are at the moment, always holding before them the world larger than the one they now inhabit, always recalling them to the wounding loves they have rejected.

Conventional worship, when it can take place, has its limitations. Sermons are dangerous unless they speak directly, briefly and meaningfully to the present needs of the men. Prayer and reading of the Scripture with individuals or small groups is frequently helpful to the men and often requested by them. Most meaningful is the ancient cultus of the Christian faith, those venerable actions in which Christians acknowledge and appropriate the redemption wrought in Jesus Christ. Men who have newly found communion with each other, and who long to continue in communion with their loved ones at home, are now hungry for the Bread of Life which brings communion with God. The bread and the cup, however hastily or informally served, are desired and accepted by the men and bring strength beyond any other ministry.

Finally, the chaplain himself is not immune to the anxieties of man in battle. He will recognize in his own response to combat some of the dynamics here outlined. This should neither surprise nor daunt him; indeed, it may well be an open door to that identification with the needs of his men which along enables him to serve. "Awareness is identifying yourself with the hopes, dreams, fears and longings of others, that you may understand them and help them", writes a modern sage. That awareness comes most deeply and sympathetically when the chaplain is one with his men in their common need. It is then indeed from his weakness, not in his own strength, that he can minister to the frailties of men in battle.

MILITARY CHARACTER GUIDANCE: MARINE VERSION   1949

by
Lt.Col. Charles L. Banks, USMC
and
LCDR Glyn Jones, CHC, USN

<u>In that Gregory F. PAYNE, 456987, Private, United States Marine Corps,</u>

<u>attached to . . . . did, on or about May 10, 1950, without leave from</u>

<u>proper authority . . . . for a period of twenty seven days . . . . .</u>

<u>To be confined for a period of ninety days and to lose forty dollars</u>

<u>per month, total loss of pay amounting to two hundred and forty . . . . .</u>

Could Military Character Guidance have prevented this?

Molding the character of men is as old as military history. Victory has frequently hinged on the success with which armies and navies have converted civilians of every degree into efficient fighting men.

Various methods have been used during the years. Eighteenth Century European armies turned their men into military automatons by flogging for minor offenses, awarding the death penalty for trivial violations, promising loot, plunder and rapine as rewards and suppressing initiative and imagination by dull, unremitting drill. In an age when the ability to think was a disadvantage to the private soldier, these methods sufficed for their purpose.

From time to time, however, there emerged unusual military combinations, whose success stemmed from different methods. It has always been noticeable, for example, that <u>religious motivation</u> has produced a fierce and able fighting man. Cromwell's Ironsides symbolize the relentless drive of the Christian soldier, while the fame of Moslem troops needs no gilding.

Then there have been military organizations whose enduring reputations have been built on their <u>esprit d' corps.</u> Since the early part of the 17th century, when the British Army began to recognize the distinctive achievements of individual units, such distinguished organizations as the Black Watch, the Grenadier and Coldstream Guards, the French Foreign Legion and our own Marine Corps have founded their greatness on unit pride, achievement and tradition.

<u>Sir John Moore,</u> the victim of Corunna, was an able imaginative soldier who was one of the first to break with the degrading training methods of his day. Faced with the high-spirited legions of Napoleon, Sir John recognized the inadequacy of contemporary training methods for coping with the revoluntionary fervor of the victorious French. After long and repeated efforts, he was finally permitted to organize and train a brigade of light troops to accompany the British Army in its prospective invasion of Europe.

For three years he was given his head with the Light Brigade, and at the end of that time had produced one of the finest fighting organizations Europe had ever seen. Based in the South of England, the Light Brigade lived permanently in the field, and behaved day and night as though they were in the presence of the enemy. Individual marksmanship, scouting and patrolling, intelligence work and outpost duty, living off the country—these were the daily lot of the Light Brigade. The soldier of the Light Brigade carried a light weapon, wore a uniform which blended with the green of the country and learned to operate as an individual as well as in units as small as a modern squad. All of this is SOP to the modern soldier. In Moore's day it was the ranking heresy because most conventional leaders did not believe that ordinary troops could absorb that kind of training.

Sir John obtained his men from the same sources as the rest of the British Army. The bulk of them came from the depressed social classes; some were discontented Irishmen, Scots and Welsh, and many were criminals. It was obvious to him that the training methods of the British Army could not produce the type of man needed for the Light Brigade. So, for three years, he worked at the almost hopeless task of changing the character of men of the most depraved type. Though he did not live to see the day, the Light Brigade became the spearhead of that extraordinary Peninsular Army which was to whip Napoleon's Marshals in order and finally to shatter the last hope of the Master of Generals himself.

Moore's methods were surprisingly modern. He insisted that his officers live in the field with their men, instead of enjoying the flesh-pots of the cities until the eve of battle. He abolished flogging, and allowed the death penalty only for the same serious offenses which require it today. His experience with looting and rapine told him that troops went out of control whenever they were permitted, and he forbade such indulgence, under threat of the most severe penalty. Moore taught his officers and NCO's by his own example to treat the common soldier as a human being. Kindness and consideration were the atmosphere in which his men worked. They were encouraged to consider themselves as partners in every enterprise with their officers and Commanding General. Small unit and individual training stressed initiative and resourcefulness.

Above all, the men were taught self-respect. In a day when drunkenness was an accepted commonplace among soldiers, Moore's troops learned to look down upon intoxication as a failure in self-control. In his own example their General was to his men a model of the highest moral character, of deeply ingrained courtesy and of great personal and moral courage. In accordance with Clausewitz's dictum that the best troops were those which reflected the social and moral character of their nation, Moore inculcated into his officers and men the solid moral virtues of the English yeoman, the same qualities which lay behind England's bulldog insistence on fighting Napoleon and Hitler to the death.

The same moral fibre was built by different methods into another famous organization, the Army of Northern Virginia. Created of superior military raw material, this Army was severely handicapped by its initially poor organization, by such demoralizing practices as the election of officers and by an excessive independence, from the military standpoint, among its personnel.

The basic moral power of these troops derived from their religious faith. Letters of the period are naturally and unquestioningly couched in religious terms through-out. Such redoubtable warriors as Lee, Jackson, Stuart, Pender and the Hills sincerely thought and wrote in terms which would be used today only by the clergy. Most of their men came from devout homes, and responded readily to the appeal of religion.

In the winter of 1862-63, when the eventual doom of the Confederacy was apparent to many, a profound revival of religion swept through the winter quarters of the Army of Northern Virginia. The consequences of that experience on the fighting qualities of the men and on their subsequent behavior in adversity during the Reconstruction were so notable that Dr. Douglas Freeman cites them as bulwarks in the South's survival of that terrible period.

Again, then, it is seen that the effectiveness of an army is largely related to its moral character. Troops which could fight on for almost two years and a half while defeat impended are unusual at any stage of history, and the achievements of the Army of Northern Virginia are part of the proud heritage of today's American fighting man.

Recognition of this truth has by no means been lacking in the Marine Corps or other components of our armed forces. For years individual commanding officers have experimented with certain phases of such a program as Military Character Guidance.

Awareness of its importance lay behind the inception, after the war, of the U. S. Army's "Chaplain's Hour" program. Based on the moral principles commonly accepted by the American people, this program is an official part of the indoctrination of all Army personnel. In like fashion the post-war British Army has been improving a similar plan called "The Padre's Hour" which was instituted during the recent war. Without a doubt these programs constitute a modern response to the persistent dilemma which Marshal Foch answered when he remarked, "Intellect, criticism——Pah! A donkey who has more character is more useful".

The Marine Corps, as its history indicates, has always recognized the importance of character in the constitution of the elite fighting man. The basic mode of creating it has been the second type mentioned above; esprit D'corps built on professional excellence, tradition and almost continuous fighting service during its existence.

The Corps has recognized, however, the importance of the first type of morale, and has attempted to build it by such activities as athletics, educational service and welfare programs. Enthusiastic command backing has assured the success and increased the moral impact of such activities as the Marine Corps Institute, Marine teams which have won all-Navy championships, and savings and insurance plans which have improved the economic and domestic lot of the individual Marine.

The warm response of the individual Marine to this kind of approach indicates that it may well be expanded in other directions with every expectation of improving the soldierly qualities of our personnel. Furthermore, it is obvious that this approach complements, without competing with, the traditional methods which have worked so well in the Corps. The better the man, the more significant is his esprit d' corps and pride in tradition.

This suggests the need of a specific practical program to develop within the men of the Marine Corps the habits, patterns of thought and attitudes of good moral character. To have meaningful results, such a program would have to operate on a Corps-wide basis. It should have a carefully conceived philosophy consistent with the highest moral principles avowed by the American people.

It should aim toward specific objectives within the Marine Corps environment. Methods of presentation should be congenial to the spirit of the Corps. Most important of all, it should become an integral part of Marine Corps life and training, not merely another extra-curricular activity.

This is a description of <u>the Military Character Guidance Program</u>. The philosophy, objectives, methods and organization of such a program can now be examined.

<u>The primary requisite of a good Marine is that he be a good man.</u> It follows, then, that effective indoctrination at this point requires a type of appeal over and above those of mere physical fitness or financial welfare. An approach must be made on moral and psychological grounds as well.

<u>The essentials of good military character are those of good moral character;</u> reverence, obedience to the moral law, loyalty, respect for duly constituted authority, personal integrity and the development of proper habits for living in the military community. Stemming from these qualities of the moral life are such important individual characteristics as self-reliance, initiative, desire for advancement and the development of good judgment. Most important of all, once the basic standards of moral living are set, is the development within the individual of self discipline. Considering the Marine Corps' insistence on good leadership, it can be seen that these aspects of moral character all are necessary in the personality of the well-rounded leader.

It would appear that any military Character Guidance Program should aim at certain <u>objectives</u>. First of these, undoubtedly, should be the constant presentation to Marines of the basic moral principles by which they should live and through which they may achieve the most satisfactory personal lives. Then should be presented the application of these principles to the concrete circumstances of life in the Marine Corps. <u>Not only should such a program deal with indoctrination as to principles</u>: <u>It should actively seek to mold attitudes</u>. Therefore it would aim at the development in all Marines of proper attitudes toward themselves, their subordinates, their superiors, and the military service itself. A prime objective at this point would be a correct emotional orientation in patriotism.

Although other programs specialize in keeping the Marine informed about Naval and Marine Corps policies and directives, it is conceived that such a program as this can and should supplement their work. A good Military Character Guidance program must strive to deal with the Marine not only as a Marine but also as an American citizen in the military service. Americans are used to "getting straight dope" in their newspapers and radio stations, and the Marine deserves the best we can give him in that line.

A final, though by no means unimportant, objective of such a program as this is the development of personal acquaintance between Marines and their Chaplain, their company commanders and battalion commanders.

A Military Character Guidance program conducted spasmodically in some places and ignored in others must necessarily be of limited effectiveness so far as the Marine Corps at large is concerned. For such a program to have vital impact on the Corps as a whole, it must become an integral part of the training of all Marines.

The natural place to begin, then, is the Recruit Training Depot. Here, where the new Marine is at his most impressionable stage, it can be driven home unforgettably that the Corps expects him to be a superior man. Furthermore, upon his transfer to the Fleet Marine Force or other duty, he will need no adjustment to the program as he finds it. He has learned to expect it.

Of crucial importance to the orientation of the recruit is the quality of his Drill Instructor [or Company Commander]. It is obvious that the effects of any program for the recruit can be seriously vitiated if his first instructors do not illustrate in their dealings with him the soldierly qualities which recruit training seeks to inculcate. Therefore, it is essential that all men assigned to duty as Drill Instructors be thoroughly indoctrinated for the work. And a vital part of such instruction would be carefully planned exposure to the Military Character Guidance program prior to assuming duties in Recruit Training.

Equally important to the proper conduct of a Military Character Guidance program is the attitude of the command under which it operates. Needless to say, no plan which makes a moral and psychological appeal can succeed without the enthusiastic support and cooperation of the command. That is especially true of such an approach as this, since it deals with a basic command responsibility, the moral welfare and morale of the personnel of the outfit.

Assuming, however, that the command fulfills this responsibility by instituting some such program as this, it does not follow that the wishes of the Commanding Officer will be adequately carried out. If the Commanding Officer will order a man transferred or a weapon moved from one place to another, he can count on prompt, effectual compliance. At that point he is dealing with things. Here he is working in another milieu. His order to conduct this particular type of training will be carried out in some fashion, but the effectiveness of compliance no longer depends merely on a mechanical process. Achieving the objectives of this kind of indoctrination depends largely upon the attitudes, rather than the professional knowledge, of the officers in whose organizations it is attempted.

It is important, then, that the Military Character Guidance Program be presented to junior officers in the curriculum at Basic School. The purpose of offering the course there is properly to indoctrinate the officers as to the desirability, the objectives and the methods of operating such a system among the troops under their command. A field officer and a chaplain experienced in the program should be available to present it to each class by lecture and demonstration.

The success of the whole project in the local command relies upon the attitude and enthusiasm of the JO and his proper utilization of the program toward solving the morale and disciplinary problems in the platoon.

At the inception of the program there will be many senior and junior NCO's who are skeptical of its purposes and value. Obviously this must be overcome or the effectiveness of the project will be sabotaged from below by the indifference and unfavorable attitude of the leaders closest to the men.

It is important that the NCO's be indoctrinated as to the purpose and the methods of the program. The thoughtful, professional non-commissioned officer will not only accept the plan, but will cooperate enthusiastically with it, if it is justified to him on the basis of its practical effect on the discipline and behavior of his men. The best type of NCO commonly tries to teach his men the subject matter of such a course as this, in any case, and will find this program a re-enforcement of practices which he has already established in his dealings with his troops.

The indoctrination of the NCO should take two forms. Before the program is set in motion, it should be explained thoroughly to all officers and senior NCO's by the Team: the Battalion Commander and the Chaplain. At this session ample time and opportunity should be provided for questions and suggestions. The conclusion of this meeting should find all hands talking the same language and in basic agreement with the philosophy behind the plan.

Again, the Senior NCO should be required to attend the regular meetings of the program. He will, of course, profit personally by the experience of considering his daily military life in a moral perspective. There will be other windfalls, as well, from the standpoint of his professional effectiveness. He will be able to discover how and what his men think on the basic questions of life. If he is an intelligent listener, he will be able to find the reasons behind the behavior of many of his problem children. Experience of the program so far has shown that, after a few sessions, Senior NCO's become interested and enthusiastic participants.

Not only should NCO's be correctly oriented toward the program by indoctrination and participation; they should from the beginning be given to understand that they have much to offer in its successful operation. The officer conducting the session should, whenever possible, call upon the experience and viewpoint of the senior NCO's to support his conclusions. Principles and points of view which may be discounted when made by officers will be immensely impressed on the minds of the men when supported by the local prestige of the senior NCO.

Granting the importance of cooperation from the command, the junior officers and the NCO's, there are two people who are the keystone of the whole effort, and without whose enthusiasm, cooperation and special point of view the program is doomed to failure. These two---the Battalion Commander and the Chaplain---may be designated the Team, and should constantly so think of themselves.

The Battalion Commander and the Chaplain have interests which run parallel to each other, and which, if coordinated, can do much to reenforce each other. The primary interest of the Battalion Commander is the military efficiency of the organization. He legitimately supports any activity which, no matter how indirectly, contributes to that end. He knows that a general moral improvement among his troops has direct bearing on their military efficiency in that it improves morale, creates a more dependable soldier and reduces such knocks in the military engine as disciplinary infractions, venereal disease and bad attitudes.

The Chaplain, though sympathetic to the aims of the Commander, is primarily interested in his men as individuals. His basic mission is to make better men. He is interested in moral development for its own sake, and carefully nurtures the virtues wherever he finds them. At many points the Chaplain sees deeper into the lives of the men than any other officer. By training and education he is equipped to offer the individual Marine a kind of service which cannot be duplicated. Furthermore, the most successful the Chaplain is at his work, the greater his contribution to the aims of his Commanding Officer.

It is obvious that the objective is to harness together these parallel aims. That is one of the functions of the Military Character Guidance program. It follows, then, that this program is more than a series of lectures periodically delivered to the troops. It is part of a larger process, a process which continues even on days when no sessions are held.

The Character Guidance approach applies, for example, to the Battalion Commander's Mast office hours. While great progress has been made within the past few years in dealing with disciplinary offenses, particularly from the standpoint of salvaging chronic offenders, much remains to be done on what could be called preventive discipline. It is at this point that the Company and Battalion Commander have most to offer. At a man's first appearance before his commanding officer the process of diagnosis should begin; regardless of the nature of the offense or the particular punishment awarded, the task of discovering WHY HE DID IT has priority.

It is here that the Battalion Commander and the Chaplain are talking the same language. Very frequently the Battalion Commander can refer the man to the Chaplain. In every such case, the Chaplain should consult with the man's Platoon Leader and Platoon Sergeant. Then he is prepared for a talk with the man. Not infrequently a referral in another direction is indicated: to the Medical Officer, the Psychiatrist, or such welfare organizations as the Red Cross or Navy Relief Society. It is incumbent on the Chaplain to give the Battalion Commander a frank and specific recommendation in respect to the particular individual, including therein such pertinent information as he may have obtained from the Platoon Leader or Platoon Sergeant.

Of practical importance in the positive approach of the Program is the presentation to the men themselves of the specific kinds of problems encountered at office hours. This is a kind of propaganda which leads to the formation of correct attitudes toward particular kinds of offenses, and from time to time offers positive solutions to the causes of these offenses.

It is apparent that these procedures are based on mutual confidence between the Battalion Commander and the Chaplain. They imply also a high degree of loyalty in both directions. The Chaplain who tacitly assents to an unfavorable description of the Battalion Commander by one of his men is sabotaging any hope for progress. The Battalion Commander who fails to use the professional capabilities of his Chaplain or tolerates the so-called "weeping chit" attitude toward the Chaplain among his officers or men is missing the boat. While this kind of relation in the Team is essential, it is interesting to note that the Military Character Guidance Program itself, by multiplying the contacts between the two, tends to develop the necessary mutual confidence and cooperation.

The first step in organizing the program is its inclusion in the quarterly regimental, or unit, training schedule. Lower organization training schedules, of course, are based on those of the parent unit.

The second step is a meeting of all officers and NCO's, at which the program is thoroughly explained to them. The importance of this beginning has previously been discussed in connection with the place of the junior officer and NCO in the scheme of things. At this meeting the Commanding Officer and Chaplain should carefully outline purposes, objectives and methods of the program, so that there can be no misunderstanding among the officers whose troops it will affect.

It is believed that the best results are obtained when each organization of Company size is covered for one hour every two weeks. When meetings are held with groups larger than one hundred and fifty men, it is found that the response of the individuals is stifled and the greatest benefit of the program is dissipated.

Experience indicates that certain administrative difficulties may be solved without being allowed to arise. Company sessions should be scheduled, for example, on days other than when they have large detachments for special working parties or guard. The program must be flexible, organized for field or barracks.

The methods of presentation are those which are congenial to the American mind and the American way of doing things. The basic means is discussion. In practice, it has been found that a method evolves as the Chaplain and men become accustomed to each other; the college professor would call it a combination lecture-discussion presentation.

Preaching is a pitfall to be avoided. The Military Character Guidance program is not to be construed as a means of offering the Chaplain an opportunity to preach to the men. Preaching is important in its place, but this program is not its place. Nothing would be more harmful than to give the men the idea that the Chaplain was going to preach to them even if they didn't go to church. Neither is this program a presentation of religion in and of itself. The Marine's religious life is presumed to be cared for by the direct religious ministration of the Chaplain on other occasions. This is not the place for doctrines peculiar to any sect, denomination or church. Above all, personnel must not receive the impression that they are being propagandized or proselityzed on behalf of any religious group.

Character cannot be superimposed on the personality. Good or bad, it is a natural growth within the person. It is important, therefore, that the men discuss freely and fully the subject of each meeting, so that active participation will assist them in developing wholesome ideas and attitudes.

In general, the Chaplain is the specialist available on matters of morals. However, there are many subjects relevant to these objectives on which company officers and the Battalion Commander can speak with great authority and experience. The importance of officer participation and leadership in certain phases of the program cannot be over-stressed. In addition, it is possible under some circumstances, particularly near large cities, to obtain especially qualified civilian leadership for particular aspects of the program.

There is no reason why the program should be limited to lecture-discussion. When available, pertinent and desirable, such visual aids as posters, slides, comic books and movies can be used. The discussion element should remain a constant, however, even when these methods are used to supplement it.

An occasional objection to including this program within the training schedule of the working day is that it interfers with other essential training. That is a serious objection, if true. When properly conducted, however, the Character Guidance program takes the time of one company for only one hour every two weeks. Furthermore, it is apparent that any practical result it may have will decrease the number of men who are missing training for disciplinary reason, absence from duty station for unauthorized reasons, confinement, venereal disease and malingering.

From the positive standpoint, it is apparent the success the program achieves will be in the direction of better morale, increased individual initiative, improved understanding of the military service and more positive attitudes. At the individual man develops these qualities he enters more fully into the rest of the training program, and not only learns faster, but also wants to learn for the right reasons.

For the past six months a program of this type has been conducted in units of the Second Marine Division at Camp Lejeune. Many of the conclusions stated above have been drawn from the experience gained in the experiment.

By the very nature of the case, it is difficult to make a specific estimate of the practical results of the experiment. It would appear to have had a positive influence toward raising morale, reducing disciplinary problems and contributing toward an effective performance of duty. On the other hand, it is difficult to isolate this contribution from other important factors. For example, the type of command personnel and philosophy which will organize and sustain such a program as this will also provide many other aspects of enlightened leadership. Such a command, even without this program, would develop superior morale and performance among its men in any case. The best recommendation for this type of program is that it was enthusiastically supported by that type of leadership.

In the execution of the program throughout the Second Marine Division, the basic subject matter is the same in every unit, though the use and treatment of the material will differ with the individual Commanding Officer and Chaplain. The program is based on the fundamental moral principles accepted by the American people, the Ten Commandments of the Hebrew-Christian tradition, but its approach is based in the concrete situation and not in abstract presentation. It is a matter, not of presenting ethical theory directly, but of applying moral laws to the actual circumstances of the officers and men of the military service. The following are typical subjects for one quarter:

1) Foundations of American Freedom
   Roman Law
   English Common Law
   The Hebrew-Christian Tradition

2) How We Got Our Constitution.   3) How Should a Marine Use His Money?

4) What Are the Pre-Requisites of a Happy Marriage?

5) How Should a Marine Deal With Liquor?   6) The Marine Improves Himself
                                                Through Education
                                               (Stressing opportunities within the
                                                 service)

A very helpful source of material for the program in the Second Marine Division has been the U. S. Army publication "The Chaplain's Hour". In practice, however, it is important that some of the subject matter should be raised directly from the personal problems of the men, and that a "life-situation" approach be taken wherever possible.

Perhaps the average military man will say that is is not the business of the armed forces to teach an old dog new tricks, that the basic character of the Marine has been set before the Corps ever has a chance to influence him. A moment's reflection, however, shows that one of the prime functions of any military organization is to change the character of a man from that of a civilian to that of a ~~Marine~~ professional fighting man.

A recruit training depot is only the first step in a long process of developing the military character. The greater part of military life is given to teaching procrastinators to be prompt, irresponsibles to accept responsibility, men who have no self-respect to respect themselves, to follow their superiors and to lead and care for their subordinates.

→ That means that —

~~We~~ are in the business of Character Guidance in any case. The only questions are what kind of character we want to build and how we shall go about it. ~~This article has presented one method, a system that is now working in a large Marine unit, and that will work in any unit that sets about it seriously.~~

Engaged in a war for the human mind. ~~Our enemies have~~ thus far excelled us in this struggle. We must begin to concern ourselves now ~~as much~~ about the intellectual and spiritual vulnerability of our men. Napoleon said "The moral is to the material as 3 to 1."

It will do us no good to have the finest weapons, if the men who possess them are fair prey for an alien destructive philosophy.

The military test of any program is simple — it is "Victory." To win a modern war we must be sure that the human weapon is as strong and fit for the work as the tank or ship he will use.

Submitted to Gen. Pollock 2 Nov. '53

    The most important problems of the commanding officer lie in the field of human relations. If he fails there he cannot succeed anywhere; neither the excellence of his tactical theory nor the efficiency of his material equipment will save him. It is the human element which creates the greatest difficulties and offers the strongest possibilities with respect to the success or failure of your command.

    The Marine Corps has provided you with specialists to assist in building the human element of your command to its highest peak of personal and professional proficiency. The Medical Officer, the Classification Officer, the Dental Officer and the Psychiatrist have clearly defined roles in this process. We are well aware of their important contributions in this field.

    The place of the Chaplain is less clearly defined. Perhaps that is intentional, since the Chaplain's effectiveness depends on factors which are intangible. He is committed, for example, to an interest in you and your men for your own sakes, regardless of any incidental profit to the working of your organization. He is a hard man to classify. For that reason, I suggest a general principle and three simple procedures which will enable you and your command to benefit from the professional knowledge and experience of your Chaplain.

    First, the general principle. Give your Chaplain the feeling that he is on your team. Respect his estimate of the importance of his religious work. That is all you need do to win his warm cooperation.

    Now the three procedures. First, confer regularly with your Chaplain. The frequency and length of the conferences will depend on circumstances, but they should be regularly scheduled even if you have nothing in particular to talk about. A weekly quarter-hour with the Chaplain over a cup of coffee will give you the climate of "grass roots" sentiment on the line and in the barracks, will reveal problems in sufficient time for you to nip them in the bud and will serve as an excellent barometer of morale. Not only will the conference tell you about the command: it will tell the command about you. It is an excellent means for giving the troops the "feel" of your personality and for extending your personal influence to the private in the rear rank. It is not a substitute for personal contact with your men but it is an excellent augmentation of your personal relationship with them.

    Next, use your Chaplain in a program of preventive discipline. The Chaplain should attend all your office hours, interview all offenders and investigate social and personal factors connected with your disciplinary cases. Official investigations generally uncover the <u>occasion,</u> or immediate reason, for the offense but the Chaplain can frequently discover the underlying <u>cause.</u>

In due course, after your team has become accustomed to working in harness, your disciplinary picture will gradually change. There will be a reduction in the number of "repeaters" as well as in the number of offenders appearing at office hours. More problems will be settled in the platoon leader's office before they assume a disciplinary stature. More men will consult with the platoon leader or the Chaplain before committing themselves to unwise courses of action, with a resultant decrease in AWOLs and venereal cases. Slowly but surely, the dominant emphasis of your disciplinary activities will shift from the punitive to the preventive.

Third, support and improve the Character Guidance program in your command. Though the Chaplain gives most of the instruction in this activity it is not his program. The responsibility for safeguarding and improving the moral welfare of your men lies directly on you as their commanding officer. The Commandant has promulgated this program to assist you in meeting that responsibility. The Chaplain is the agent through whom your command responsibility is fulfilled in this field. It is your business to use him and to support him in every activity which works positively to improve the discipline, the moral fibre and the morale of your command.

Office Memorandum · UNITED STATES GOVERNMENT

TO: Chaplain Jones
FROM: Chaplain Salisbury
SUBJECT:

DATE: 12 Feb. 1952

We hope that the C. G. will concur so that your wishes may be carried out.

L.W.S.

11 February 1952

Dear General Silverthorn:

As required by the Chief of Naval Personnel, I am writing to you to inquire whether or not you will be willing to accept Captain Herbert P. McNally, CHC, USNR on your Staff.

Chaplain McNally has recently been selected for Captain and is a trained educator. He is a priest of the Jesuit Order and was for a time the Vice President of Fordham University. With the accent upon training and Character Guidance, it is believed that Chaplain McNally will be able to contribute greatly to your program in that field.

Commander Glyn Jones, CHC, USN, your present Post Chaplain, indicated to me when he was detached from this office that it was his desire to serve under some senior, experienced chaplain. He has indicated this desire to others and I believe that the arrival of Chaplain McNally will make for a fine team of chaplains who will work together to accomplish the mission of the Recruit Training Depot.

Upon the receipt of your reply, Chaplain McNally will be nominated for duty there if you concur with this suggestion.

With all good wishes to you and your family, I remain

Faithfully yours,

S. W. SALISBURY
Rear Admiral, CHC, USN

Major General M. H. Silverthorn, USMC
The Commanding General
U. S. Marine Corps Recruit Depot
Parris Island, South Carolina

cc: Chaplain Jones

31 January 1972

The Editor
Boston Globe
135 William T. Morrisey Boulevard
Dorchester, Massachusetts

To the Editor:

As a regular Navy chaplain retired after almost a quarter century of service I read with interest Dr. Louis Mutschler's contention that cadet cheating at the Air Force Academy is nourished by the institutional lie which surrounds them. Wide acquaintance with members and former members of service academies faculties and staff has persuaded me of their high personal integrity and morality. On matters relating to the academies, however, these otherwise highminded men virtually surrender their personal morality to another of lesser standard. Too many alumni of these service schools alma mater is not simply a religion; it is the religion.

Dr. Mutschler mentions the place of required chapel in this syndrome. About two years ago the ACLU represented a cadet from West Point and several midshipmen attacking this practise as an infringement on their constitutional right to freedom of religion and as an offense against the establishment cause of the First Amendment. I was privileged to testify with Father (now Representative) Robert F. Drinan, S. J. in support of these young people.

The defense of the government in this case, Anderson v. Laird, was and is that religious services at West Point, Annapolis, and the Air Force Academy are "purely secular exercises carried out for purely secular purposes". The secular purpose avowed is the training of officers in understanding the religious sentiments of their men, yet it is difficult to the point of impossibility for a cadet or midshipman to transfer from the service of his original choice to that of another religious persuasion. Ostensibly a Roman Catholic officer would learn about the sensibilities of his Protestant, Orthodox, and Jewish men by attending Mass under compulsion for four years. It is frivolous to suppose that any honor code can survive in an atmosphere of such dishonesty and cynicism.

In the meantime the priest at Annapolis is under the delusion that he is celebrating Mass for a religious purpose. The Military Ordinariate of the Roman Catholic Church, and the endorsing agencies of other religious bodies, assume that their chaplains are commissioned for religious purposes and not to provide "purely secular exercises for purely secular purposes."

- 2 -

Be these matters as they may, the government has won its first test in Anderson v. Laird. By judgment of a U. S. District Court at Washington D. C. religious services at all service academies are now legally defined as "purely secular exercises conducted for purely secular purposes".

Anderson v. Laird has been argued on appeal and the judgment will soon be entered.

                        Sincerely,

                        GLYN JONES

COMMANDER IN CHIEF
UNITED STATES NAVAL FORCES, EUROPE
FLEET POST OFFICE
NEW YORK, NEW YORK

IN REPLY REFER TO:
FF1-3/15
1611
7 September 1961

Rear Admiral George A. Rosso, ChC, USN
Chief of Chaplains
Navy Department
Bureau of Naval Personnel
Washington 25, D.C.

Dear Chaplain Rosso:

    It is only fair to suggest that this letter is a likely candidate for your circular file. It does, However, deal with a problem which is familiar to all of us. I am encouraged to send it, moreover, by the attitude of several senior members of our staff with whom I have discussed the work of NAVEUR chaplains.

    The question is the adequacy for their purpose of fitness reports submitted on chaplains. The issue rose here while I was shepherding through the staff various instructions, notices and other written materials pertaining either to my job or to our chaplains. In due course it struck me that, before my proposals could get off the ground in many instances, it was necessary to educate people as to what a chaplain is and what a chaplain should be doing. This effort was generally well received and frequently generated considerable discussion. (It always snows the line to learn that we're all volunteers and that we have a higher percentage of officers at sea than they!) Several of these officers pursued the logic of our discussion to its conclusion: that chaplains should be evaluated in terms of their actual function. Most of them agreed that chaplain fitness reports rarely reflect in depth their capabilities in primary duty. Some of them wondered whether, as reporting seniors, they had done justice to their chaplains or to our Corps.

All of us know the objective of the Navy fitness report system. BUPERS has worked hard and wisely to refine the entire system of evaluation and selection. Its effective function depends on certain fundamental postulates:

    1. The assumption that a reporting senior is technically competent to pass judgment on professional performance.

    2. The existence of universally applicable criteria.

    3. The objectivity of criteria.

    4. Standardized objective procedures of evaluation used by selection boards.

The present system, by itself, does not achieve its purpose with respect to the Chaplain Corps. Chaplains constitute a special case for which the present report does not provide.

    1. Reporting seniors are not technically competent to evaluate the professional performance of chaplains. It is as sensible to require a chaplain to judge the logistic, tactical and strategic abilities of a line officer as it is to ask a line officer to evaluate the professional performance of a clergyman.

    2. It is precisely with regard to a chaplain's _professional_ performance that the personal orientation of the reporting senior intrudes uniquely into the evaluating process. The religious opinions of a reporting senior introduce no particular bias into his evaluation of line officers. Those opinions may well introduce degrees of ignorance, of reservation, or even of hostility into his estimate of the _professional_ duties of the chaplain. An agnostic reporting senior is quite as unable to be fair to his chaplain as a Christian Scientist reporting senior to his doctor. This is not impugning integrity but merely stating the unavoidable consequence of preconceptions brought by the reporting senior to his task of evaluation. Our reporting seniors differ not only about the priority to be given a chaplain's primary duty but even, in some cases, about the very desirability of its performance.

    3. The present fitness report does not contain criteria which would make possible a considered judgment by the reporting senior on the professional performance of his chaplain.

    4. Chaplain Corps selection boards do not receive evaluations in the professional area which enable them to fulfill their function.

This unfortunate situation subverts the selection process in our Corps. The dynamics of the present system clearly portray this result and the reasons for it.

    1. Lacking defined criteria for judging chaplain professional performance, the reporting senior is reduced to a judgment based on his personal preconceptions. This subjective factor is so wildly various as to nullify the universality and objectivity sought for reports by the Bureau.

    2. In the absence of such professional criteria reporting seniors stress the tangible and measureable in the area of chaplain performance. These are rare in the professional area but common in peripheral areas. Emphasis gradually builds, therefore, on material evidences of the chaplain's success as tour officer, project officer on fund drives, etc.

    3. Some chaplains consequently receive outstanding or mediocre fitness reports for reasons not related to their performance as clergymen.

    4. Chaplains are human. They are strongly tempted to concentrate their activity in those areas which are rewarded by good fitness reports. This legitimate concentration, under present circumstances, subverts the professional standards of our Corps.

    5. Chaplain Corps selection boards, lacking adequate professional evaluation data in the record, face Hobson's choice. They can "go by the record" and cause all manner of injustice to chaplains and expense to the Corps. Or they can try to compensate by introducing into the process still another subjective factor, "service reputation". This device does permit an approximation of justice in the circumstance but only by sabotaging the Bureau's effort to standardize the selection process.

The brevity of this statement excludes certain qualifications which could be made. Nevertheless, it can scarcely be denied that the inadequacy for chaplains of the present report has introduced very considerable subjective factors into several stages of the process. Neither the reporting procedures nor the selection procedures are addressed to the actual service required of this system by the Chaplain Corps and which is provided by this system for the line.

Abolishing the present report in the case of chaplains is not a solution. First, for all its shortcomings, this report represents a legitimate function of command. Moreover, within certain limits the present report is useful to us. No other evaluator in the world can equal the American naval officer in integrity, fairness, objectivity and concern for the good of the service. Most civilian bishops would profit from non-partisan estimates of their clergy by laymen of experience and character comparable to those of our reporting seniors.

What we need, it appears to me, is a procedure which is economical in operation, which does not compromise the present fitness report and which copes with the difficulties we now experience. The establishment of a "Professional (or Technical) Performance Report" as a supplement to the present fitness report would surely contribute to these ends.

The operating mechanics of such a report can be sketched in broad outline.

1. Institution.

    Personnel and facilities for establishing such a report are available in the Bureau. Criteria relevant to the chaplain's professional function and to his personal fitness for this particular ministry should be stressed.

2. Subjects of the report.

    All chaplains under the rank of captain should be the subjects of this report.

3. Reporting seniors.

    Reporting seniors should be chaplains of captain rank selected from the echelon of supervision nearest the operational chaplain. The emphasis would be on selection for this duty of type command, division, wing and training command supervisory chaplains rather than on district or fleet chaplains.

4. Submission.

    Annually through official channels, to the Chief of Naval Personnel, with copy to the command of the chaplain reported on.

5. __Conditions of Reporting.__

   Derogatory or unfavorable comments should be discussed prior to inclusion, both with the chaplain concerned and with his commanding officer.

6. __Use.__

   The proposed report should be included in fitness report jackets for use by all boards. When utilized by selection boards it should receive a pre-determined weight factor in relation to the present report. It should also be considered by boards selecting Rear Admirals of the Chaplain Corps.

The proposed report offers the following advantages to the service, to our Corps and to individual chaplains.

1. It will provide, for the first time, evaluation of the chaplain in terms of his primary function by a technically competent reporting senior.

2. It will improve the chaplain selection process by providing selection boards with estimates centrally relevant to their purpose.

3. An essential ingredient in the efficiency of the present report for line officers is the fact that reporting seniors and selecting seniors are all from the line and share the same general standards. The proposed report would give the same homogeneous character to Chaplain Corps participation in the reporting-selection process. "Speaking the same language" at both poles of this procedure is of the greatest importance to a fair and effective selection process.

4. The proposed report would limit and institutionalize the subjective factor "service reputation". The Chaplain Corps is small enough to permit considerable control at this point. Vizualizing the dynamics of this factor highlights some of its advantages.

   a. Without exception technical reporting seniors and their standards will be known to selection boards. This permits a truly informed, rather than a haphazard, consensus on the standards of reporting seniors.

   b. The knowledge that their reports are read by their peers will exercise a moderating influence on technical reporting seniors. This should be noted in the event that fear of denominational bias raises its ugly head.

   c. Of course, this factor would strengthen the Bureau's effort to standardize procedures and criteria.

5. The proposed report would give chaplains the protection of evaluation on professional performance.

6. Conversely, the proposed report would protect the Chaplain Corps against chaplains who seek advancement at the expense of their primary function.

7. The proposed report would enhance the task and the status of the technical reporting senior.

    a. It would give him an instrument of supervision.

    b. It would define to subordinate commands his legitimate sphere of interest in, and responsibility for, chaplains.

    c. It would improve the quality of supervision.

8. Without diminishing command authority over the chaplain, the proposed report would strengthen the technical control necessarily exercised by the Chief of Chaplains.

9. The proposed report will provide the Chief of Chaplains with an official, organized body of information based on professional estimates for use in the general conduct of his technical control over the Chaplain Corps.

10. The proposed report will enhance the value of the present report by providing a context within which its estimates will be more meaningful.

11. The fitness report, per se, involves unavoidable administrative output in connection with its institution, with evaluation of its effectiveness and with preparation and issuance of revisions. Beyond that administrative investment the proposed report would impose a minimal workload. The number of reporting seniors is small. The relative number of officers-reported-on is small. Demand on the line and other corps in administering this report would be comparable to that now required in connection with quarterly reports.

12. The existence of the proposed report would have considerable educational value.

    a. It would encourage commanding officers to learn more about the professional functions of the chaplains.

    b. It would stimulate commanding officers to utilize their chaplains in ways consistent with their primary duty.

    c. Passage of this report through channels would be in itself an educational experience for all levels of command.

    d. It would educate chaplains, if that were needed, to the priority placed by higher authority on their primary function.

The length of this may persuade you that sin in NAVEUR is under control if I have time for this kind of thing. Sin unfortunately continues to abound among us and I continue to do my best against it. I am moved, however, by one or two specific instances of this problem in our command to afflict you with these thoughts. I know, too, that you are not averse to considering ideas from the field, however far in left field they may be. I send this, then, as "grist for the mill" in the hope that some part of it may one day be of benefit to the Corps.

    Very respectfully,

    GLYN JONES
    CAPT, CHC, USN
    FORCE CHAPLAIN
    CINCUSNAVEUR

16/GJ:pas
22 May 1962

Reverend A. Ray Appelquist
Executive Director
General Commission on Chaplains
100 Maryland
Washington, D. C.

Dear Ray:

During your recent visit to San Diego you indicated that the General Commission may soon be a stronger influence in support of the Chaplaincy. In that hope I venture to discuss with you a fundamental problem of the Navy Chaplain Corps which requires the active intervention of the endorsing agencies and of sympathetic Congressmen for its solution.

I refer to the fact that our Corps does not occupy a position in the Naval organization comparable to those of the Army and Air Force Chaplain Corps. The USA and USAF Chiefs of Chaplains are placed organizationally directly under the Chief of Staff or the Service Secretary. Our Chief is directly under the Bureau Chief you would call G-1. He heads a Division in the Bureau of Naval Personnel which is on a par with such other divisions as Welfare, Retirement, Officer Promotion and Enlisted Detail. This organizational structure reflects the accepted official opinion that religion is a personal service equated with insurance, athletics, personal affairs and library supervision.

The Navy takes quite a different position with respect to such other professional personnel as doctors, lawyers, civil engineers and business men. Doctors have their own Bureau of Medicine and Surgery. Civil Engineers have their Bureau of Yards and Docks. Supply officers have their Bureau of Supplies and Accounts. Lawyers have the Office of the Judge Advocate General, which is on the EXOS level directly under the Secretary. Only the Chaplaincy is considered a simple, uncomplicated profession which can be governed quite capably by the layman who happens to be Chief of Naval Personnel, be he atheist, agnostic or believer.

In this circumstance the Navy Chief of Chaplains has not the slightest shred of authority for coping with the multifarious problems of his ecumenical flock. He is empowered to manage the internal affairs of his Washington office. Otherwise he can do no more than recommend policy to the Chief of Naval Personnel. Though he is a Rear Admiral and an Assistant Chief of Naval Personnel, the Navy Chief of Chaplains cannot authorize for himself a set of TDY orders from Washington to Baltimore. He is the only Chief of technical services who is selected for his post by one man on the Bureau or "G" level.

The Chief of Naval Personnel is required by law to select a Chief of Chaplains from the two flag officers of our Corps.

The sad consequences of this system to our ministry are apparent. Let me cite a few.

1. The Navy Chaplain is frequently assigned to duties which, either by their character or their demands upon his time, militate against his ministry. If you want specific evidence on this score I can provide it ad nauseam – ranging from the employment of Chaplains as social workers by the Navy Relief Society to their utilization for months at a time as housing officers in advance of a destroyer squadron's foreign deployment. Enclosed is an instruction I originated (signed, incidentally by a four-star admiral who is a former Chief of Naval Personnel) in an attempt to stem this tide of abuses in my area of responsibility. The Navy Chief of Chaplains has been unable to promulgate this kind of policy for our Corps as a whole. Individual Chaplains, especially aboard ship, are therefore treated as jacks-of-all-trades to the serious detriment of their ministry.

2. This system raises to leadership in our Corps undistinguished, mediocre men who are strongly conformist in character. Our present Chief – a Roman Catholic – is a happy exception. I recognize that Erastianism is in most cases an indispensable precursor of formal success in the Chaplaincy. Its effects in our Corps, however, have been compounded by the Navy Chaplain Corps organizational placement. It should not be enough, in considering men for Chief of Chaplains, to commend their habitual "yea" saying and to rejoice that they have not run away with even one choir singer.

3. Organizational placement represents to military people the precise relative importance of an activity. The Pentagon telephone book (or the Navy Department's) exactly reflects this hierarchy of value. Unfortunately, it also indicates with some exactitude the authoritative and financial capabilities of an office for fulfilling its mission. The Navy Chief of Chaplains, for example, does not in a strict sense have his own budget. He participates, on a divisional basis, in the budget of the Bureau of Naval Personnel. This means that his budget loses at every point in the fiscal process. First, it is radically pruned at the point of submission in the interests of every other division in the Bureau. Naturally it shares prorated losses, and sometimes even more, en route through the Comptroller and BuBud to the Senate and House Committees. Again – as a portion of a Bureau Budget – it suffers when across-the-board cuts are made, because it represents a flexible (and reduceable) cost in contrast to such so-called fixed costs as travel on orders, etc. The budget of our Chief in 1949 was $25,000. When it was reduced 20% in an across-the-board cut, the Welfare Division behighly gave us $5,000. This budget of our Corps has increased ten fold since that day, but even this represents no more than the budgets of two – perhaps three – large city churches. Need I say more?

The Congress has been willing on two occasions in the past 16 years to correct this inequity. The effort failed on one occasion because of limited backing from the churches and on another in spite of strong support from the endorsing agencies. The latter attempt was frustrated because the Chief of Naval Personnel recalled to active duty a personally impressive, obsequious retired Chief of Chaplains - Thomas - to testify that all was well in rebuttal to the contentions of the endorsing agencies. It is very important to success in this enterprise that the testimony of former Chiefs of Chaplains be impugned on the ground that they have personally profitted from an invidious process.

I cannot pretend to advise you on the tactics of a movement in this direction. You may be receptive to certain comments. First the objective is that our Corps be established on the EXOS level and that it be authorized within the staff process to develop its own policies, to defend its own budget, and to promulgate program. Second, achievement of this objective - which is merely parity with the Army and Air Force - requires coordination and cooperation among all endorsing agencies. In my opinion - and you must recognize this is a limited view - this effort deserves priority over a move to correct the USA-USAF penchant for equal Protestant - RC selection to the top jobs. You have my complete support at that point - I think only that its place is after this problem. Third, achievement of this objective requires strong Congressional interest and support. Fourth, the pressure should be applied not to the Navy, which will successfully resist by time-honored means, but to the Secretary of Defense, who can accomplish the needed reform by requesting appropriate legislation. Finally, the time to move is now. The Secretary of Defense convened some three months ago a committee to submit recommendations for reorganization of the Defense Department. Such a change as this should be considered and approved by that committee. That could well happen if the committee were spurred by active intervention from endorsing agencies and evidence of strong congressional interest.

You stated in San Diego that such letters as this would be handled by your office as anonymous communications. This is acceptable to me, for I have no desire to achieve notoriety or to increase my reputation as an enfant terrible. On the other hand, I want you to feel perfectly free, if that will help the cause, to attribute your source. I have no ambitions that can thereby be injured. Nor do I write from a position of moral superiority. What I have described, given these conditions, is merely a predictable exercise in group dynamics. Our Chiefs of Chaplains have been victims rather than victors, men who have behaved as will as most humans under this kind and amount of temptation. I don't think this project can begin by assigning blame - there is enough for everybody. We can right this wrong only by the intrinsic merit of our argument. That will suffice if the matter is pressed with vigor.

Thank you for your patience in reading this. I enjoyed seeing you in Quantico - and was happy you found a tie. Perhaps we have reached the point where men are surprised to find a Baptist without a tie - is this good or bad? Please do what you can to help us.

Cordially,

GLYN JONES
CAPT, CHC, USN
Senior Chaplain

Chaplain's School Address

3/4/77 Newport

I am honored by the invitation to be with you today. Almost exactly thirty-five years ago I entered Chaplains' School. I left after a month without graduating to join the First Marine Division, which had already been committed to "duty beyond the seas". As I pondered these remarks, memories of my Navy life flooded back. Great commanders under whom I served - Chesty Puller in the First Marine Regiment, John Snackenberg on the Yangtse Patrol, Arleigh Burke with destroyers. Great priests and rabbis and ministers who were my colleagues - Joshua Goldberg and Sam Sobel; Francis Timothy O'Leary, Frank Sullivan and George Rosso; Roland Faulk, John Zimmerman, Bob Coe, Pat Rafferty, your Officer-in-Charge.

But let me not reminisce. Old Navy men are avid tellers of sea stories. Around the Officers' Club bar we are great liars. We are not to be believed. The good Lord listens benignly and makes allowances. For all our experience, my generation is irrelevant to the Navy you will serve. I was in uniform during three wars, but the world has since changed. The senior course in this school testifies that you have a better, more competent Corps than ours and that we have little wisdom to offer you. But I have my orders and must have at it.

My thoughts, then, pass over the new developments since our time and seek out the perennial, that which has not changed and which will probably remain. The changeless and unalterable in our Navy ministry is its ambiguity. We chaplains seem everlastingly to be hung on one or another horn of dilemma. As servants of the Prince of Peace we are members of a war machine. As citizens of a land dedicated to separation of church and state we are churchmen employed by the government. Committed by moral conviction to freedom of conscience we participated until recently in the conduct of compulsory worship. Though believers in voluntarism and in human freedom we were yet part of a system which, in defiance of the Constitution, inflicted involuntary servitude upon thousands of young citizens who had not been duly convicted of any crime.

I say we are caught up in ambiguity. Some of our anomalies have been resolved and others will be, but it is unlikely that the paradoxical center of our calling can be done away. That is the equivocal character of power. This seems to me true throughout and especially in three areas. So, like a first year seminarian's sermon, my little talk offers three points and each begins with the letter "P", then a conclusion that starts with a "C:. And, for what it is worth, I say it to my shipmates, the graduates of today's class.

I

First, pastoral power. To a pastor the Navy is a field white for the harvest, such a magnificent opportunity as the civilian clergyman can scarcely believe. Men and women who shun the clergy at home will come to you easily and naturally. They will candidly discuss with you their most intimate problems and will expect you to accept them without condemnation. You can minister to them fully and unreservedly. Yet there is a certain polarity here which we can scarcely avoid.

On the one hand we are pastoral counselors. We are ordained to be shepherds of the flock. We are commissioned to be custodians of sacred mysteries which communicate to the depths of man's being. We are repositories of ancient skills for the cure of souls. We call upon divine power for the help and healing of broken and sinful men. We care for people as pastors who are servants.

On the other hand, we are beneficiaries of an explosion of knowledge in the behavioral sciences. In some ways man now understands himself as never he has before. He wields human skills of analysis and therapy unknown a century ago. In all this there seems little need to invoke the divine, since man appears to be his own measure. He seems to be in command as a master.

Need these two approaches be occasion for contradiction? Whether or not they should be, they are. Our increasing competence in psychological skills enables us to act on a simple, finite level in helping those who need only human assistance. As this type of counselling becomes an increasingly larger part of our work, it begins to redefine us and our role. I observed a few years ago several retired chaplains who had departed the ministry in order to practise a simplistic but sometimes useful therapy called Transactional Analysis. I understand that there was a similar trend among civilian clergy. These men opted for one pole of the tension. They retrogressed from pastor to pop psychologist, from servant to master.

But the mysteries will not go away, because they correspond to inscrutable, unfathomable depths in ourselves. There come times when the recondite and the gnosis collide. Then the pastor may lack learning. More frequently the psychologist fails to address the entire dimension of man. Here is an unbelieving Jew, for example, who sickens whenever he eats pork. He goes to a TA specialist who is baffled. Does either plumb the obscurities of man's unconscious mind which contains primal symbols? Can either reach the decisive depths in personality of which we are not consciously aware? Well, that is what religion does in unifying the conscious and unconscious elements of man. It is the arcane space in which priest and pastor unite and reconcile men, often without a complete understanding of the forces they dispose.

Willy nilly, we must counsel. Let us learn all the behavioral sciences have to teach us. Even so, let us be aware of the antinomy of seeking to heal persons. Let us be shepherds. Let us remember that mystery in the client which is not amenable to simple human powers. Let us avow the power of the symbol, which will not respond to the cognitive stimulus of Psychology 101.

II

There is ambiguity as well in political power. Life cannot be lived without it. Yet, as Lord Acton observed, "Power corrupts, absolute power corrupts absolutely". Here we are, then, belonging to a community prepared to exert power with utmost violence, while we must use political means to govern ourselves and to accomplish our mission.

Men have tried in many ways to resolve the ambivalence of power. They have sometimes defined power as not-power. Some Christians, in particular, have sought to dream the problem away by eschewing the use of power. But there is no way to define power out of existence. Power will not go away. The Gospel itself is about the victory of a particular kind of power. The effectiveness of your ministry will depend, to some extent, on the use of legitimate power.

It was true when you were with the church. Because the church is human it is a political organization, and it functions through the distribution of power. Baptists are quite as political as Catholics, as the former pastor of the Plains,

Georgia, Baptist Church can today attest. I see no reason to apologize for governing ourselves as Christians or Jews through the peaceful application of power, however mistaken we may be in particular instances.

So with our participation in the Navy's distribution of power. It is a legitimate process which carefully defines, allots and limits authority. To be effective ministers we must master the skills of applying power to advance our influence and service in this community. We must certainly know the 13th Chapter of I Corinthians, but that will be of little use unless we also understand the necessity of completed staff work and the importance of obtaining the commander's signature on an instruction or order to get done what is needed for the welfare of our men and their families.

Nor should we ignore the necessities of power in the larger arena. Placement within the organization determines the resources of authority, personnel and money available to any community for accomplishment of its mission. The Chaplain Corps is placed within the Bureau of Naval Personnel to be administered along with recreation, libraries, officer's clubs and reserve personnel. We belong to a company of the demeaned. For many years some of us urged that the ministry of religion in the Navy, because of its constitutional sensitivity and the need of its moral integrity, should be administered not by military command but by the civilian authority. This is not to denigrate military command. All operational chaplains should be under it. Yet it is another matter entirely to place a great profession under military authority alone. The doctors exercise their technical control of medicine through a bureau. To assure religion in the Navy its proper autonomy our Corps should be placed directly under the Secretary of the Navy as is the Judge Advocate General.

The attempt continues to correct the organizational placement of our Corps. I recently learned that the Chief of Chaplains, while remaining under the Chief of Naval Personnel, has been given another hat at the level of CNO. This has little improved his power position, beyond placing him under two line admirals rather than one. It reminded me of Joe Lang, who found a skunk in his cellar. He laid a trail of peanuts through the cellar door, and by the next morning the animal had eaten his way out. When Cora Smith found a skunk in her cellar she remembered Joe's achievement and laid down her trail of peanuts. When she looked next morning she had two skunks.

Something like that has happened to our Corps. I'm not calling CNP or CNO skunks, for they are distinguished men and naval officers. I'm merely describing an exercise in the use of power, a perfectly legitimate one, in which the Chaplain Corps has been beguiled into enjoying its Babylonian captivity under an illusion of freedom. But the ministry of religion is not a function of personnel administration. Nor is it a branch of naval operations. Even the churches, ever forgetful of their Navy clergy, will eventually rebel against the definition of Christian and Jewish faith as only an aspect of the Navy's capacity to plan and to make war. For too long rejection and misunderstanding of political power have consigned our Corps to a position of poverty and humiliation in the organization of the Navy. It is time that we accepted the place of legitimate power in life and began to seek and to use it.

III

Again, there is the confrontation between pietist and prophet. Chaplains are supposedly pietists and not prophets. Indeed, that noble old word "Chaplain" has the connotation in some sophisticated quarters of a naive, submissive clergyman conducting meaningless little rituals to satisfy the power structure and to defend the status quo. The quintessential "Chaplain" in that meaning of the term has been poor Dr. Billy Graham, who, in all innocence and simplicity, preached in the White House, carefully avoided questions of justice as he addressed the prayer breakfasts of the establishment, lent his unwitting sanction to all manner of corruption and subversion, and dignified with his presence the jackals of Nixon's imperial presidency. He had gone forth as a sheep in the midst of wolves but he had not been wise as serpents.

There are several things wrong with that understanding of the Navy Chaplain. It assumes that Navy commanders resist the ethical element in religion and censor the preaching of their clergy. It suggests that the Navy is blind to moral insight and determined to prevent its application. It proposes that Chaplains are prone to temper their judgments and shave their convictions in order to gain promotion. These assumptions about our commanders and our people are caricatures of the Navy and its chaplaincy. Let us confess, nevertheless, that they are temptations which Navy people share with the world at large. My Lai, the Phoenix program, the Jensen court-martial and acquittal, the long segregation of our stewards' branch show that military people are not immune to human frailty. We need the prophet, as does the rest of mankind.

For two centuries the Navy has produced prophets. Some have been chaplains, who fought against flogging and liquor aboard ship, who believed in education for enlisted men, who stood against discrimination of race and sex, who struggled for freedom of worship. Some have been Navy laymen of all ranks and faiths, acting on their own convictions, without whom chaplains could have accomplished little. These were the clergy and laymen who, long before blessed John XXIII, sincerely and artlessly practised ecumenism because it was Christian and Jewish, and practical and right. They were pietists, perhaps, but they were also prophets.

The Navy needs prophets today. We are learning that history offers us ever and again new moral problems. Forty years ago, when I was earning my living by playing in dance bands, my fellow musicians were the drug culture. Now much of our community is the drug culture: youngsters on pot, oldsters on Valium and booze. The pietists criticize clergy for preaching the "social gospel". Well, since the prophet Amos, what other kind of gospel has there been? Those who would limit God's work to the saving of individual souls are partisan and unbiblical. Their limitation was illustrated during a parliamentary debate of World War II. When Mr. Greenwood rose to speak for the Labor opposition, Mr. Amery cried out to him from the Conservative benches, "Speak for England!" Well, so must you speak not only for a party but for the nation of mankind, for the entire people of God, for the whole of the Gospel. Celebrating and sharing the Good News are social actions. There is only a social gospel, including every individual, and no other. You are called to the fulness of that prophetic ministry.

IV

You are called... However we may put it that is the important thing: we are the called, the avowed, the professed. Notice carefully the career officers and men of the Navy and you will see that they show many characteristics of religious profession. They are men under orders ready for an ultimate fate. So we, counselling, politicking, prophesying in the community of the called are not our own. We are men under orders from synagogue and church, from Moses and Christ.

Frustration and darkness accompany the call of God. He has poor tools for the job, but He proves us and tempers us and makes us His own. I was blowing a trumpet in the roadhouses of prohibition, casually preparing for the law, when He laid a hand on my shoulder. No one would believe it, least of all my colleagues. I wrote my father a long explanation of my vocation, but he promptly telegraphed his reply: "Come home immediately. Are you well?" He suffered existential disappointment, the kind which one man recalled from his early youth when he had crawled under a tent to see the circus only to find himself in a revival meeting.

The Lutherans are a stiff necked people of the Lord but they hold before us, among other things, the great truth that God does not stop calling the professed. Every invitation to a new parish, every set of orders, is a new call which He makes through the needs of His people. While I was detail officer of the Corps this truth reminded me that, while my impulse was to run the whole shebang, I was only an instrument of the deeper purposes of God. "Ho, Assyrian, rod of mine anger..."

Moreover, the nearer the need, the more authentic His call. Chesterton made this point in observing that if he had direction of the church the newly ordained would start in as bishops and then gradually work up, as their competence was demonstrated, to the high office of parish priest. The parish priest is the first called. He is the most tried. To him will be given the power for his is the greatest need. "...God gives power only to men who need it. He does not waste power. He gives it to those who have tackled something so big, so overwhelming, that their own resources are quite insufficient. Tackling a task too big for human power is the opening of a door through which comes the rushing of a mighty wind as of Pentecost." A task too big for human power - the healing and saving of one soul, the healing and saving of a nation, the healing and saving of a world!

In our hands is the puissance of the holy. You remember how it appeared to the early Hebrews. To them the holy was a twofold physical force like electricity. It was either the mysterium tremenduum, the awesome, clarity of goodness, or the mysterium fascinans, the seductive, demonic power which could kill at the touch of the ark. In racism and chauvinism, in sexism and evil and hubris, the demonic holy is active in our world. From time to time we succumb to its seduction.

But against it we wield the power of God. That is our Good News. There is power and the power is on. Years ago a village in the state of Washington was prepared for the advent of electricity. All the houses and businesses had been wired, and everyone waited for the dynamos to turn. In one home the switches had inadvertently been left open and this evening, when the power was turned on unexpectedly, lights flashed on in every room. Immediately the man of the house ran down the main street of the village shouting the good news he could not keep to himself: "The power's on! The power's on!" That is the trumpet peal of the gospel. May it be the good news you pray and proclaim, that you live and love: "The power's on!"

Elgin Jones

16/GJ:jlw
26 November 1962

Rear Admiral George A. Rosso, CHC, USN
Chief of Chaplains (Attn: Pers J13)
Bureau of Naval Personnel
Washington 25, D. C.

Dear Chaplain Rosso:

This is an exploratory letter through which I hope to elicit your views with regard to new chapel construction at this Training Center. It stems from your new system and philosophy of centralized priority, planning and funding for chapels.

It cannot be doubted that the Naval Training Center needs chapels to accomplish the stated mission of the command. The basic questions, as we see them are these: how many chapels, where located, in what priority as measured by the needs of other commands. The last question must be answered, of course, by you in terms of the large picture which is denied us.

Our basic planning is for a population of 20,000 recruits, of 6,400 students and 3,500 permanent personnel. We consider our present North Chapel adequate to provide for the worship of the student and permanent population, only a small percentage of which is aboard on Sundays. It is not adequate for such other purposes as religious education, chaplain office space and religiously oriented meetings (youth groups, communion breakfasts, sodality and womens' meetings, etc.). Chaplains now have offices in sacristies.

The recruit planning figure is for recruits in two separate training areas: Camp Nimitz for primary training with facilities for 5,060 and an advanced training area with facilities for 15,000. To care for these men we now have one chapel with a seating capacity of 450. The great bulk of recruits attend church in theaters, classrooms and the outdoor boxing arena (sometimes it rains!) It should be noted that these men, for the period of their training, are not allowed to leave the base for worship ashore.

Our initial and tentative evaluation indicates that considerations of available land surface will count heavily in the decision on what number of chapels to build. In our particular situation SECDEF criteria for siting of chapels by area population are not relevant. An adequate number of stock chapels to serve this population would require a land area which is already pre-empted by other essential construction. For this reason it does not appear likely that the SECDEF standard chapel will meet our needs.

It seems to us that our situation calls for the following construction:

1. <u>Camp Nimitz</u>. One 1,000 seat chapel which would accommodate all Roman Catholics at one mass and all Protestants at three services. Camp Nimitz recruits now must march to mainside for church. Construction of this chapel would therefore contribute toward achieving the current aim of conducting Camp Nimitz as a self-contained entity. Convenient and appropriate land surface is available alongside the estuary for this chapel. It is possible that the standard 600 seat chapel modified to provide an additional 400 seats in balconies can meet this requirement. If this solution is feasible the religious education building in the package can be used as recommended below.

2. <u>Advanced Training</u>. Since space is available for only one chapel, it is considered that this should be a structure seating 2,500 men about a central altar and containing appropriate side chapels and oratories one of which should be especially prepared for Jewish worship.

3. <u>Religious Education Building</u>. The religious program for schools and permanent personnel is seriously limited by the lack of a religious education building. This building should be sited next to North Chapel and should conform to its architectural style.

We are now consulting with the command toward the end of placing our required construction on the Center's Shore Development Plan. The ideas presented above are merely our rough initial thinking in this area. I shall welcome your suggestions and guidance as we develop these concepts into a finished plan.

                                          Very respectfully,

                                      GLYN JONES
                                      CAPT, CHC, USN
                                      Senior Chaplain

16/GJ:hrf
1301
20 December 1962

Rear Admiral George A. Rosso, CHC, USN
Chief of Chaplains (Attn: Pers J)
Bureau of Naval Personnel
Washington 25, D. C.

Dear Chaplain Rosso:

This is to apprise you of certain developments aboard this Center which may affect your future decisions involving assignment of chaplains.

As you know, at the time of my reporting our NTC chaplains were gathered in several sizable concentrations - 10 in one building in the Recruit Training Command, 6 at one building in Service Schools and smaller groups at the North Chapel and in my office. This distribution struck me as resulting in a relatively low effectiveness. In May, therefore, we began a process of decentralizing our chaplains with the assignment of one man as AdCom Ship's Company chaplain and the reassignment of Service Schools chaplains to plexuses of schools. The general results of this policy have been highly satisfactory. The volume of counselling has risen, new and productive relationships have been formed and individual chaplains are now positive influences in their respective circles. Comments from officers-in-charge of various Service Schools have been particularly favorable.

We shall embark in early January upon the same policy in Recruit Training. We shall begin slowly, but it is anticipated that complete decentralization of chaplains into battalions will have been accomplished by May. We foresee many advantages from the end product: reduction of friction between the chaplains and small unit leaders, extension of a personal pastoral ministry to battalion and company commanders and other permanent personnel and a more direct participation by chaplains as clergymen in the recruit training process. More importantly, this will increase the chaplain's influence through the Company Commanders upon the recruits themselves.

To this point we have tended to place more experienced chaplains in the decentralized Service Schools Division, where they minister on a quasi-independent-duty basis, while sending new or less experienced chaplains to Recruit Training, where constant direct supervision is available. The forthcoming decentralization of chaplains in Recruit Training radically challenges this policy. Beginning with the initial phase in January, we shall have a rising need for experienced men in Recruit Training which will peak at completion of the change. At that time Recruit Training chaplains will encounter a situation of great delicacy requiring mature decisions under difficult, almost experimental conditions.

This is particularly the case since the training personnel (battalion commanders, company commanders, etc.) view this development as a dangerous innovation. We shall then be in the business of winning our way and justifying our presence. For the first several months, at least, inexperience will be very costly to the entire enterprise. It will so continue until the situation has been accepted and chaplains are allowed as many mistakes as anyone else.

I recognize several fixed necessities which limit your response to this situation. The number of transfers on-and-off the Training Center is not large. We have a continuing responsibility to accept chaplains of certain denominations who cannot readily be assigned elsewhere. You must have some place to send graduates of the Chaplains' School.

Denomination is not a serious consideration as we see our problem. It would be helpful, however, if it were possible for you during the next six months to replace our departing Chaplains' School graduates with more experienced men. We estimate that this unusual situation will have been resolved by the middle of next summer, that the new organization of chaplains in Recruit Training will have won its way to acceptance and that chaplains on their first duty will be perfectly adequate for the demands they will then encounter.

You know, I am sure, that we shall cheerfully accept whatever you find it necessary to do. I hope that this information will be helpful to you in making your decisions.

Very respectfully,

GLYN JONES
CAPT, CHC, USN
Senior Chaplain

COMMANDER IN CHIEF
UNITED STATES NAVAL FORCES, EUROPE
FLEET POST OFFICE
NEW YORK, NEW YORK

CINCUSNAVEUR 1743.1B
1
16 NOV 60

CINCUSNAVEUR INSTRUCTION 1743.1B

From: Commander in Chief, U.S. Naval Forces, Europe
To: DISTRIBUTION LIST

Subj: Chaplains and Religion

Ref: (a) Article 0709, U.S. Navy Regulations, 1948
     (b) Article 0711, U.S. Navy Regulations, 1948
     (c) Article 0807, U.S. Navy Regulations, 1948
     (d) Article 1355, U.S. Navy Regulations, 1948
     (e) Article C-12201(2), BUPERS Manual, 1948
     (f) Article C-12203, BUPERS Manual, 1948
     (g) Article C-12206, BUPERS Manual, 1948
     (h) Section 2401, CHAPLAINS' Manual (NAVPERS 15664-B)
     (i) Section 2402, CHAPLAINS' Manual (NAVPERS 15664-B)
     (j) General Order No. 21
     (k) BUPERSINST 5390.1
     (l) BUPERSINST 1730.6
     (m) COMSIXTHFLTINST 5000.1D, para 703.1

1. **Purpose.** This Instruction implements in the NAVEUR area certain requirements of references (a) through (l) with respect to chaplains and religion.

2. **Cancellation.** CINCUSNAVEUR Instruction 1743.1A of 15 Nov 1957 is hereby canceled and superseded.

3. **Information.** The Force Chaplain, CINCUSNAVEUR, is available to all NAVEUR commands for consultation on moral and spiritual matters and on the work of the chaplains. His mailing address is:

   Force Chaplain
   Commander in Chief, U.S. Naval Forces, Europe
   Fleet Post Office
   New York, New York

4. **Discussion.**

   a. References (a) and (b) define as command responsibilities the provision of Divine Services and care for the moral and spiritual well-being of naval personnel. Reference (c) vests the chaplain, under the Executive Officer or Chief of Staff, with responsibility for performing all duties related to the religious activities of the command.

   b. Every Navy chaplain is a volunteer. He is an ordained clergyman commissioned in the Navy to represent a particular religious body.

CINCUSNAVEURINST 1743.1B

An applicant for the chaplaincy must have completed 120 semester hours at an accredited college or university and 90 hours of graduate work in theology. He must, moreover, provide the Chief of Naval Personnel with written evidence of his clerical status and with an ecclesiastical endorsement which remains in effect at the pleasure of the endorsing agency.

    c. The primary duty which alone justifies a clergyman's presence in the chaplaincy is the ministry of religion. His professional training, his ordination and his singular sacramental faculties qualify him uniquely and irreplaceably for this work. His task is not merely an exercise in conducting stated ceremonies. The Navy has commissioned him, and his church has endorsed him, to a full ministry of pastoral care, of religious education, of sacramental service and of preaching directed toward gaining and deepening the religious commitment of his men.

    d. The ministry of Navy chaplains is traditionally a broad, rather than a narrow, service. While chaplains may be assigned collateral duties related to their primary function and utilizing their specialized professional training, several factors argue strongly for increased concentration of NAVEUR chaplains on their primary duty. Among these are the facts that there are no chaplain billets allocated for the care of dependents and that there are no chaplains assigned to certain outlying stations or to small ships. Nevertheless, available chaplains must extend their ministry to dependents and to units without chaplains. Moreover, the Navy's active effort to strengthen the moral fibre of its personnel, especially amid the complex problems they face on foreign duty, requires maximum application in their profession by the limited number of chaplains. Finally, diversion of the chaplain from his religious ministry, or his assignment to tasks incompatible with the religious calling, may also compromise his relation with the church which endorses him for naval service.

4. Action

    a. Commanders and Commanding Officers:

        (1) In accordance with reference (b) will cause Divine Service to be held on Sunday at convenient times and places. The Commander in Chief heartily concurs with the intent of reference (n), which states, "Unless absolutely necessary, operations at sea that interfere with Divine Services shall not be scheduled between 0800 and 1130 on Sundays."

        (2) Governed by reference (e), will provide opportunity for personnel to observe the Sabbath on another day than Sunday.

        (3) Will provide the services of their chaplains to ships without chaplains, and will encourage exchanges by chaplains of different faiths in order to provide the broadest possible religious coverage.

        (4) Consistent with the exigencies of the service, will encourage observance of religious holy days for personnel of the various faiths and

will seek, as far as possible, to permit compliance of personnel with dietary requirements of their respective denominations.

    (5) In accordance with reference (j) may employ their chaplains as advisors in the Naval Leadership program.

    (6) In compliance with reference (l) will require that religious lay-leaders, if needed, function only by command selection and appointment and under supervision of a chaplain.

    (7) Will insure that the chaplain is not assigned to the following duties: to receive or to retain custody of any funds other than an officially constituted chapel fund; to function in relation to naval personnel as a loan-agent or money-lender or in any capacity where he can decide that loans are to be granted or withheld; to bear arms or to serve on a coding board; to conduct social events at which intoxicating beverages will be served; or to other duties which, by their character or their cumulative demands upon his time, inhibit the chaplain's performance in his primary duty or hazard his ecclesiastical standing.

  b. Chaplains:

    (1) Will regularly consult with the Executive Officer and/or the Chief of Staff with regard to moral and spiritual matters affecting the command.

    (2) Will inform their commands about the spiritual needs of units without chaplains and, as directed, will provide such units with their ministry.

    (3) Will exert every effort to secure a ministry for personnel of other faiths than their own.

    (4) Will indoctrinate and supervise religious lay-leaders selected and appointed by commanding officers.

    (5) Will assist, as directed, in the Naval Leadership program.

4. **Reports**

  a. Chaplains will submit reports in compliance with reference (g).

  b. Chaplains attached to SIXTH Fleet units will send information copies of their quarterly reports to CINCUSNAVEUR.

H. P. SMITH

DISTRIBUTION LIST: (CINCUSNAVEUR 5216.1A)
LIST II, III, IV and VI

COPY

Personal File
G.J.

EN4/P17
Pers J121-fwg
Serial T-1918

27 November 1951

MEMORANDUM

From: J121
To: J
Via: J1a

Subj: Rank Structure and Assignments of the Chaplain Corps;
Comments and Recommendations concerning

1. Selections by recent promotion boards have created an increasingly serious problem in assignments of chaplains by aggravating the already disproportionate rank structure of our Corps. Recent changes in the Reserve Recall Program, involving acceptance of LCDR volunteers, the involuntary recall of LTs senior to 1 January 1946 and the elimination of LTs(jg) and LTs upon whom the Navy has no special claim beyond the fact that they hold commissions, tend further to subvert the rank structure of the Corps. Indicative of this tendency are the following facts:

   (a) Promotion of recently selected Commanders will give us one hundred two Commanders on duty to fill sixty authorized billets.
   (b) Promotion of recently selected LCDRs will bring our strength in that rank to two hundred seventy-nine on active duty.
   (c) As of 1 November there were one hundred twelve LTJG chaplains on duty, with that number to be further reduced by the January, 1952, selection unless procurement is radically increased in this rank.
   (d) Acceptance of volunteer LCDRs and involuntary recall of about forty inactive Reserve LTs senior to 1 January 1946 will give the Chaplain Corps approximately three hundred fifty LCDRs on duty as of 30 June 1952 out of an estimated on board strength on that date of eight hundred plus.

2. The implications of this state of affairs are obvious. Chaplain Corps billets are heavily concentrated toward the lower ranks, as is normal for the Navy at large. It is apparent, therefore, that a substantial proportion of our CDRs and LCDRs must be assigned in junior

27 November 1951

rank billets. Such assignment is uneconomical, destructive of proper rank relationships within individual commands and limits the variety of age, experience and physical condition necessary to accomplish the mission of the Corps at the various levels of command. Assignments will tend to place chaplains in billets where they are senior to their Executive Officers. The physically demanding billets, such as destroyers and Marines, must be filled by older men unfitted for such rigorous duty. It must be remembered that in many billets (e. g., CVs) the senior chaplain is subjected to physical demands far in excess of those made upon line officers of similar rank, while at the same time he is older than his line running mate. Morale among regular Navy chaplains has already noticeably declined because of the recall of certain senior reserve chaplains. Many of them have much less active duty experience than more junior regular Navy chaplains, have been rapidly promoted after recall and frequently stand in the way of Regular Navy chaplains for assignment to supervisory billets. As an example, one Reserve LCDR was promoted to that rank after serving a total of eight months on active duty since his commissioning.

3. Control over this situation could be exercised in the following ways:

   (a) A higher degree of attrition in Reserve selection. This method cannot be utilized unless (1) the law is changed or (2) selection boards select fewer reserves than the law allows.
   (b) Return to the recall, voluntary and involuntary, of only those LTs(jg) and LTs who will not make LCDR for one year after return to active duty.
   (c) Radical increase in new procurement, with bulk of new active duty increment to come from that source after exhaustion of current resources of LTs(jg) and LTs from the reserve.
   (d) Return to inactive duty without their consent all reserve chaplains, LCDR and above, least capable of performing the duties in the higher ranks, and acceptance of the principle that such returns to inactive duty must be utilized as one means of maintaining a practical rank structure within the Corps.

4. Toward implementing sub-paragraph (4) of paragraph 3, the following specific recommendations are respectfully submitted:

   1. That reserve chaplains currently on active duty for more than one year who fail of selection to LCDR, CDR and CAPTAIN be ordered to inactive duty. It is pointed out that the criterion for reserve selection is suitability for retention on active duty. Failure of selection, therefore, indicates unsuitability for retention and is sufficient ground for involuntary release from active duty.

27 November 1951

2. It is further recommended that reserves promoted to LCDR, CDR and CAPTAIN be involuntarily released from active duty when an excess in those ranks over the number of billets to be filled takes place. Such involuntary release should, when applicable, coincide with the date of expiration of the minimum required period of service.

5. These recommendations are only partial solutions. Since selection boards are limited by law to specifying that reserve promotion is dependent upon suitability for retention upon active duty, maintenance of high performance levels in the senior ranks of the Corps must depend upon administrative action. Maintenance of a rank structure which bears some relation to the mission of the Corps also requires a radical reorientation in procurement policies and practices. Consideration of the following is seriously recommended:

(a) Constitution of a board in the Chaplains Division to evaluate yearly all reserve LCDRs and CDRs toward the end of returning to inactive duty all who cannot be utilized in billets of their rank.

(b) Expansion of the Corps to the size where it meets the actual need of the service, thereby creating more LCDR and CDR billets. As an indication of the degree of expansion needed, CNO states that one thousand three hundred chaplains could be placed on duty on 1 July 1952 if the personnel are available.

(c) The previous paragraph indicates the scope of our procurement problem. Procurement planning on this dimension will meet only the present need. It is apparent that, in addition to meeting the present need, procurement must also provide substantial replacements in the lower ranks for those reserve chaplains who wish to return to inactive duty upon completion of the minimum required period of service. Planning for NSTC must be in addition to the foregoing. It is apparent that our procurement planning is not oriented to these dimensions of our need.

(d) Radical revision of Chaplains Division thinking about the Chaplain Corps Reserve. There is presently available no analysis of our Reserve component which would give any estimate of personnel availability for M-Day. It is seriously doubted that the estimated one thousand five hundred now in the Reserve component represents that number of potential accessions in case of need.

27 November 1951

Furthermore, no breakdowns in terms of age, physical condition and other pertinent factors as to utility of the reserve are currently available.

(e) The changes required in the Recall Program by Pers Ell will have a bad effect upon the rank structure of the Corps. When publicized they will have the unfortunate effect of giving the Reserve component and the chaplains in the field the idea that this office is vacillating and uncertain in its policies. Bureau reversal of published Division policies lowers the prestige of this Division within the Bureau. Chaplain Corps policies should be cleared in detail for conformity with Bureau policy prior to promulgation.

(f) Personnel problems of the Corps should be considered by all desks concerned. Consultations with Pers Ell on the recall program involves directly chaplain assignment and distribution, since the form and nature of the recall program depend entirely upon the needs of the Corps. It is felt, therefore, that the Head of the Distribution Branch of the Bureau prior to his decision should have been acquainted with the particular problems of J121. It is in the nature of the desks involved that J121 has a better understanding of the importance of the Reserve component to assignment and distribution than J122 could have of the implications of assignment and distribution to Reserve recall planning. This will be true no matter who as an individual is assigned to each desk.

(g) All consideration of the personnel problem should take account of, and exploit, the increase in the mission of the Chaplain Corps caused by the promulgation of Joint Ltr ChNavPersCMC dtd 24 October 1951. There is widespread lack of understanding at several levels of the Bureau and CNO of the implications of the Character Guidance Program on future PAPs of the Chaplain Corps. Much of this responsibility rests with J121, but should be shared with the other desks.

GLYN JONES

MM/TS-2
Pers J121-fwg
Serial T-1726

16 October 1951

MEMORANDUM

To: Pers J

Subj: Navy Relief Activity by Chaplains

Ref: (a) Survey of April, 1950

1. Reference (a) revealed that chaplains at the following activities were employed in Navy Relief work by assignment for the following percentages of their work-time:

20% of work time

NRS, Charleston, S. C.
Naval School, General Line, Monterey, Calif.
NAS, Moffett Field, Calif.
Naval Shipyard, Mare Island, Calif.
NS, Orange, Texas
NOB, Kodiak, Alaska

25% of work time

NS, Green Cove Springs, Florida
District Chaplain, 13th Naval District
NS, Bremerton, Washington
NAS, Jacksonville, Fla.
Naval Supply Corps School, Bayonne, N. J.
NTC, Great Lakes, Ill.
NH, Great Lakes, Ill.
District Chaplain, 1st Naval District

30% of work time

District Chaplain, 6th Naval District

35% of work time

NH, Oakland, Calif.
MCAS, Cherry Point, N. C. (2 chaplains, each for 35% of work time)

16 October 1951

USCG Academy, New London, Conn.
NH, Portsmouth, N. H.

40% of work time

Assistant District Chaplain, 12th Naval District
USNA, Annapolis, Md.
NH, St. Albans, N. Y.

50% of work time

NSyd, Hunter's Point, San Francisco, Calif.
District Chaplain, 8th Naval District
Sr. Chaplain, NAS, Pensacola, Fla.
NAS, Atlantic City, N. J.

More than 50% of work time

NAS, Memphis, Tenn.
NAS, Corpus Christi, Texas
MBks, Camp Lejeune, N. C.
NAS, Pensacola, Fla. (in addition to one spending 50% of work time)
NTS, Newport, R. I.
Assistant District Chaplain, 5th Naval District

2. In several of the above activities Commanding Officers have attempted to restore their chaplains to performance of primary duties by employing qualified civilian social workers as Executive Secretaries. A number of requests from Commanding Officers for authority to employ such personnel have also been denied by the National Board, Navy Relief Society. In the cases where such requests were granted there has been no appreciable diminution in the chaplains' participation in the work load where the chaplain has retained office in the local Auxiliary.

3. It is estimated that about thirty-five chaplains in the continental United States spend 20% or less of their time in Navy Relief work.

4. The tremendous increase in the workload of the Navy Relief Society since 25 June 1950 has been directly reflected in the time expenditure of our chaplains. A report received yesterday from JLh, upon his return from touring all Districts in Conlus, states that our chaplains are becoming "increasingly more involved" in Navy Relief Activities. This is taking place while the requirements of the religious ministry to Naval personnel have multiplied many-fold and while the strength of the Corps has risen since July, 1950, only from four hundred thirty-four to six hundred fifty-two. In the meantime, inquiries as to the shortage and

16 October 1951

activity of chaplains (cf. Ltr. Mr. and Mrs. E. Wunderlich, dtd 5 September 1951 to Chief of Naval Personnel, Ltr. of Mrs. Walter Krile, dtd 5 September 1951, to the President, etc.) are increasing in number and intensity.

5. Implementation of SecDef memo of "Protection of Moral Standards" dtd 26 May 1951 by Chief of Naval Personnel-Commandant of Marine Corps Joint Ltr. 51-627 of 31 August 1951 has so increased the scope of the mission of the Chaplain Corps that inroads upon the work time of the Corps by Navy Relief assignments now render it impracticable for this Corps any longer to plan in terms of accomplishing the assigned mission.

GLYN JONES

MEMORANDUM

4 September 1951

From: J121
To: J
Via: J1a

Subj.: Reassignment, Request for

1. It is respectfully requested that I be relieved of my present duty and reassigned wherever the needs of the service require.

2. It is proper that the Chief of Chaplains should know the reasons underlying this request. They are as follows:

   1. Disagreement with Personnel Policies
      a) Correction of Maldistribution of Chaplains
      b) Toleration of Civilian Influence on Assignment of Chaplains
      c) Evasion of stated policy re relief of Chaplains at request of Commanding Officers
      d) Support of Chaplains in the Field
      e) Creation of Equitable Formula Governing Denominational Quotas of Chaplains

   2. Disagreement with General Chaplains Corps Policies
      a) Collateral Duties
      b) Navy Relief

   3. Developing Tension in the Office
      Serious differences of opinion over planning and policy with respect to personnel have led to undesirable tensions within the office. While I feel it my duty to raise my voice in conference with respect to what I regard to be questionable policies and lack of intelligent planning, it is increasingly apparent that the differences of opinion are not so much over particular questions of policy as they are over fundamental approaches to Chaplain Corps philosophy. In that event it is important that the Chief of Chaplains have represented in his office a general agreement on such questions as the nature and function of the Chaplain Corps and its place in the organization of the Navy.

3. In making this request I wish to reaffirm my personal and official loyalty to the Chief of Chaplains and gratefully to acknowledge his constant and unfailing personal consideration.

GLYN JONES

EN4/P16-3 - Pers J-aj
Ser T276 - 21 Sep 51

FIRST ENDORSEMENT on Pers J121 of 4 Sep 51

From: Director, Chaplains Division
To: CDR Glyn JONES, CHC, USN 135097/4100
Via: Assistant Director

Subj: Reassignment, request for

1. Returned, approved.

S. W. SALISBURY

24 May 1965

From: CAPT GLYN (N) JONES, CHC, USN 135097/4100
To: President, Chaplain Corps Selection Board convening 25 May 65
Subj: Request for Non-Selection

1. It is requested that I not be selected by the Board now convened to recommend a chaplain for promotion to the grade of Rear Admiral.

Very respectfully,

GLYN JONES

THE SECRETARY OF THE NAVY

Washington

The President of the United States takes pleasure in presenting the SILVER STAR MEDAL to

LIEUTENANT GLYN JONES, CHAPLAIN CORPS
UNITED STATES NAVAL RESERVE

for service as set forth in the following

CITATION:

"For conspicuous gallantry and intrepidity while accompanying the First Battalion, Third Marines, during the landing operations at Cape Torokina, Bougainville Island, on November 1, 1943. Although the beach was heavily defended and the battalion engaged in violent combat, Lieutenant Jones voluntarily exposed himself continually to hostile fire in order to search for the wounded and move about among the fighting men in the front lines to reassure and encourage them. On the second day of the battle, when a cemetery had been selected and Lieutenant Jones was conducting burial services, a Japanese sniper singled him out as a target and fired five rounds, one bullet striking the ground not two feet away during the offering of a prayer. Completely disregarding his own personal safety, the chaplain continued his ceremonies calmly and with unfaltering voice. His courageous conduct and inspiring leadership under extremely difficult conditions contributed in large measure to maintaining the high morale of the battalion and were in keeping with the highest traditions of the United States Naval Service."

For the President,

Secretary of the Navy

THE SECRETARY OF THE NAVY

Washington

The President of the United States takes pleasure in presenting the BRONZE STAR MEDAL to

COMMANDER GLYN JONES
CHAPLAIN CORPS
UNITED STATES NAVY

for service as set forth in the following

CITATION:

"For heroic achievement as Regimental Chaplain, attached to a Marine Infantry Regiment, First Marine Division, Reinforced, Fleet Marine Force, during operations against enemy aggressor forces in Korea from 23 September to 1 October 1950. Throughout this period, Commander (then Lieutenant Commander) Jones repeatedly exposed himself to intense enemy small-arms, machine-gun and mortar fire to visit and encourage the members of the front line units during the attack. By his courageous and untiring efforts, he served to inspire all personnel with whom he came in contact. His initiative and steadfast devotion to duty were in keeping with the highest traditions of the United States Naval Service."

Commander Jones is authorized to wear the Combat "V".

For the President,

Secretary of the Navy

INDEX

to

Series of Interviews

with

Captain Glyn Jones, CHC, USN (Ret.)

ACKER, Capt. Frank: p. 273-4;

AMERICAN CIVIL LIBERTIES UNION: p. 373 ff; p. 380;

AMERICAN RED CROSS: p. 143-4;

ANDERSON, Admiral George: Commander, 6th Fleet, p. 287-8;

ARMED FORCES STAFF COLLEGE: Jones has tour of duty there (1956-7), p. 258-274; the Sunday morning Bible Class, p. 261-7; the softball team, p. 271-2;

BARROW, Lt. Gen. Robert: incident in Seoul involving the North Koreans, p. 172, p. 187;

BROWN, Major General W. C. (Big Foot), USMC: p. 132-3;

BURKE, Adm. Arleigh: becomes Com DesLant - instructs Jones to ask for additional chaplain billets, p. 247-9; p. 250; p. 255-7;

CAMP LE JEUNE: Jones assigned to 3rd Marine Division, p. 25; p. 29;

CAMP PENDLETON: chaplains trained there eventually in combat methods, p. 74, p. 105; the complex problems involved in preparation to send the first division to Korea, p. 163-4;

CAULDWELL, Col. Speed: trained his men in jungle warfare, p. 47-8;

CHAPEL ATTENDANCE: Jones and his effort in this area - at Mt. Hermon School, p. 160-2;

CHAPLAINS CORPS - DETAIL OFFICER: Jones takes up duties in Washington (1950), p. 205 ff; Jones raises question of rank structure in the Corps, p. 209-210; Jones raises question of Navy Relief Society and the Chaplain, p. 211-12; Jones objects to the Corps being under BuPers, p. 213; the request for detachment of insubordinate chaplain, p. 232-3;

CHAPLAIN'S SCHOOL - Norfolk, Virginia: Jones sent there for indoctrination, p. 23; Jones' physical fitness qualifies him for assignment to the Marine Corps, p. 24; the course of study at Norfolk, p. 25-6; on sermons, p. 96;

CHAPLAIN'S SCHOOL - Williamsburg, Va.: Jones assigned there after coming back to States in 1944, p. 71-3; problems with denominationalism, p. 75-6; new dimensions added to understanding of chaplain in combat, p. 77-8; p. 81 ff; Jones evaluates qualifications of a chaplain student for duty with marines, p. 88; what was done to prepare a chaplain for battle experience, p. 104-5; necessity to open school again with the Korean War, p. 205-6;

CHIANG kai-Chek and the KUOMINTANG: p. 120-1;

CHIEF OF CHAPLAINS: Jones' argument against the office being under BuPers, p. 213-4; private correspondence with Chief from chaplains in field, p. 304 ff; p. 324; Jones on the correct position of Chief, p. 306-9; the Chief and BuPers, 310 ff; disadvantage in the situation, p. 312 ff; the Chief and Congressional Committees, p. 313-4; p. 322-3;

CHIEF OF CHAPLAINS - OFFICE OF: Jones persuaded to remain on active duty - accepts assignment in Washington - lists 25 points he wanted action on there, p. 345 ff; Jones persuades Chief to send Annual Report to SecNav, p. 350;

CHIEF OF NAVAL PERSONNEL: Jones' argument against the Chief of Chaplains being under him, p. 306-10; prognosis for the future, p. 311-12; Adm. Semmes as Chief puts a chaplain in Chief of Chaplains office to oversee situation - forces resignation of Chaplain Dreith, p. 351-2; p. 354-5;

CHINA: Conditions in China, post WWII, p. 118-21;

CHARACTER EDUCATION: p. 160-2;

CHURCHILL, Sir Winston: p. 19;

CINCUSNAVEUR: Jones ordered to staff as chaplain in London (1959) with duty assignment to Naval Administrative Command, Naples, p. 274 ff; relations with the 6th Fleet, p. 287-8; p. 291; Jones reports to London from Naples on permanent basis (1960), p. 297; becomes Fleet Chaplain, p. 298; manner of keeping Chief of Chaplains informed, p. 303-4; Jones hospitalized, p 324 ff;

CITIZENSHIP EDUCATION: Jones' article in the Junior College Journal (Sept. 1952), p. 156; the program at Parris Island (1952), p. 156 ff; p. 219 ff;

CIVIL LIBERTIES: Jones' interest in this subject, p. 367;

COE, Chaplain Robert: lifelong friend - suggests Navy Chaplaincy to Jones, p. 21; studies at Harvard at same time as Jones, p. 123-4; p. 239;

COMDESLANT: Jones ordered to staff of RADM C. C. Hartman (1954), p. 240; program for lag leaders is strengthened, p. 240-1; Adm. Burke instructs Jones to write for additional chaplain billets, p. 247-9; Burke as CNO again presses for chaplain billets, p. 249;

COMPULSORY ATTENDANCE AT CHAPEL: p. 335; Jones begins to agitate at Naval Training Center, p. 335 ff; BuPers mentions effect upon the Naval Academy and the issue is joined p. 338 ff;

CRAVEN, Chaplain John: becomes a great success in the Marine Corps, p. 86-7; p. 93;

DESTROYERMEN: a characterization, p. 246-7;

di GIACOMO, Father James: p. 161-3;

DRAFT, The: Jones' ideas on the subject, p. 363-5;

DREITH, RADM Floyd: Chief of Chaplains - wanted Jones to serve in Washington, p. 346-7; p. 352;

ECUMENICITY - and the Navy: p. 136;

FARELLI, Father: Italian priest in Naples who cared for scugnizzi, p. 282-3; p. 285;

FAULK, Capt. Raymond, CHC, USN: District Chaplain, San Diego, p. 331; Jones consults him on compulsory training, p. 337 ff; p. 348;

FILARIASIS: prevelance in Samoa, p. 48-50; U.S. had no great knowledge of it at outset of war, p. 50; disabling effect on the Eighth Marines when committed to combat, p. 50-51; p. 65; Jones stands up for his afflicted men at hospital in Noumea, p. 67-8; Jones gradually loses his infection on Guadalcanal, p. 71;

FITCH, Chaplain Bob: assigned to the WAVES at Hunter College, p. 78;

FITNESS REPORTS: p. 317-21;

FRASER, Admiral Sir Bruce: p. 116;

FREE PRESS IN AMERICA: p. 375 ff;

GUADALCANAL: p. 61 ff; p. 64;

HARTMAN, RADM C.C.: ComDesLant (1954), p. 240-1;

HARVARD UNIVERSITY: Jones has a year at Harvard U - mind enrichment, p. 122-4;

HASKINS, Col. Jack: p. 175-6;

HEMPHILL, Chaplain Eddie: p. 278;

HERSEY, Lt. Gen. Lewis B.: Director of Selective Service, p. 364; p. 366;

HOWE, Chaplain Harris: p. 205; wanted Jones to relieve him as detail officer in the office of Chief of Chaplains - tried to get him away from First Marine Division, p. 166-8; p. 195-6;

INCHON, Korea: 1st Marine Division briefed on proposed landing while enroute to Japan, p. 170; Jones account of the landing, p.171 ff

INTERVENTIONALIST: Jones becomes an interventionalist in his convictions and preaching - 1940 - p. 14-17;

JACKSONVILLE, Florida: p. 39-40;

JOHNSON, VADM Felix: skipper of the transport PRESIDENT ADAMS, p. 60-61;

JONES, Captain Glyn: personal background data, p. 1-5; sudden decision to enter ministry, p. 5-6; education for ministry, 7-8; first assignment, p. 8-10; marriage, p. 20-21; contacts malaria and filariasis, p. 65; p. 66-67; repatriated to U. S., p. 68 ff; San Diego Naval Hospital, p. 324 ff; retirement, p. 353-6; reflections on his career, p. 357 ff.

KELLY, Chaplain Frank; a Roman Catholic - Reserve Chaplain - most successful in the Marine Corps, p. 88-89;

KELLY, RADM James: Deputy Chief under Chief of Chaplains Dreith, p. 347; p. 349-50; p. 352; p. 354-5;

HMS KING GEORGE V: stationed in Far East, p. 116

KLAMATH FALLS, Oregon: location of hospital for treatment of filariasis, p. 70; p. 109-110;

KOBE, Japan: 1st Marines go there for trans-shipment to Inchon landing p. 171;

KOJO, Korea: 1st Batt. of 1st Marines sent through Kojo, p. 184; attack by the North Korean division (the Diamond Hill Gang), p. 184-5; Jones' story of the Master Sergeant and his meeting with Jones first on Bougainville and then at Kojo, p. 185;

KRULAK, Lt. Gen. Victor H.: p. 179-80; his diversionary operation on Choiseul, p. 179-80;

LAY LEADERS: The Chaplain Corps at ComDesLant, p. 240-5; in the 6th Fleet, p. 290-1;

USS LOS ANGELES: Jones assigned to her in late 1945 - destination China, p. 111-112; demobilization, p. 113; addition of two hundred brig rats from Okinawa, p. 114 ff; coping with declining morale, p. 117-9;

SS LURLINE; p. 44;

LYONS, Chaplain Vaughan, p. 278;

MacARTHUR, General Douglas: his plans for Inchon landing p. 170; p. 174; p. 180;

U. S. MARINES - FIRST ENGINEER BATTALION: Jones departs for overseas with battalion - Lt. Col. Riley in command, p. 43-44; training in jungle warfare on Samoa, p. 47-8; jungle diseases, p. 48; state on morale on Samoa, p. 55; to Guadalcanal via New Zealand, p. 57 ff; Jones armed for landing on Bougainville, p. 63-4;

U. S. MARINE CORPS - CHAPLAIN: Jones on indoctrination, p. 27-8; the kind of authority a chaplain can exercise in Marine Corps, p. 34-5; as illustration - story of several marines and their jail sentence in Jacksonville, p. 35-8; a second illustration - the SeaBee still on Guadalcanal, p. 38-9; attitude of various marines towards the chaplain and his role, p. 40-1; tendency to conduct a very simple worship service, p. 41-2; comment on existence of fear as marines prepare for departure from U. S. p. 42-3; training on board LURLINE enroute to Samoa, p. 45; policy of arming chaplains because Jap snipers concentrated on men wearing Red Cross arm bands, p. 63-4; p. 181-3; Jones at Chaplain's School - asks to get back to Marine Corps, p. 73-4; contrasted with duty as a navy chaplain, p. 81 ff; what the marines look for in a chaplain, p. 84; examples of Navy Chaplains who achieved success in the Marine Corps and why, p. 86-7; necessary characteristics of the Marine Chaplain, p. 89-91 chaplain as a counsellor, p. 99-100; the ministry on the battlefield, p. 101-2; how a chaplain deals with fear, p. 103-5; leadership training and intellectual acumen, p. 105-8; Col. Puller and the hassle with BuPers over appointment of Jones as division Chaplain, p. 167-170; the chaplain in combat, p. 97 ff; calling of reserve chaplains for Korean conflict, p. 205-7; Jones' work with junior chaplains at Parris Island, p. 218-9; Jones welcomes obligation at Parris Island to write fitness reports on juniors, p. 229-30; incident at Parris Island involving an insubordinate R.C. Chaplain, p. 230 ff; p. 239;

U. S. MARINE CORPS DRILL INSTRUCTORS: p. 217-8; p. 223-5; p. 228; p. 235-6; p. 238;

U. S. MARINE CORPS EDUCATIONAL CENTER - QUANTICO: Jones reports there Oct. 1953 - to produce source material for character education movement, p. 236-9;

U. S. MARINE CORPS - FIRST DIVISION: Jones attached to First Division for duty in Korea, p. 162-3; many chaplain applications for duty with this division, p. 206-7;

U. S. MARINE CORPS RECRUIT DEPOT - PARRIS ISLAND: Jones (rank of Commander) ordered there, p. 215 ff; Lt. Gen. Silverthorne, p. 216; Jones arranges to have chaplains farmed out to training battalions, p. 216-8; Citizenship Education program, p. 219-20; Jones' difficulties with an insubordinate chaplain, p. 230 ff;

U. S. MARINE CORPS - SECOND DIVISION: Jones ordered to this Division (Aug. 1949), p. 145; Jones institutes discussions on moral leadership, p. 146; regimental baseball team, p. 147-8; Mrs. Jones' story of departure of Division for overseas, p. 191 ff;

MORAL GUIDANCE COMMITTEE - at PARRIS ISLAND: p. 222 ff; the question of men confined to the brig, p. 225-7;

MORAL LEADERSHIP TRAINING: in the 2nd Marines, p. 146; p. 149; how discussion was achieved, p. 149-56; p. 159; idea originally developed in the army, p. 159;

MOUNTBATTEN, Admiral Lord Louis: p. 116;

MT. HERMON SCHOOL: p. 363;

NAPLES, Italy: Jones account of certain activities in Naples, p. 277; the chapel council, p. 219; his relations with several orphanages, p. 283-4; visits to 6th fleet, p. 287-8;

NAVAL ACADEMY CHAPLAINCY: p. 342-3;

NAVAL AIR STATION - QUONSET POINT: Jones serves as Protestant Chaplain - problem with fraternal organizations, p. 126 ff; how naval fliers differ, p. 131 ff; Don Bryon and his clambakes, p. 135-6;

NAVAL TRAINING CENTER, San Diego: Jones becomes senior chaplain (March, 1962) p. 332-3; Jones' efforts to get a new chapel, p. 335-7;

NAVY CHAPLAIN: Jones becomes a chaplain - March, 1942, p. 21; p. 23; the men who wanted only combat duty, p. 79-81; Navy Chaplain duty contrasted with that in the Marine Corps, p. 81 ff; the Chaplain in combat, p. 197 ff; calling up reserves for the Korean conflict, p. 205-7; need for a chaplain to stand by his convictions, p. 208-9; rank structure in the Corps, p. 209 ff; p. 233; lay leader program at ComDesLant, p. 241; Jones' discussion of moral power of chaplain - in contrast to command power of inspection, etc., p. 289-90; the position of chaplains under BuPers, p. 310 ff; attitude of denominational churches, p. 314 ff; Fitness Reports, p. 317 ff; the Navy Chaplain in the modern world, p. 386-90;

NAVY RELIEF: at Quonset Point, p. 139-40; the changed situation of Naval Relief in WWII and afterwards, p. 140-1; Jones' new policy instruction - torpedoed by VADM Vincent Murphy, p. 141-2; p. 211-212;

NEWPORT (R.I.) CHAPLAINS SCHOOL: p. 363 ff;

NEW ZEALAND: the appeal of the islands to the U. S. Marines, p. 57-60;

NEYMAN, Chaplain Clinton: his efforts to develop a curriculum for training of clergy in the Chaplain's Corps, p. 26-7; p. 72-3; p. 77; p. 96-7;

NOREM, Captain Wesley, USMC: p. 359;

O'CONNOR, RADM John, CHC - Chief of Chaplains, p. 361;

O'LEARY, Chaplain Francis T.: Roman Catholic Chaplain at NAS, Quonset Point, p. 126 ff; p. 138; p. 193;

PARRIS ISLAND: see entry under CITIZENSHIP EDUCATION.

POWER: in the Church and society - Jones on the subject, p. 315 ff; p. 322-3;

PREACHING: Jones on value of, p. 96-9; preaching on the battlefield, p. 101-2;

PROMOTIONS: Jones on promotions in the Chaplains Corps, p. 93-6;

PULLER, Lt. Gen. Lewis (Chesty): Jones served as his chaplain in First Marines, p. 132; p. 163 ff; his complete support of the chaplain to the First Marine Division, p. 163 ff; insurance for the marines, p. 164-5; p. 166; his help in retaining Jones as Chaplain to First Marines, p. 167-170; in Seoul, p. 178-9; p. 180; he sends relief to the marines at KOJO, p. 186-7;

RAFFERTY, Captain Pat: Baptist chaplain on Noumea, p. 68; p. 109-110;

RIBBON CREEK INCIDENT: p. 223-5;

ROOSEVELT, President F. D.: p. 17; p. 19;

ROTA, Spain: p. 294-5;

ROTRIDGE, RADM Cy, CHC: p. 353;

RULE OF LAW: p. 371 ff;

SACRAMENT, The: on the battlefield, p. 102-3;

SALISBURY, RADM Stanley (Stan): Chief of Chaplains (1951) p. 211, p. 247;

SAMOA: First Engineers Battalion arrives, p. 46;

SAN DIEGO NAVAL HOSPITAL: Jones sent there as a patient, p. 324 ff; his interesting experiences, p. 326-30;

SEABEES: Jones' story of the Still they constructed on Guadalcanal, p. 38-9; a battalion with the 19th Marines, p. 38;

SECNAV: Jones argument that Chief of Chaplains should be under SecNav, p. 307-8; Jones induces Chief (1962) to send Annual Report direct to SecNav, p. 309-10;

SEMMES, VADM Benedict J. Jr.: as Chief of BuPers forces resignation of Chief of Chaplains Dreith, p. 351-2; p. 354-5;

SEOUL, Korea: the taking of Seoul, p. 172 ff;

SILVERTHORNE, Lt. Gen. Merwin: USMC - in command at MCRD, Parris Island (1952), p. 216 ff; p. 222; his conviction about the Moral Guidance Committee, p. 227; his attitude in case of the insubordinate chaplain, p. 232; p. 265;

U. S. SIXTH FLEET: Jones serves as Chief Chaplain to fleet in Naples, p. 287-8;

SMITH, Adm. H. Page: CincUSNavEur, (1959), p. 274; p. 297; p. 324;

SOVIK, Captain Ansgar: assigned with Jones to the Marine Corps, p. 24-5;

SULLIVAN, Chaplain Frank: A Jesuit who becomes Marine Corps Chaplain, p. 29-31; p. 45-6; his famous sermon, p. 56; p. 357;

THOMAS, Captain D.I.: Naval Training Center Commander, San Diego (1962) p. 332; Jones involves him in compulsory attendance requirements in BuPers Training Manual, p. 337 ff; BuPers reacts, p. 338; p. 343-4;

VANDEGRIFT, General A.A.: his cordon defense, p. 54;

VICTORY, Brig. Gen. Randall: with the 2nd Marines - approves of Jones offering ethical instructions, p. 146;

WELLBORN, Vice Admiral Charles: Commandant of Armed Forces Staff College, p. 259; p. 272;

WONSAN, Korea: the 1st Marines land - deployed in semicircle around the city, p. 183-4; p. 188;

WOONSOCKET, Rhode Island: Jones becomes pastor of the First Baptist Church (1940), p. 12 ff; they want him back after the war is over, p. 22;

WORKMAN, RADM R.D. - Chief of Chaplains: p. 73-4; p. 86; p. 88; his ideal for the rounded chaplaincy, p. 92-3; p. 239;

www.ingramcontent.com/pod-product-compliance
Lightning Source LLC
Chambersburg PA
CBHW080625170426
43209CB00007B/1516